UNTHINKABLE

Other books by Harry Keeble with Kris Hollington

Crack House

'A true life account of an honest cop's successful
effort to stamp out crack houses on his turf, this is a fact-filled,
very readable and at times disturbing book. Raid it and
weep ... truly shocking. Much like its subject
matter, this is gripping stuff'
5 stars, *Maxim*

'In his blistering book, *Crack House*, hard-nosed cop
Harry Keeble tells how, for nine bone-crunching months, he and his
men rampaged through London's seething drugs underworld'
5 stars, *News of the World*

Baby X

'Powerful and moving. I didn't think I could be
shocked anymore until I read *Baby X*'
Cathy Glass

'The subject matter is obviously heavy ... But the pace
crackles from case to case – with Harry's fight to save neglected
and abused kids taking him around the world'
5 stars, *News of the World*

Terror Cops

'This is the first time a counter terrorism officer
involved has written the inside story of Operation Overt.
And it's a truly fascinating insight into the lives of terror cops,
and the painstaking evidence-gathering that went into
this large scale operation. A terror-ific read'
5 stars, *News of the World*

UNTHINKABLE

THE SHOCKING SCANDAL OF THE UK
SEX TRAFFICKERS

KRIS HOLLINGTON

SIMON &
SCHUSTER

London · New York · Sydney · Toronto · New Delhi

A CBS COMPANY

First published in Great Britain by Simon & Schuster UK Ltd, 2013
A CBS COMPANY

1 3 5 7 9 10 8 6 4 2

Simon & Schuster UK Ltd
1st Floor
222 Gray's Inn Road
London WC1X 8HB

www.simonandschuster.co.uk

Simon & Schuster Australia, Sydney
Simon & Schuster India, New Delhi

A CIP catalogue record for this book is available
from the British Library.

ISBN: 978-0-47111-455-7
ISBN: 978-0-47111-456-4 (ebook)

Typeset by M Rules
Printed and bound by CPI Group (UK) Ltd, Croydon, CR0 4YY

CONTENTS

INTRODUCTION

The system currently in place to protect vulnerable children from sexual exploitation is so inadequate it is almost as if a sexual predator had designed it. It is contributing to the trafficking and abuse of children instead of preventing it.

That we are only now starting to wake up to the full extent of sexual exploitation in the UK is thanks in no small part to the pioneering journalism of Andrew Norfolk from *The Times*, whose articles brought the scandal of on-street grooming of children by organised groups to the attention of the wider public.

Andrew reported on the investigation, trial and conviction in May 2012 of nine men who had exploited up to forty-seven girls in the Rochdale area of north-west England. Since then he has continued to investigate this topic, pushing it into the national news, forcing the launch of official inquiries into how gangs such as the Rochdale Nine were able to operate unchecked for years.

It wasn't easy. *The Times* was forced to battle injunctions from children's safeguarding services and often had to rely on confidential sources to uncover the truth. Which raises the question: why do those services that are there to protect our children want to hide the truth, when the truth is vital to saving children from horrific abuse?

Time and again, the heads of children's safeguarding boards (CSBs), police and social services have published wishy-washy press releases, admitting the smallest possible amount of culpability, i.e., 'We didn't do anything because we weren't aware' but 'lessons have been learned' and 'actions have already been taken to rectify the problem'.

These lazy, meaningless, blame-dodging phrases are designed to hide the truth, to allow those responsible for the current crisis in child protection to carry on as if nothing has happened, to continue without taking responsibility or even explaining in any detail what went wrong, and what has since been done to put things right, so that the same mistakes will never occur again.

It is perhaps for this reason that many people did not want to speak to me during the writing of this book. Take the police, for example. Besides contacting individual officers across the UK, I asked police services for official comments and received a collection of press releases stuffed full of stock phrases. Even those police services that have made tremendous leaps forward in battling sexual exploitation didn't want to talk. This is because they know this issue has, so far, been a total disaster for them.

The same goes for social services. And although many social workers would like to come forward, they are afraid to expose wrongdoing. As Community Care reported in November 2012: 'Recent research by the British Association of Social Workers portrayed a climate of fear and intimidation in many social work departments, with almost half of practitioners surveyed saying they would be reluctant to speak up if they had concerns.'[1]

Fortunately there were other sources I could turn to, sources that suffered from a different kind of fear – for their physical safety, as well as for continued funding, and it is to them that this book is dedicated.

I am referring to outreach workers, those brave and selfless people who work for charities large and small, public and privately funded, doing all they can to help those most in need. Because of their entirely justified concerns, they have asked that the locations of their offices be disguised, as well as their identities and the identities of the girls they worked with.

If the locations of some of the centres dedicated to helping girls at risk of sexual exploitation are revealed here, there is a chance that those using their services or the workers may be victimised. It has already been well documented (see most of Part II of this book, for example) that once predatory gangs know the location of children's care homes, they target them hoping to snare victims. Also, when the name and location of one of the kebab shops at the centre of the Rochdale case was revealed, it was attacked by a mob, even though its new owners had changed its name and appearance.

There is a danger that even a fake description of a hotel, pub or takeaway might sound like a real one, with the result that certain organisations with aggressive tendencies will decide to exact 'revenge'. For this reason I have avoided embellishing locations with too much environmental description.

The solution is one I am familiar with from working on five books with Harry Keeble from the Metropolitan Police, three of which were about his work with a child protection unit in East London. With the exception of names that are in the public domain, I have protected identities by changing names and altering some background details. Those cases that are a matter of public record have been reported in their original detail.

So, in Unthinkable, 'Ennett House' (introduced in Part I) is not the real name of the building where Miranda, Natalie, Mary and Beatrice work. And those are not their real names (neither is Chief Superintendent Brannigan, in Chapter 34, whose name has been changed so as not to help identify the location of Ennett House).

But the building exists, is based in London, and is under the supervision of an established children's charity. All other building names and organisations described here (such as Middlegate and the London Refuge, for example) are real.

I also spoke to many other outreach workers across the southeast and in the north of the UK. I spent an unforgettable week with 'Ben' as he took me into the heart of this twilight world. Together, patrolling more than one estate, we found needles and other drug detritus; spoke to addicts, dealers ('Fat Bob' in the book), ten-year-old runners ('Andy'), caretakers, police detectives ('Eddie'), council workers and 'Alan', the police community support officer.

Ben also introduced me to victims of vulnerable takeovers, young girls (some of them single mums) living alone in small council flats who found themselves targeted by drugs gangs who moved in, had taken over the property and, in several cases, forced the girl into prostitution.

'Sylvia', who sometimes joined forces with Ben, was amazed to see a writer taking an interest in her drop-in centre for recovering addicts, and was incredibly generous with her time and knowledge. She introduced me to a number of recovering addicts and revealed the growing anger and frustration of the impoverished. It was Sylvia to whom 'Sarah' turned when she made her desperate attempt to break free of exploitation (see Chapter 21). Sylvia's drop-in has since closed, thanks to cuts in funding. The recovering addicts are now on their own.

I could not speak to the youngest victims in this story directly. Apart from many obvious ethical reasons (I would not want to exploit them in order to tell a good story, for example), a few of them are still in care.

In all newspaper articles and serious case reviews about child sexual exploitation, no one is identified: no police officer, social worker, outreach worker or child. This is to protect the child. And I have followed the same procedure here.

The only exceptions are cases like that of Laura Wilson (her story is told in Chapter 29), who was murdered and whose mother backed *The Times* to fight the case to expose the attempts by the Rotherham Safeguarding Children Board to conceal the circumstances surrounding her death. Where real names are used, I give their full name.

As for the gangs, 'Vinnie' was an unpleasant reality, as was the 'Hideous Man' (Chapter 32), who, abhorrent as he was, also needed to be protected. It was not a pleasant experience but, if we are to learn to defend ourselves from the enemy, we must know how they think.

For the Hideous Man interview I must thank another courageous charity worker, who looks after ex-offenders and attempts to re-educate them so they don't fall back into their old ways. Understandably, this person wants to keep their location and identity under wraps for fear of repercussions from extremist groups.

The trial described in Chapter 25 is one of many that ended in a similar manner. Reporting restrictions have been observed and it is vital to take a look inside the courtroom to see exactly how appalling and unfair to victims the current system is.

The stories the outreach workers told me were intense, detailed and deeply personal. This method, I hope, gets closer to the larger issues than any other (after all they are closest to the problem and are not restricted like the police and social services) and will help to bring home the horror of what has been happening in towns and cities across the UK for decades. This method also helps to expose the increasing difficulties charities face as they try to do their jobs while the world seems to be falling apart around them, thanks to vanishing resources, the result of poorly considered cutbacks.

This method also, I hope, brings home the fact that these girls are real people. They have personalities, hopes and dreams like you and I and, as Hilary Willmer, whose charity (see Chapter 31) helps the parents of children who have been sexually exploited told me: anybody's child, rich or poor, can become a victim.

Part I introduces Ennett House, the outreach workers and the girls who go there for help, explaining how some of them ended up in care homes.

Part II deals with the horror that is unleashed on these girls while in the 'care' of the State and then shows how the care system is trafficking girls. Although they ended up in care in the Rochdale area, these girls were not part of the now infamous Rochdale case, which saw nine men convicted (which is dealt with in Part III). There were other gangs, and many more victims from the same area.

Part III deals with the larger, national picture, and reveals many other scandalous truths about the care system, including efforts made to hide the extent of the scandal. This section also contains the stories of more charities, offenders and parents of victims.

Part IV concludes the girls' stories from Part II. It describes the situation as it stands in 2013 and what might be achieved, if we are willing.

I can only hope that I have done justice to the stories of the abused children in this book. Their bravery cannot be praised enough. The scandal of sexual exploitation and of the care system is, as this book's title suggests, unthinkable. It is about time the unthinkable is finally believed, confronted and dealt with. Writing this book made me angry. I hope reading it makes you angry too.

Kris Hollington, February 2013

Sexual exploitation of children and young people under 18 involves exploitative situations, contexts and relationships where young people (or a third person or persons) receive 'something' (e.g. food, accommodation, drugs, alcohol, cigarettes, affection, gifts, money) as a result of them performing, and/or another or others performing on them, sexual activities. Child sexual exploitation can occur through the use of technology without the child's immediate recognition; for example being persuaded to post sexual images on the internet/mobile phones without immediate payment or gain. In all cases, those exploiting the child/young person have power over them by virtue of their age, gender, intellect, physical strength and/or economic or other resources. Violence, coercion and intimidation are common, involvement in exploitative relationships being characterised in the main by the child or young person's limited availability of choice resulting from their social/economic and/or emotional vulnerability.

National Working Group for Sexually Exploited
Children and Young People

Localised grooming is a form of sexual exploitation – previously referred to as 'on street grooming' in the media – where children have been groomed and sexually exploited by an offender, having initially met in a location outside their home. This location is usually in public, such as a park, cinema, on the street or at a friend's house. Offenders often act together, establishing a relationship with a child or children before sexually exploiting them. Some victims of 'street grooming' may believe that the offender is in fact an older 'boyfriend'; these victims introduce their peers to the offender group who might then go on to be sexually exploited as well. Abuse may occur at a number of locations within a region and on several occasions.

Child Exploitation and Online Protection Centre (CEOP)

PART I

1885

'But,' I said in amazement, 'then do you mean to tell me that in very truth actual rapes, in the legal sense of the word, are constantly being perpetrated in London on unwilling virgins, purveyed and procured to rich men at so much a head by keepers of brothels?'

'Certainly,' said he, 'there is not a doubt of it.'

'Why,' I exclaimed, 'the very thought is enough to raise hell.'

'It is true,' he said; 'and although it ought to raise hell, it does not even raise the neighbours.'

> *Journalist William T. Stead interviewing Howard Vincent,*
> *Criminal Investigation Dept, Scotland Yard,*
> *Pall Mall Gazette, 1885*

Stead details how teenagers are being groomed or kidnapped and forced into life as sex slaves, and quotes a brothel keeper: 'I have gone and courted girls . . . and made them believe that I intended to marry them, and so got them in my power to please a good customer.'[1] The series creates a moral panic. The age of consent is raised from thirteen to sixteen. The brothels remain. The abuse continues.

CHAPTER ONE

FIRST DAY NERVES

Name: Natalie
Age: twenty-eight
Profession: outreach worker
Location: London 2006–present

London inhales each morning, drawing in workers through road and tunnel, filling its city lungs.

I squeezed out of the crowded Tube and joined the flow of rush-hour crowds pouring out onto the street. New job, first day. Tired after a restless night. Excited, nervous, uncertain.

My new employer: Ennett House, an outreach charity, trying to help the sexually exploited children of London's inner city.

Katya had brought me here. Katya, fifteen years old, blonde, blue-eyed, small for her age, had turned up at a central London A&E department, bleeding between her legs. She was covered in bruises. The doctors told me she'd been beaten and bruising on her arms was consistent with being held in a crushing grip.

'There's something else,' the doctor added. 'There are signs of old internal injuries, a lot of scarring.'

'You're saying this isn't the first time.'

'There's a significant chance that she will never be able to get pregnant.'

Katya didn't want to talk. The doctor called the police who issued an EPO, Emergency Protection Order, which meant she would go into their care for seventy-two hours, giving us time to find out what had happened and to make her safe.

I looked at Katya and tried not to think about all the other children's files on my desk. I forced myself to focus. The sooner I worked it out, the sooner I could make her safe.

I loved my job as a child protection social worker, even though I often found the work daunting. You sometimes have to argue with people double your age and with ten times your experience; you have to make life-changing decisions and live with your mistakes and the limitations of a system that sometimes leaves children at the mercy of evil.

That was the hardest part. I found it near impossible to accept the fact that we couldn't help every child on our radar. At the same time, this failing fuelled my determination to carry on.

A home visit told us that her two younger brothers, twelve and thirteen, were both well cared for and clean, as was her home. Her parents, from Czechoslovakia, seemed normal enough, although they didn't trust social services, wouldn't undertake assessments, and claimed to be as baffled by their daughter's behaviour as we were. We were persecuting them unnecessarily, they said. They loved their daughter very much.

'The only problem we have is we can't control her,' her father told me with a shrug. 'She does what she wants, when she wants to.'

Katya looked closer to ten than fifteen. She was sweet, quiet and polite and chatted as I tried to build up rapport, talking about school, her likes and dislikes, music and so on.

As we talked, I kept getting distracted by strange beeping sounds coming from the top pocket of Katya's jacket.

'What's that noise?'

Katya shrugged.

'It's coming from you. Is it your phone? Is it playing music or something?'

Katya said nothing and pointed at it apologetically, shrugging her shoulders.

I waited for an explanation. Nothing.

'What is it then?' I asked.

Katya made waving noises as if to make me stop talking about the phone, to change the topic.

'May I see it?'

She took it out of her pocket. She was in the middle of a live call.

Someone was listening in. Her abuser was right there, listening to us.

I got to my feet and started to pack up my papers with added volume. 'OK, Katya, we're going to your foster placement now.'

As I noisily gathered my things I hissed, 'Turn it off.'

She obeyed and immediately looked worried.

'What's wrong?'

'I have to leave it on whenever I'm with someone else, otherwise I'll get into trouble.'

'Well you've been with us for a long time now, so you can say the battery in your phone has run out and you don't have your charger with you.'

Katya looked relieved, smiled and said, 'OK.'

'Why do you have to keep your phone on?'

'It's my job.'

'What job is that?'

Silence.

Legally, I couldn't take the phone from her.

The foster carer was not so constrained, however. She looked at Katya's phone that night and I passed the account number to the police.

It was registered to a nineteen-year-old Afro-Caribbean man with a record of violence and drug dealing, who'd been

arrested – but never charged – for sexually assaulting girls under
sixteen.

I confronted Katya first thing the following morning.

'We've found the guy who owns that phone.'

Silence. She looked petrified.

'Where did you meet him?'

She spoke quietly: 'After school.'

She was in love, she said. He had given her food, clothes, alcohol, cannabis and the phone and made her safe, told her she was
beautiful, mature, old enough to hang out with men like him.

Then he raped her.

Afterwards, he told Katya she was really good at sex.

Men came to the flat. He told her to have sex with them. She
owed him for all the things he had done for her. She would have
sex with them if she loved him, he said, and if she wanted to keep
her phone and other 'presents' as well as have access to a ready
supply of booze and skunk.

Katya obeyed.

She still loved him now. Katya thought being abused this way,
being raped, was 'sex'. She thought she was in love.

Katya had no experience, so did not know any different. Her
abuser had taken advantage of her naivety to trick her into
becoming his slave. She would learn he had taken her love and
trust and abused it for his own evil purpose. It would be a long
time before she trusted another man.

'Were there ever any other girls in the flat?'

She nodded.

'There were others, doing the same as you?'

She shook her head.

'They hung out, smoked and drank.'

'How many?'

'Three.'

He'd been grooming them slowly. Katya was less streetwise and had fallen fastest.

'What will happen to him?'

'We'll see.'

This man had raped her and had passed her on to his friends to rape her. She would never be able to have a baby, yet still she did not see him as a bad man.

Katya went back to her foster carer, for the moment. I gave the address to the police. They said they would pull surveillance from CCTV cameras on the estate where the man lived.

I went to tell the parents. How do you tell a mother and father that their daughter has been raped and turned into a slave, right under their noses?

Be clear, calm and direct.

'Your daughter has been seeing an older man. She says they have had sex. He has given her alcohol and cannabis. She's had sex with other men in his flat.'

They stayed silent.

'I'm sorry. She's safe now, but she has been hurt. It is possible she will never have children.'

Her mother started to cry. Her father had a hand over his mouth. I tried to answer their questions and offer them hope for their daughter's future.

The police got CCTV footage of Katya coming and going from the block where her pimp lived. He was charged with rape and assault and this time he was prosecuted.

Katya stayed with the foster carer, not far from her parents. She would return soon; for the moment she needed help to remove this guy from her head, to change her thinking, give her insight into what had happened, time to process and deal with the emotions.

This was the first time I'd heard of something like this, a pimp controlling a girl with a mobile phone. During the investigation I asked around, to see if anyone else had been through a similar case.

That was when I found Ennett House, an outreach centre that specialised in helping children who'd been sexually exploited.

'Oh yes, we've certainly seen that phenomenon, more than a dozen times I'd say,' Miranda, the centre's manager told me over the phone. 'Some girls have to take photographs of where they are and send them to their pimps.'

I couldn't believe this could happen, that so many girls could end up so hopelessly brainwashed to the extent that they were being remote-controlled.

But Miranda told me there were many more.

'I know this is a bit cheeky,' Miranda said, 'but you sound interested in what we do, and a position has opened up here. Why don't you come in for a chat?'

I was curious. As much as I loved my job, perhaps this was the opportunity I didn't know I'd been waiting for.

Ennett House did not look particularly welcoming. It was a nondescript concrete block on the corner of a busy central London crossroads. The windows were covered and the front door would have looked at home protecting the vaults of the Bank of England.

The lock buzzed, and I stepped into another world. The interior was warm, soundproofed and bright, with colourful photos on the walls.

I liked Miranda immediately. She was half Irish, tall, slender, in her early thirties, open, honest and warm-hearted. Miranda had worked in media and then mental health, raising a family along the way, before a friend mentioned Ennett House twelve years ago. She came to have a look, saw the amazingly positive and effective work that was going on, and never left.

'This is my life's work,' Miranda told me, as we took our seats in a cosy counselling room. 'The work we do is unique, vital and a constant challenge. We never know who's going to come knocking at our door. Even I'm still surprised at some of the cases we get. And, being in the inner city, we have no shortage of girls turning up. This is definitely where all the action is.'

'Do girls just turn up often?'

'Yes. Happened to Beatrice just yesterday. Very sad story, very sad indeed. A hopeless case, some would say. More often, girls are referred to Ennett House via social workers, teachers and police officers. Here, the girls receive the intense support that nobody else can provide; often we're substitutes for failed parents. We're also big sisters, friends and mentors who help them through the system into the real world with, if all goes to plan, a chance of a better future.'

Miranda continued: 'I love it most when we save so-called hopeless cases. Children that everyone else has given up on. Some of these so-called no-hopers have finished school and gone on to find good jobs. I'm still in touch with some girls from a decade ago. Most of them are incredibly thankful and talk about wanting to "put something back". Some have built careers in nursing, policing, social services and the legal business.'

I smiled. I knew many social workers who had chosen a career in care after being helped by the service when they were young – myself included.

'We can't save them all, of course. And right now, we're down to just two practitioners and myself, the manager, so if you do decide to work here you'll go straight in at the deep end; I'm afraid case files are already waiting.'

'I'm used to that.'

'Then there's lots of home visits to check the girls' progress, welfare and that they're going to school – and that means getting them out of bed every now and again. You'll also visit schools, care homes and hostels and take part in group sessions.'

'All sounds good to me.'

'Do you have time to meet the rest of the team?'

'I'd love to.'

We climbed the stairs to the first floor and entered an open-plan office.

'Natalie, meet Mary and Beatrice, Mary and Beatrice, this is Natalie.'

Mary: thirty-something, looked younger, white, short blonde hair, petite and single. Like me, she had a background in child protection and had been at Ennett House for two years. Her desk was covered in photos.

I'd soon learn that she had a huge family with six brothers and was auntie to about twelve nieces and nephews. She was always arriving with presents and cards ready for some family member's birthday.

Beatrice: black, mid-twenties, massive build with the loudest, most boom-tastic voice I'd ever heard. She'd previously worked in local social services with refugees and children, and had been at Ennett House for five years. She was married and had two young children.

Then there was me: twenty-eight, white, curly light brown hair, green eyes, five feet five, sixty kilos, single and an ex-smoker with a penchant for red wine.

'Beatrice knows everyone around here,' Miranda said, 'from criminals to social workers.'

'I know everything, honey,' Beatrice said cheerfully. 'Where the gangs draw their territorial lines, where they like to hang out, who's dealing what, which schools have the worse gang problems, the "good" and "bad" council estates. You need information, you just ask.'

'Thanks.'

'This line of work is incredibly rewarding,' Mary said. 'I can't see myself ever leaving. Before I came here I hadn't realised just how bad things were, and how badly these kids were being let down.'

'What made you come?'

'When I was a social worker I saw a homeless teenager, fourteen years old, put into a children's home where she ended up under the spell of another girl who inducted her into a gang. She got into crack and ended up selling her body.

'Her parents weren't perfect but they weren't drug addicts or alcoholics. If someone had helped her before she ended up in care, if we'd been quick enough and had enough time, then her life might have turned out very differently. I'll never forget her. She made me realise that a different approach was the way forward.'

I nodded. 'So, the dreaded question: how big are your caseloads?'

'Right now we have about ten each,' Mary said. 'You've got some waiting for you, that's if you decide to take the job, of course.'

'Come on,' Miranda said. 'Let's leave these two and finish the grand tour with a cuppa.'

We went back downstairs and through a long corridor to the back of the building. There were a couple of private counselling rooms, a lounge, bathroom and kitchen.

Miranda put the kettle on.

'Everything is designed to make the girls that come here feel at home. Bright colours on the walls, soft furnishings, proper kitchen and bathroom. The key thing here is to be persistent. We keep ourselves linked to these girls any way we can, whether by text or carrier pigeon.

'Many of them are mouthy, resentful and distrustful of adults.

They're defensive because they've had to be. Some are aggressive and set up fights with their peers. These aren't the happy slap variety; they knock out teeth and break bones.

'At the same time their minds are fragile. There's much they don't understand. Most of the time they don't know they're being sexually exploited. Often they think they are in control of the situation, that they are manipulating it to get what they want.

'Their world is very small. Most of them have never left their borough – unless it's in a taxi, travelling to and from a hotel – and have no plans to. They live in the greatest city in the world yet they've never been to St Paul's or walked over Tower Bridge. They have experienced every kind of neglect: familial, educational, cultural, you name it they've suffered it.

'We have to keep our ears open, too. For example, drugs are pretty much a closed world to us, young people simply don't want to talk about them, but every now and again they let slip a little something, a name, address, which one of us may have heard from another girl. That kind of info is important, so we talk about all of our cases and, if it merits, we let the police know.

'If we hear the same male name coming up with different girls then that's obviously important. Same with addresses, hotels, etc. The same addresses do tend to pop up. The girls mention them in passing and it's important that we try and pick up on these.

'My main worry at the moment is that we aren't able to follow girls for long enough. I understand the reasoning behind the six-month time limit but it makes life really hard. This kind of work is long term. We have to stand by these girls for years, so when they've fallen down again we can say: "We're here, let's have a fresh start." We just need to be there like a normal parent, big sister, responsible adult would. They need somebody who's going to stick around and will always be there for them.

'Of course, this is easier said than done, especially when you're dealing with a fifteen-year-old threatening to stab someone and is swearing like a sailor at the top of her voice.

'I see from your CV that you've worked with girls trafficked from abroad to work as prostitutes. But working with local girls who are victims of sexual exploitation is harder, in terms of getting a positive reaction. Girls trafficked from African and East European countries usually leap at a chance of a new life, free of their pimps, so they study like mad. In their countries education is expensive, here it's free and we take it for granted.

'Girls from abroad have often come from towns and villages with a strong community at its heart: they have a model on which to build when they're rescued. The English girls don't. They have such complex and insecure attachments and have suffered such a lot of parental neglect that their perceptions of the world are massively skewed – so much so they often defy belief. They often don't see that they're being exploited; they'll tell you they're in love with their pimp.

'We do lose some, to drugs and to the gangs. That's the way it goes and you have to be able to deal with that. It's hard, you spend months with them and you can't help but get attached, so it's crushingly awful when they fall from our wagon and end up back in the arms of some pimp. When it happens, we talk about it. We're in this together, the girls and us.'

Miranda handed me a tea.

'So, when can you start?'

1908

The 1908 Children's Act includes measures to prevent the seduction and prostitution of girls under sixteen. It is used to convict a woman in 1912 who 'deliberately set herself to bring about the defilement' of her eleven-year-old daughter who was found with a paying client 'in a position of outrage'. The mother is sentenced to twelve months' imprisonment. Her daughter is placed in a care home.[2]

The Waifs and Strays Society publishes a report that says a large part of the problem of 'moral temptation' comes from care homes, where 'corrupt' girls influence others and lead them into a life of vice. Venereal disease is rife in children's homes. It is mistakenly attributed to contamination through the shared use of towels and lavatory seats.[3]

CHAPTER TWO

GIRL NO. 1

'She's a lying fucking whore bitch and if she says any different then I'll ...'

On the other side of the coffee table was Mika, thirteen, Asian, bone thin, hollow-cheeked and on the downward slope of some unknown narcotic's high, possibly speed, her right leg a bouncing blur.

Mika was the wildest girl I'd ever tried to talk to. She looked about ten but spoke like a savvy eighteen-year-old. Her social services record, which began when she was five, was the size of a phone directory, meriting its own cabinet drawer.

Police officers had found her half naked and insensible in a hotel room in West London. No witnesses, no CCTV and with Mika saying nothing there was nothing they could do except to beg her to please stop swearing so much and kicking the back of the seat as they drove her home.

Now she was raging against her social worker.

Mika wanted to make one thing absolutely and 100 per cent crystal clear: she was not a victim.

To anyone who'd dealt with her in recent years, Mika was a hopeless drug addict, interested in nothing but immediate self-gratification, i.e., her next fix of crack, smack and whatever else she could get her hands on, anything from speed to weed. She was known to every police officer in the borough, every one of whom was truly sick of her, thanks to an unending stream of missing person reports, all filed by social services.

They'd tried to work with her at first, to get to her pimps and the men who were raping her, to offer her help but she'd refused, time and again, kicked, screamed, spat and swore. Now, if they weren't duty-bound to react, some officers would have loved to let her be, or would have delighted in charging her with wasting police time.

More than one officer described Mika as feral.

'She's the most streetwise, dirtiest, toughest little shite I've ever had the misfortune to try and get in the back of a car,' one officer told me. 'After she bit my hand I went straight to casualty for a tetanus top-up. I was only half-joking when I asked for a rabies shot as well.'

Mika spoke in a clear, high-pitched voice at twice the normal speed, and used disturbingly effective logic to describe her relationship with the care system: 'Social services say I should be home, so report me missing when I run off. But when the cops bring me home my dad beats me. So I leave. Social come round see I'm not there, report me. The cops bring me home again and Dad beats me. I'm better off without anyone's fucking so-called "help", thank you very fucking much.'

Her father was a short, overweight and violent bully with no time for his daughter. He had wanted a son, not a daughter. Once his wife gave birth to a boy, he saw no point in raising Mika.

Mika didn't like to talk to the police or social services but actually quite liked us. Once she understood we respected her confidence and that we could talk about anything, legal or not, she was happy to sit and chat. Her boundaries had collapsed to the extent that she had no trouble talking about her horrifying sex-capades without hesitation or embarrassment, as if they were just another day in the office.

My predecessor had made a clear note on Mika's file: 'Do not mention the words "sexual exploitation", or try and describe what it is to her. Engagement will be brought to an abrupt, if not violent end.'

We were in the middle of our first meeting and, so far, it had gone quite well. After Mika had calmed down about the social worker's 'suggestion' that she'd been raped, we moved on to other aspects of her chaotic life.

'Do you have any other family?'

'I lived with Gran and Grandad for a bit but that meant I could just run away without the beatings.'

'Why did you run away from them?'

'Oh pleeease, they're sooo old. Still act like they're off the boat even though that was donkeys ago. Not got a fucking clue. I was too into street life.'

'That's when you started hanging out with older boys?'

'Yeah. Started getting high. Fucked a boy on the top deck of a night bus.'

Mika had just turned thirteen.

Under thirteen and any adult who'd 'had sex' with Mika, whatever the circumstances, would be charged with rape, no question. Over thirteen and any adult was free to claim 'mistaken belief' as a defence, that Mika had told him she was over sixteen or even more simply that he thought she was over sixteen.

And, his hypothetical defence lawyer would no doubt argue, that Mika 'gave herself willingly' and 'made all the running' (these are actual quotes, the first from a defence lawyer, the second from a judge).

All the responsibility is placed on the thirteen-year-old girl.

Sentences are lighter for sexual crimes committed against children over thirteen as opposed to under-thirteens. For example, for a single offence of rape by a single offender, the starting point is ten years custody for a victim under thirteen. Over thirteen and it drops to eight years, then to five years if the victim is sixteen or over. The distinction seems unnecessary to me. It is equally bad if a man rapes a twelve-year-old or sixteen-year-old, yet the law defines it as 50 per cent less bad to rape a sixteen-year-old.

That's if one is able to get a conviction past a judge in a case of 'he-says-she-says'. The law is weighted in favour of 'reasonable doubt', which is fair enough, but makes such an argument futile and pointless if the perpetrator is genuinely guilty.

I've seen dozens of under-sixteens with their lives in tatters, while their pimps and rapists remain free to abuse fresh young victims, and I can't help but feel as though there's something badly wrong with the law. I believe passionately in justice but the justice system is not perfect. It is old and unwieldy; a patriarchal system with chauvinistic roots steeped in hundreds of years of history, it is slow to change.

'So what happened in the hotel?' I asked Mika.

'Had sex with this guy and he held me down, innit. He put his hands round my throat and squeezed, like this.'

Mika made a mock performance of being strangled. She laughed.

'Fucking weirdo,' she said. 'He wanted me to say all kinds of stuff but how could I with his hands round me throat?'

Bruises marked the position of her attacker's fingers.

She didn't see it as rape. She really couldn't see any of what she was doing as wrong.

Mika didn't want to change.

I was supposed to write an assessment that showed how Mika was doing, and the levels of risk. This would be shared with police and social services.

I could have summed her up in just one word: doomed.

Trying to get anyone in authority to show an interest in her was, it seemed, an impossible task. Councils, social services and the police tend to focus their attention on under-tens who are suffering child abuse from their family members – which is understandable. It's often easier to solve, at least in the short term (move the children to safety, find evidence, arrest the suspect).

Older children, especially over-thirteens like Mika, are still being demonised as willingly plunging headlong towards their own doom and therefore don't attract the same level of effort. This misconception remains extremely common. Mika's case was just as horrific as any other. Investigating would not only help her, it might help others being used by the same gang, and it would almost certainly prevent Mika from leading any of her peers down the same path.

In 2010, less than 30 per cent of London councils were able to confirm that they met their dual responsibility of working towards protecting children from sexual exploitation and collaborating with police to prosecute abusers.[4] Discussions about foster carers, care homes and secure homes were in progress, with the police very strongly in favour of a care home a long, long way from the Metropolitan Police's boundaries.

For now, we remained Mika's best bet. At least she was talking to us and we were able to dispense advice (she hadn't known about contraception until I explained it to her, and was fascinated) and let her know help was there, should she decide to take it.

Mika, meanwhile, was able to offer plenty of advice and opinion on everyone and anything, including local terrors the 'Area Boys'. Originally based in Nigeria, the Area Boys street gang had been active across London for some years and now took on members from all nationalities.

'The Area Boys, and all the others, they do it to themselves. They self-police, keep themselves restricted to a few streets. They would give the cops double trouble if they stopped fighting one another, ignored the postcodes and got organised. Then they could make some serious dosh.'

'You're not in one of the gangs then?'

'Nah. Not me. They won't have me. I'm out of their league anyway.'

Although Mika came across as a tough know-it-all, there were glimmers of another side. As her comedown took hold, her bouncing leg slowed.

'And what about drugs?'

'What about them?'

'Why do you take so many?'

She thought for a moment. 'That's funny. No one ever asked me that before. Hadn't really thought about it.'

She thought a little longer.

'You know that feeling when you're sick in your stomach and you want to puke?'

'Yes, of course.'

'Well, I feel that, but over my whole body. Like my whole body is about to shake itself to pieces. Every second I'm straight. The only way to make it stop is to take crack, smack, bump*, whatever. If I do enough, it goes away.'

I stared at her for a moment, surprised at this sudden insight.

Mika leapt up. 'Talking of which, I need to go score meself something white and rocky, know what I'm sayin'!?'

'Fine, I'll come with you.'

---

*ketamine, a powerful tranquilliser

1913

A charity documents how young rape victims as young as eleven are made to stand on chairs before magistrates, the press, the clerks and solicitors and tell them, in a clear voice so everyone can hear, the full details of what has happened to them.

A judge tells a sixteen-year-old girl who was forced into prostitution she is 'depraved' and suggests she should be 'restrained'.

The charity describes the treatment of child witnesses in the courtroom as 'highly inappropriate'.[5]

Nothing is done.

CHAPTER THREE

BEGGING FOR HELP

Mika looked at me in disbelief as we walked.

'Seriously, Natalie, you ain't comin' with me to score crack. There's no way.'

I thought our first meeting had gone well but I was keen to spend as much time as possible with Mika – I had a feeling it might be a while before I saw her again.

'That's all right. I'll just tag along until we get close.'

It was a sunny day, and people were marching back and forth to Tube stations, bus stops, offices. By day this part of the city belonged to the high-flyers, market boys, students, artists and tourists. By night it belonged to the pimps, dealers, prostitutes and users.

We passed people from dozens of different nations, all chasing dreams.

Mika grew uncomfortable as we drew close to an estate.

'Seriously, Nat,' she said. 'You can't come with me.'

'I know,' I said. 'I just want you to come back and see me soon, OK?'

'Yeah. You guys are all right, bit weird, but all right.'

I said goodbye, watched tiny Mika wander off to score, and walked back in the direction of Ennett House. I stopped to take some cash out of the hole in the wall, not daring to check my balance, hoping I had enough till payday.

'Got any spare change, please?'

The girl was wearing ill-fitting dirty jeans, tight black T-shirt. She had short dreadlocks, spotty skin and red, rheumy eyes. She looked school age.

Time for an on-street intervention.

'Can I help you?'

'What?'

'You're begging for change, aren't you? I work at Ennett House just around the corner. You know it?'

She nodded.

'You hungry? Have something to eat, a cup of tea, a rest, come on.'

She shrugged. 'S'pose.'

We started to walk.

'I'm Natalie. What's your name?'

'Gloria.'

'How come you're begging?'

Gloria shrugged. 'Need the money.'

I smiled. 'Obviously. For what?'

She shrugged again.

We turned a corner and reached Ennett House. I took Gloria straight through to the lounge, put the kettle on and made tea.

She sat on the soft bright-green sofa across from me. Chin in hands, elbows on knees pressed together. She looked so tired. There's something about young faces that have seen too much, some set of micro-expressions that you're only supposed to get when you're grown up, that at certain moments make children like Gloria look so much older.

Beatrice came in and stopped in surprise.

'Gloria? What are you doing here?'

'You know each another?'

'It's been, what, two years? You must be seventeen now.'

'I found her begging on the street on my way here.'

'What happened to rehab?'

'Closed down halfway through, so I went home.'

'Oh good grief, not another one. So what's happened to you, Gloria?'

Gloria stared at her tea.

'Something happened all right. I don't want to do it no more. But that means I have to beg to get what I need.'

Beatrice sat down next to Gloria. She spoke gently. 'You know you can tell us, right? We don't judge. We understand. We're here for you whatever happens.'

'I was kind of raped.'

'Kind of?'

'Yeah, I was in bed with Darren, my boyfriend, when these other guys came in the room. Darren looked like he was expecting to see them, you know? I jumped up, tried to get dressed, told them to get out but then Darren said to stay.'

Gloria said she was 'kind of' raped because she didn't try to stop them. She was high, naked and outnumbered eight to one.

'You know what?' Gloria said. 'I just wish, more than anything in the world, that I'd never tried crack. But I did and I can't stop. Mum says I sold my soul for that drug and she's right.'

Gloria's first so-called boyfriend put crack in the joints they'd smoke together, so she got the taste. She soon got lost chasing the God-like high.

It wasn't long before he told her she had to pay; she couldn't have it for free forever. She exchanged sex, moved stuff around for dealers and then started dealing a bit before becoming a hopeless addict, selling sex for rocks.

Gloria had come here, looking for help. Miranda managed to get her into a live-in rehab centre.

'And now it's closed?' I asked.

'Yeah, a while ago now,' Beatrice said. 'There's one left, I think, and that's on the critical list.'

Middlegate was the last remaining publicly funded specialist drug rehabilitation centre for teenagers in the whole of the UK before it closed for good in 2010. At the time, they were desperately trying to find homes for the children who had nowhere else to go.

There are no publicly funded specialist drug rehab centres for under-eighteens left in the UK.[6] Considering most addicts discover drugs like heroin and crack during their teens, this seems ludicrous. According to the British Crime Survey, sixteen- to twenty-four-year-olds report the highest levels of drug use.[7]

To begin with their young bodies can take the punishment and the disintegration is, for a while, gradual, so they're less likely to develop major physical problems, and are very hard to find – unless they end up in the criminal justice system.

In 2011 the government's National Treatment Agency for Substance Misuse reported: 'Any substance misuse among young people under eighteen years old is a cause for concern ... fortunately, the number accessing specialist services continues to fall.'

Indeed. Accessing specialist services is difficult when they've been taken away.

There are adult rehabs, but many don't take under-eighteens, simply because they require a different kind of care to adults, and have many other underlying issues – such as child sexual exploitation – that require specialist knowledge.

Treatment for addiction often comes too late, when the user is older, when they can't 'handle' the drugs anymore, when their minds and bodies have caved in, exhausted not only by the effects of their addiction but from all the lines they've had to cross to maintain it. By then it's harder to get them free of the drug. Heroin users are given methadone, and one long-term addiction is exchanged for another.

By the time they're free of methadone they might have been using for twenty years and understandably find it hard to build a 'normal' kind of life.

Intervention with teenagers is hard work and expensive – with a team of specialist carers and therapists, Middlegate cost £3,620 per week per person, so £43,440 to complete the twelve-week course. But every year councils already send thousands of children into private care homes that cost an average of £4,807 per week (around £250,000 per year), spending a total of £1 billion.[8]

And centres like Middlegate worked wonders. More than 90 per cent of the residents stayed clean – and that's hundreds of children over many years. Middlegate saved the UK millions of pounds.

Many people don't believe that teenagers are able to sustain a class A drug addiction. A police officer once told me that a teenage girl could not possibly have a £150-a-day habit because there was no way she could earn that sort of money – more than the officer's basic salary.

On the face of it, this seems logical: let's say addicts spend, conservatively, £100 a day, so they have to find £30,000 to £40,000 a year to fund their habit. So how on earth is a teenager going to manage to make this kind of money?

Through crime.

The easiest way for boys (more often than not) is theft or burglary. Brand-new items sell for one-third of their market value. If they're used, then it's one-fifth. So the average addict has to steal at least £150,000 worth of goods every year. According to the Home Office, there are 306,000 registered drug addicts in the UK (that's the ones we know about). So it works out at 306,000 × £150,000 = £45.9 billion.

Most official estimates (the University of York, for example) put the value at a conservative £20 billion, perhaps taking into account that not all addicts have to steal to support their habit and that girls have another option open to them.

But consider also that, for the police, chasing burglars is expensive. House-to-house inquiries, crime reports and intelligence matching takes about four to five hours to complete, with £500 spent on forensic submissions. Then there's the community support officer and the victim-support team, who all pitch in a few hours at a cost of £500. This means the police can spend £185,000 a year chasing just one drug-addicted burglar. If they get the burglar to court, a trial costs about £10,000 per day. A single burglary trial typically runs for one to two days. If one burglar stopped taking drugs, it could save the country over £300,000 in just one year.[9]

Burglary and theft take time and are better suited to heroin, a slow-release drug, so addicts only have to 'work' once or twice a day to find the cash they need for their next fix. You have to find a suitable property, wait until the right moment and then, once you have the goods, you have to find someone to sell them to, or find a dealer prepared to accept stolen goods in return for drugs.

Crack is far more addictive than heroin and the effects wear off after just a few minutes, so users need to earn cash quickly if they're to feed their addiction. Burglary takes too long. Mugging, on the other hand, takes a minute, hence the spikes in street robbery often seen in proximity to crack houses.

The easiest way for girls to support their habit is to sell their bodies. Often, girls work directly from a crack house, at the very least as close to their dealer or pimp as they can, so they have quick access to drugs and can directly swap sex for a fix.

A front-line police detective told me that in his experience 90 per cent of crime is committed by 2 per cent of the population; 99 per cent of that 2 per cent are addicted to drugs. If we help them get off drugs billions of pounds could be saved.

Letting people use drugs is far, far more expensive than pre-venting drug use or treating addiction through a three-month stay in a rehab centre. And if they get better then they're still young enough to finish school, get a job and pay taxes for the rest of their working lives.

Then there's the cost to parents. After I'd taken on Gloria's case, I got to know her mother. She was in her mid-thirties, wore M&S cardigans and long skirts. She'd raised two daughters on her own after the father vanished. The first sailed through school, col-lecting plenty of GCSEs, then A levels.

'Gloria was right behind her,' she said. 'Then something knocked her off course. I don't know, the wrong crowd I think. I didn't know she was doing drugs for a while. I mean you never imagine your daughter – she was so good. Is so good.'

All of her efforts were directed at saving her daughter. She had to leave her job; it was impossible for her to focus. She says: 'When the police and social services couldn't help, I tried every-thing else I could, advice groups, church, charities, outreach.'

There are hundreds of advisory and counselling charities that can help young people understand drug misuse, offer advice and treatment in the community where they live. The problem is that an addict will tell you what you want to hear but as soon as they leave they go and see their friends, who are taking drugs, and they want to get high.

For class A addiction, rehab really is the only way. If someone's really struggling to get clean, if they're physically dependent, or their community or home environment is too risky, they need to go to rehab. They have to be removed from any area where they can access drugs and put somewhere where they have no choice but to be clean for a long time.

The government's National Treatment Agency (NTA) admits that there are no longer any rehab centres for substance addiction but states: 'There are plenty of residential places for children in need – care homes or secure estate ... There's no problem sending a child with a substance misuse problem into one of these homes where they can get treatment for their problem alongside other problems.'[10]

This is incorrect. There are many problems with this approach.* And just try keeping a teenage crack addict away from drugs in a refuge. No matter how experienced workers in refuges and secure units are it's impossible. Besides the addict, they're trying to stay on top of runaways, violent offenders, antisocial behaviour, sexual exploitation, and so on.

The NTA is also keen to stress that community treatment is the dominant therapy for most addicts (roughly 120 adult rehab centres compared with 1,300 community clinics) for sound scientific reasons, and that rehab should be a last resort. According to a spokesman for NICE (National Institute for Health and Clinical Excellence): 'There's no independent evidence that rehab is any better than other treatments. It says very clearly that it has a role to play in most serious cases, but doesn't recommend it as matter of course and says community treatment is the best bet.'[11]

But for children like Gloria, their community is made up of pimps, clients, dealers and fellow addicts. They do not want children like Gloria to succeed.

'I was back home when my mobile rang,' Gloria said.

She hadn't changed the number. It was her pimp. He told her he missed her. He had some new stuff in and would give her a free bag.

She was found by some older sex workers a few days later, bombed out of her mind, trying to sell her body. Gloria ran away when they called the police.

---

*There's a whole chapter on care homes coming up

A few weeks later, police officers were called to find Gloria, her pimp and a punter brawling in the street. Gloria had 'clipped' the punter. After she was raped, she didn't want to sell her body anymore, so she offered sex, asked to see the colour of the man's money, snatched it and ran. She wasn't fast enough and he'd given her a beating before her pimp arrived to rescue her. She was arrested; she gave a false name and address. She was bailed and never returned.

She showed us her leg – a white and pink serrated scar. A stab wound. A dealer had attacked her for refusing to work to pay off her drug debt.

'I don't want to sell myself anymore,' Gloria said. 'That's why I was begging.'

She wept.

I wanted to help. Despite her mum's best efforts, Gloria wasn't getting better staying at home. But with the rehab closed, where could she go to break free of her addiction?

The answer, everyone thought, was in care.

1922

An influential study reveals that children as young as seven are offering sex for pennies in cities across the UK. Another children's charity worker writes: 'Some of the youngest on my lists have become habitual little courtesans for the sake of sweets or for the money with which to buy them.'[12]

The *Weekly Dispatch* reports that a young army officer on leave was 'accosted 16 times, sometimes by those who appear to be near children' trying to sell him sex. The officer is quoted as saying: 'No healthy lad could long withstand this kind of temptation,' and then the paper adds: 'It is a true saying. They cannot and we should not expect it of them. It is up to us to remove the temptation from their path.'[13]

The 1922 Children's Act removes legal protection for girls under sixteen involved in prostitution. The popular view is that children are sexually exploiting adult males and are therefore not entitled to protection.[14]

CHAPTER 4

THE GIRL WHO DIDN'T EXIST

The B&B didn't look that bad from the road.

Inside, rats scurried between walls, civilisations of bugs lived in the mattresses. And then there was the damp. It felt colder inside than out. My breath continued to condense in the entrance hall. Screaming and shouting came from above, a full-on row between, I presumed, husband and wife.

A child was playing on the first-floor landing below a sign that forbade, amongst many other things (such as unauthorised visitors), playing in the corridors. The door next to her was open. A bed filled the room, leaving a hair's breadth of walk-around space. A young woman was sitting on it, smoking and staring into space.

I'd had no idea emergency accommodation could be like this. I kept going, to the second floor and knocked on Mariam's door. No answer. I turned the handle. It was open. I pushed it wide.

'Mariam?'

The room was empty. No clothes, nothing.

'Can I help you, miss?'

I jumped.

A man was behind me. Eastern European accent, boxer's face, bald, tattoos, smell of alcohol. He held a plunger in his right hand.

'I'm the caretaker. Manager's out right now.'

'I'm looking for the girl that was in this room,' I said, trying not to sound panicked.

'Couldn't tell you about that. I can't keep up with all the people coming and going.'

'But you must know. She's only sixteen, really striking looks—'

'Seventeen people are sharing one kitchen, three toilets and two baths. I spend all my time trying to unblock drains and pipes. I really have no idea.'

'Have you heard or seen anything unusual, screaming, banging?'

He looked up towards the ceiling. The row had escalated to the point that things were being thrown.

'Here, screaming and banging is not unusual.'

I took his point. Living here for any length of time would be enough to drive any family bats.

Sixteen-year-old Mariam, born in the UK, was without ID. She didn't exist. No chance of going to school, receiving benefits, getting a job, finding a home, opening a bank account.

She'd been living like this because people wanted her dead. And she'd been put here for her own safety but no one had come to check on her. Now she was missing and no one was looking for her.

One week earlier

The phone rang. It was an ex-prostitute, now running an adult sex worker service.

'I've just had a sexual health clinic call me,' she told me. 'They're looking after a Muslim girl who's just turned sixteen and got genital warts for her birthday. She's disclosed she's a sex worker and is in fear of her life.'

I grabbed my bag and made for the stairs. 'Where is she now?'

I met her in a West End café. Alone, scared-looking and model-perfect face and skin, she stood out from people staring into laptops, office workers wide-eyed on coffee and tourists dazed by the West End rush.

'Mariam?'

She nodded.

'I'm Natalie. Tell me what's happened to you.'

'I don't want to go back.'

'Go back to where?'

'To the flat.'

'Why not?'

'I love my parents. They were good to me. My father hit me some-times, but only when I'd done something to annoy him. He is a strict Muslim. He doesn't like the clothes I wear, sometimes the things I say, some of my friends and teachers and some of my schoolbooks.

'He misses home. Even though things are infinitely better for us here, he doesn't like it much. Neither does Mum. But we can never go home. After Morocco invaded Sahrawi, they fled to Algeria where they lived in a refugee camp in the desert for many years before coming here. This, to them, this is another world.

'I wasn't beaten often and my parents told me they loved me much more than they hit me. Until now, I think of my childhood as a happy one.

'I met Femi when I was thirteen. He was in my year at school. We fell in love. He wasn't from a Muslim family. This would be a huge deal for my parents. I kept it secret. We just saw each other at school. We were really in love.

'I knew the moment I stepped through my door after school that they knew. They were waiting. Mum, Dad and my older brother Bou. My brother found out through friends at school. I didn't think he would tell but he did.

'Dad asked me. I could not lie. He always knew, I couldn't look him in the eye, and then it was worse. He went to hit me and I tried to run away but Bou held me. Mum watched.

'After he stopped, they left me alone. I ran out of the front door and kept going. A friend told me to go to social services. They called the police. They picked me up and brought me to a police station. They were nice. I didn't say much. They gave me a cup of tea. Then they took me into a room for an interview.

'My dad was there. They asked me if he hit me, with him sitting next to me. What could I say? They were going to send me home. I could not escape. I could feel him staring. I said he never hit me.

'The police said I should stay somewhere else for that night, to let the situation calm down. I went to stay with an auntie and uncle, friends of my dad's.

'As soon as the police had gone, my uncle picked up the phone. He said: "Come and get her." This time, both my mum and brother held me down while Dad beat me. Dad told me if I carried on seeing this boy he'd kill me. I was ruining the family honour. Honour was more important than my life.

'They put me in a different school.

'What can I tell you? Love is as strong for me as it is for anyone else. I would leave school and Femi and I saw each other again. We were in love. Femi left school as soon as he could and got a job working for a taxi company, answering the telephone. He saved his money. We were careful. We kept it secret this time.

'I was fifteen when I found out about my husband, Abdul. My father knew his family. He owned a farm in Morocco. He was twenty-eight years old. When I was sixteen, my father said, we would be married and I would go and live with him there and we would grow barley and wheat and have lots of children together.

'I didn't know what to do. I told Femi. He told me not to worry; there was an answer for everything. Maybe he would get a place on his own and I would live with him.

'After my sixteenth birthday my mum told me to come with

her. I did not know where we were going. On the way she told me we were going to see a doctor for a check-up.

'I ended up in a small room with an old man. He asked me to undress and he looked between my legs.

'He could have lied. He knew what would happen. Why would he tell my mother? I had done nothing to him. I was just a girl. But he told her.

'I was not a virgin.

'Mum lost it. She banged her head on the wall over and over; crying and asking again and again why have you done this to me?

'As soon as we left the clinic I ran. I knew what was waiting for me. My mum and brother would hold me down and this time my dad would kill me.

'I ran and found Femi. We stayed with a friend of his from work, a really nice guy. He said we should get married; then we would have more rights, more protection. But without my parents' permission it was impossible. I was too young. I had to wait until I was eighteen.

'I had to stay hidden. Femi gave me a bit of money but I had no money to get clothes, no ID and I couldn't go to school anymore. No GSCEs. All that work for nothing. Femi said he'd get me a job with him but I couldn't because I had no ID. It was awful. But it was this or death.

'There were happy moments. But mostly I was depressing to be around.

'Femi said I should go back to social services. This time they would listen properly, he said. They were more understanding these days. They knew about honour killings and all that.

'Then he told me he had met someone else at work.

'I couldn't handle this and I ran, just like I'd ran from my mother, the same feeling of betrayal. He called for me to come back but I couldn't.

'This time I was really on my own.

'I wandered the streets, among all these people, but it was like I didn't exist. It is hard to describe how I felt then. Betrayed by Mum and Dad. I had ruined everything with them and then I'd ruined everything with Femi. I'd lost the love of my parents and the love of Femi.

'That night I slept on a night bus. The next day I walked the streets again, lost. I did not know what to do. I could not go to social services. They'd send me back to the police, the police would send me back to my father, and he would kill me.

'It got dark. I was so cold and tired. I looked for somewhere quiet and snuck onto a night bus again. I rode it until dawn.

'Then I walked close to places I knew. Maybe another friend from school would help me. I met someone. He was well known where I came from. Lots of the older kids at school knew him – he sold drugs, all kinds. He was friendly and told me he could sort me out with my own flat. In return, he would send me clients. He was totally straight and open with me. I would have a place to stay and money coming in. I didn't need any ID. Once I'd made enough money I could buy any ID I liked. He said he had lots of girls and they were all doing really well.

'I said yes.

'My flat was in an estate a few stops from the City. There was a murder board outside the block, you know one of those yellow ones with "Murder" written in large black letters, "Can you help?" But the flat was all right. Basic, but dry and warm. Bed, TV, hot running water. I got some clothes.

'Clients wouldn't usually come to the flat. They'd call me and I had to go to them to have sex. The first time was horrible. In a hotel. I'd never even been in a hotel. I had to go straight up to the room. I felt like everyone was watching me, like they all knew. A white man in a suit answered the door. It was at that moment I realised I didn't have any protection. And I didn't know what to do, how to behave. I felt so uncomfortable, so nervous.

'He was uncomfortable too. He smelled of alcohol. It hurt and I cried but he still managed. He left £100 on the table and I practically ran out once I had the money. That was my hourly rate. Half for my pimp, half for me.

'They came, about a dozen a week to start with, most from the City, then some friends of my pimp, local boys who got a special price of £50. My pimp got £40 and I kept £10.

'I hate it. I feel sick every time. I spend all day in the shower. I can't go back.'

Neither of us had touched our coffees.

Stress was killing Mariam. Left heartbroken by her family and Femi, abused by countless men, listening to her story, I was certain she was suicidal. She needed a way out.

'I don't want to go back.'

I agreed.

'To do that, we're going to have to get some help, though.'

'No! I can't go to the police, or social services. I really, really can't do that, not after last time.'

'Let me start by finding a women's refuge, so you don't have to go back.'

I could find none willing or able to take her. They were either full or nervous about her youth and situation. The afternoon was turning into evening. Time was running out.

'Please let me call children's services.'

'No!'

'I won't tell them your name. I'll just explain the situation; make sure they understand, that they get it. That this is a non-negotiable situation.'

I looked straight into Mariam's eyes.

'They'll get it. They'll have to.'

She stared back.

'It's the only option we have.'

She gave a small nod.

I called, and the social worker understood straight away, she was totally on board. The social worker took Mariam to a B&B for the weekend.

Next stop was the police.

I explained Mariam's situation and that I needed their help to go into the flat to get her things. 'They're all she's got. She has no income, she needs her clothes.'

Two officers drove me down in a marked car.

'Forgive my telling you how to do your job,' I said, as we slid through heavy traffic, 'but if you wanted to arrest this character, then you've got a great opportunity. You've got his address, witnesses to his drug dealing and pimping – we know he keeps other girls. You could follow him to other addresses, catch him in the act of dealing, take him off the streets.'

'Is your witness prepared to give us a statement?'

'I just told you what happened before with the police the last time.'

'Then there's not much we can do.'

They also told me that it wasn't that easy, that there was a lack of resources, police budgets had been cut and surveillance was expensive.

The estate could have been anywhere in London. Grey, depressing, grouped in a diagonal row of three blocks. I felt as though eyes were on us as we got out of the car. One of the two officers said, 'I hate coming here,' and his colleague grunted in agreement.

The foyer was cold but clean and vandalism free. The stairs and lifts, too.

I took Mariam's key and opened the door. The flat was almost bare. Nothing untoward. I packed her clothes, a few books, including a Koran, radio, portable TV and her toiletries. Nothing in the kitchen except for some milk, which I poured away.

We each took a bag and walked back to the car.

And that was that. No going back.

And now Mariam was missing. Her stay at the B&B had stretched beyond the weekend into the middle of the following week.

I waited for the manager to return. The building was in an appalling state. In places it smelled as though something had died below the floorboards. Rooms were like little cells; the shower looked like it would leave you dirtier than when you went in. Most of the residents were male, far older and looked to me to be in many different states of mental derangement. The manager, long dark hair, short fat body, hadn't seen Mariam for a couple of days.

I called social services. They hadn't heard from Mariam. Neither had they carried out her assessment, her Section 47. Section 47 of the Children Act (1989) is the key legislative document for children and families. It places a duty on local authorities to safeguard children, and Section 47 states that a 'Local Authority has a duty to investigate when there is reasonable cause to suspect that a child is suffering, or is likely to suffer, significant harm.'

A review of the child protection system, carried out by Professor Eileen Munro, had led to legal time limits for assessments being scrapped. The idea was that the S47 would no longer have to be 'rushed' in order to meet a deadline, giving social workers more time to spend finding out what the family most urgently needed.

Serious case reviews have told us time and again that

teenagers are a high-risk group but all too often, all through society, and most ashamedly amongst professionals, they are seen as
resilient and better equipped to cope with stress than younger
children. This meant that in some cases suicidal teenagers were
left alone in B&Bs or even sleeping on the streets while they
waited for the assessment that was supposed to set them on the
road to a safe future.

A homeless teenager needs to be assessed immediately. They
aren't likely to have much in the way of clothes or money and
people don't decide to sleep on the streets for nothing – gang violence being one reason. The longer the wait, the greater the risk.

I called the police and filed a missing persons report, telling
them to check that Mariam's parents hadn't found her first. I'd
contacted them to update them about their daughter and they'd
already lied, telling me Mariam's mother was dying and that she
needed to come home to say goodbye. Luckily Mariam wasn't
about to fall for a trick like that. I also told the police about her
former pimp. Suppose he'd found her, or she'd naively decided to
go back to him?

There weren't many places Mariam could have run away to.
She had no money. She couldn't get benefits without ID. She
couldn't get a passport because no one had known her for more
than two years and could not countersign. No one, not her teachers, family or doctor had been prepared to say that Mariam was
who she said she was.

She was alone in a world in which she didn't exist.

1936

The *Daily Express* publishes the first of a series of articles about sex trafficking. Headlined 'Mystery of Britain's Vanished Girls', it describes how increasing numbers of runaways are making their way to the big cities, particularly London, where they're preyed upon by pimps who, through threats of violence and/or peer pressure, force them into a life of vice.[15]

Mr F. Sempkins, the secretary of the National Vigilance Association, warns girls arriving in large cities to choose their girlfriends carefully, and 'avoid like the plague those who boast of boyfriends, of places they know, and good times they have'.[16]

CHAPTER FIVE

THE BENDY BUS HOTEL

'Can't get no peace in a crack house.'

Malki, sixteen, is one of London's lost children. No up-to-date record of her exists – no school, no GP, no social worker (her case has long been closed). With no address and a crack habit to support, Malki comes and goes as and when the crack demands – and like hundreds of others she doesn't know how to keep appointments (or how important such things are to social services).

Tonight, I'm worried about Malki. She's been turning up regularly at Ennett House, almost every other day, but now I haven't seen her in over a week.

'They come and go without rhyme or reason,' Beatrice said.

This is true, but every once in a while you get drawn to one of the girls that comes in. I don't know why. Hope, maybe. Or perhaps you see something of yourself in them.

Malki once told me that getting any rest in a crack house is impossible and that she sometimes slept on the N29 bus. Mariam had also mentioned she slept on the night bus when she was at her most desperate. So I've decided to venture out and take a post-midnight ride on the N29 to see what I can find.

I've told Paul, the bus driver, what I'm up to and sit near the driver's door.

'Some drivers don't let them on, the homeless, like, if they can help it,' he says.

The bus is eighteen metres long. I admire Paul's driving. I find

London's streets challenging in my little ten-year-old Daewoo. He always stops, even though he knows they don't have Oyster cards. If you slip through the doors way down at the back, Paul won't know if they can pay or not and, as inspectors don't work in the small hours, they can sleep on the Bendy Bus Hotel for free.

He stops, more homeless get on among the drunk, the shift-workers and the sober readers. They're easy to spot. Wrapped up in clothes that don't look like they've been removed for a while. Most have large bags, stuffed full. They hug their bag and drop their head immediately. It's almost impossible to believe, but the bendy buses are a moving hotel – for hundreds of people.

'Most people hate these buses,' Paul says, 'and the mayor says they're going to go next year. But when they go, the homeless are going to miss them big time. People on here aren't all junkies. They might have lost their job because of cuts, been kicked out for getting behind on the rent, or split up with their other half and just walked out. It frightens me. I don't make a fortune. If I lost my job, in a couple of months I could become one of these night-riders.'

It's February, bloody cold and I find riding the bus exhausting; as we twist, the announcements come, the noisy doors letting in cold air. Suddenly, at Camden, it fills with lively young people, drunk and high, clowning around, shouting and in two cases, singing. The sleeping don't move. If they're awake, they don't show it and they go unnoticed by the revellers who, I am certain, would be as surprised as I am to learn that there are now more than a dozen homeless people on the bus. Lost in our own thoughts and worries, it's easy to miss what's right in front of us.

Malki suffers from anxiety attacks. God knows what she goes through on here, what thoughts and memories pass through her mind. She's been using crack since she was fourteen and has a record of theft. Her situation is painfully familiar but extraordinary at the same time: parents separated, mum an alcoholic, dad – on heroin – moved in with a younger woman, also into heroin in a big way, and her little boy.

I think of her sitting here, out of her mind, watching London float past, from the lights of the West End to the cosy suburbs of Enfield; distant, alien lands.

The bus has quietened by the time Paul's snaked it as far as Wood Green. Serious sleeping time. No sign of Malki or Mariam. I decide to do the return trip and then out once more.

I'm sitting up front with Paul and watch as he exchanges a few words with one guy who actually has a Freedom Pass – the golden ticket to bendy-bus nirvana.

'I know some of them now,' Paul says. 'Some have been homeless for years, some just a few weeks. New faces all the time. Last month, when we had that snow, it was rammed in here. Not all of them homeless but some just couldn't afford to heat their homes. Others say this is better than the hostels. Some couldn't sleep for the fear of what was going on around them.

'You're out late at night. It's cold. Everything's closed, the Tube, the railways. Where's warm? The night bus. Takes an hour this time of night. Sleep's interrupted for sure but it's better than being out there.'

'You're performing an extra public service,' I said. 'Like a moving hostel.'

'I see it more like a secret club. I've got a lot of regulars and they'll look out for one another, sit close, check on each other's stuff. I feel like we're all in it together.'

I smile. The bus is being used for a totally different purpose, so far removed from what it was intended to do it's hard to believe it's true – but then hard-pressed Londoners tend to come up with the oddest solutions.

Malki's mum had thrown her out. She'd grown up hanging out with the sons and daughters of drug addicts in her neighbourhood. Playing hide and seek then going home to drug deals, strange men and women hanging about outside, chatting to the full-time look-outs (aka 'uncles') while her parents waited for the dealer to get back from wherever he'd gone.

And it wasn't long before Malki was using class As and, without money to finance her addiction and too frightened to steal, she slept with the man who became her pimp.

'He could do what he liked as long as I had rocks to put in my pipe.'

She'd been drifting in and out of crack dens for a year.

We reach Victoria. London is quieter now but still the bus fills with homeless.

'Is the 29 a special case? Is it like this on all the night buses?'

'Yeah, other drivers say it's like this.'

The charity Thames Reach interviewed 214 homeless people who used the Bendy Bus Hotel – a fraction, they said, of the total number of night-riders.[17] They were divided into thirds: British, Middle and Eastern Europeans, and immigrants from the rest of the world. The charity managed to help more than sixty into permanent accommodation.

Yet another small group doing their bit for our forgotten citizens. So many people help, yet so many more need helping.

I was on the N38 a week later when I spotted Mariam. She was so thin. She trembled with fatigue and hunger as I sat in the seat in front of her.

She cried when she saw me.

'Mariam, you can't stay here.'

She nodded, wiped her tears away. She'd decided to sell her body, stand in the street and wait, to get money for food, clothes, a mobile phone, credit and eventually a place to stay. But at the same time she became terrified, by the pimps, other girls on the streets, not to mention the men who wanted to have her, that she couldn't go back. She'd been surviving on free food from a Hare Krishna van.

'This time,' she said, 'I cannot go into a B&B.'

'Don't worry,' I said, 'we'll get it sorted, I promise.'

The next day, with Mariam sleeping in the lounge, Miranda and I hit the phones, dialling all around the UK, playing the care home lottery, hoping we'd get through at the right time, when someone had a place free in just the right area.

To my delight, I managed to secure Mariam a place in intensive supported accommodation (with staff present twenty-four hours a day) in a quiet town not far from London. She was very happy and relieved to have somewhere safe to stay at last. She received counselling and support from the workers there, one of whom was prepared to countersign her passport application.

Her new life had begun.

Over the next few months, when I got the chance, I rode on different night buses. I never found Malki, she simply vanished, as many do, but I did find, talk to and tried to help others.

For example, on the N38 (Victoria to Walthamstow) I found Marcus, seventeen. His mother had fallen prey to crack, as did his older sister, who followed her mother's example and ended up selling her body for crack. She was taken into care, leaving Marcus living with his mother in what had become a very popular crack den – what with the promise of mother and daughter sex. Marcus got ill, developed a series of infections that had baffled doctors. After he turned sixteen the police stormed through the door and he was placed in an adult homeless person's hostel – with class-A drug users all around him. It was only a matter of time before crack's God-like high blew his mind and sent him out onto the street, stealing to survive.

Sixteen-year-old Stephanie was riding the N253 (Tottenham Court Road to Aldgate). She'd been on the Child Protection Register for years. Stephanie had been bullied and beaten by her older brother. Her new stepfather did nothing to stop this and, in fact, simply joined in. The police were often called to her home to break up fights. Her mother blamed Steph for the fights and threw her out. Homeless, Steph was offered a bed for the night in exchange for sex. She started taking crack. She returned home and when her mum refused to let her in she begged for a coat. Her mum said no. A few weeks later, when the bendy bus came to the end of its route, Steph didn't move. The driver called 999 and Steph was taken to hospital, suffering from malnutrition and pneumonia. Once she'd recovered, Steph was placed in a care home. She later ran away from the care home and returned to the bus. It was safer, she said.

I found Jane on the N8 (Oxford Circus to Hainault). She was thrown out of her home after being beaten by her mother. The council's housing department put her in an adult homeless person's hostel where, encouraged by others, she turned to crime to make a living. After a short period in a youth detention centre, she disappeared from the care system and spent her nights sleeping on a bus. Since the bendy buses' departure, night bus sleeping without a travel pass has become almost impossible, except for a lucky few who rely on sympathetic drivers.

They all circulate, in the night buses, and in and out of the system.

1938

The Association for Moral and Social Hygiene reports: '... surely when the girl is only 15 and the man is 29 or 35 years of age, some emphasis might be laid on the responsibility of the man as borders on the girl.

'It seems strange that men who are 15 or 20 years older than the girl concerned ... should be told by the judge that they are more sinned against than sinning, or that he should say that the girl is a danger to all young men, or that she is of such immorality that every decent man and woman is shocked.

'In several of these cases the girl gets three years detention in a home, and the man is acquitted or bound over.'[18]

CHAPTER SIX

WAYS OF ESCAPE

On the sixth floor of the block, Beatrice pounded on the door with her fist.

'Hannah!'

She checked her watch.

'Hannah! Seriously, I'm not going anywhere!'

Beatrice was an expert in the tough-love mother role and knew the minds of the girls we worked with better than anyone. She threw herself at each new case with she-who-dares-wins determination and atom-smashing energy; woe betide any obstacles foolish enough to block her way. Beatrice had brought me along, for the experience. I kept back as she whacked the door again. It rattled on its hinges.

'Coming to this estate is always "interesting",' Beatrice told me before bending down to the letterbox.

She cautiously pushed her fingers against the flap and peered through it from a safe distance.

'Just in case of a mop handle,' she said.

'Hannah! You'll be late for school!'

Through the mottled glass I saw a figure appear in the hall and approach the door in the shuffling, floor-dragging zombie steps of the just awakened.

'There you go. You just got to be persistent,' Beatrice said. 'The message is: we're here to help and we're not going away until you agree.'

The door opened.

Hannah, fifteen, sleep in her eyes, hair like random volcanic extrusions, grimaced, turned and shuffled back down the hall, mumbling.

Six weeks earlier, at 1 a.m., a police officer found Hannah outside an all-night garage in what he reported to be a 'confused state', which didn't do her condition justice. Hannah didn't know who she was, let alone where she lived, and her trousers were soaked with blood.

She'd been gang-raped, part of an initiation by the Area Boys. Hannah, drugged with alcohol, cannabis and who knows what, could remember nothing. The police thought the gang had probably panicked at the amount of blood and dumped her somewhere near the service station.

Trapped in their postcode, with boundaries marked by streets, parks and schools, there are gangs all over London who expend great amounts of energy guarding their territories from one another. To cross the boundary is to invite physical attack from rivals. Trying to understand the world of London gangs is beyond most people, even the police can't keep up with changing members, names, loyalties, aims and specialities.

A few years ago the Block Gang (which had absorbed the Mad Souljaz, Abbey Wood Boys and associated with the still independent Ferrier Boys from Greenwich) began a gang war with the Cherry Boys and then the Woolwich Boys. The front lines were the borders between Greenwich, Woolwich, Abbey Wood and Bexley.

Add to this mix the somewhat confused ethology of Racist Attack (incorporating Young Racist Attack for under twelves) made up of white British youths who (despite dressing, speaking like and enjoying the music of black rappers) attacked any non-white, non-British gang. Hopelessly outnumbered, Racist Attack's destruction was both rapid and violent. Survivors quickly ditched their principles and sought protection by joining the very gangs they had previously poured hatred upon, and found themselves racially oppressed minority members. The Nike was on the other foot, so to speak.

During the chaos of senseless war, as the Block Gang, Cherry Gang and Woolwich Boys fought one another and, as all three gangs united against Racist Attack, innocent people suffered, none more so than eighteen-year-old university student Philip Poru, shot dead while in a car with his friend by members of the Woolwich Boys who suspected he may have been a Block Gang member. Poru, who was not from the Block Gang, was on Woolwich Boy territory.[19]

Perhaps the only thing all the gangs had in common (apart from a love of violence and mutual hatred) was how they treated the young girls who lived within their boundaries.

In 2010, London's Metropolitan Police reported that gang rape had risen from thirty-six cases in 2004 to ninety-three in 2009. Attacks by larger groups were increasing and the average age of both attackers and victims were falling. In 1999 48 per cent of victims were under nineteen. This increased to 64 per cent in 2008, with 36 per cent aged fifteen or younger.[20]

This is how girls are initiated into the gangs – whether they want to join or not. Hannah's rape was very likely filmed and photographed, useful for blackmail and humiliation. It's all about power and control.

Boys are influenced by pornography, easily accessed by anyone with Internet access.* Porn's saturation of the Internet

---

*Sixty per cent of eleven- to sixteen-year-olds have Internet access in their own rooms, compared with 30 per cent six years before. These figures appeared in a cross party parliamentary report published in 2012, which found that four out of five sixteen-year-old boys and girls regularly access porn online, while one in three ten-year-olds has seen explicit material. The government has asked the major Internet service providers to force new customers to 'opt in' to adult content as opposed to the current system of 'opting out' by installing filters. No ISP has done so at the time of writing.

has normalised scenes that would have once shocked. Gangs recreate these scenes and film everything so it looks just like what they see online. Sharing the material is expected, encouraged and praised and spreads far beyond the gang. Taking part in the act, especially in gang rape, creates strong bonds within the gang and mutual respect for one another's masculinity.

For the younger girls growing up in the same area as Hannah, the threat of rape was something they were going to have to face at some point. There was no escaping it.

Beatrice knew many of them.

Kayisha was in a thirty-strong gang, wanted to get out but saw no possible way. They threatened her eleven-year-old sister, saying they were going to do her. Kayisha could choose, 'It was either her or me.' And if she still resisted then they would go after her mum. Kayisha was 'sexed in' and in return for their 'protection' and the privilege of membership, she gave them sex and held drugs and weapons for them.

There was 'baby mother' Mia, mum of one of the gang's kids. Her mum had wanted Mia to have an abortion, so she could focus on school; she was a bright girl.

Taheisha was a 'link', not a gang member, but she would have sex with them if they demanded.

Sherryl was a sister, in the gang by default because her brother was. You had to show loyalty.

Roshawna was a 'tough girl' with an I-take-no-shit-from-no-one attitude. She could fight, cut her hair short and dressed like a man. It worked in that none of the boys wanted to try to have sex with her, but it did mean she had the perpetual problem of proving her 'masculinity' through drinking, drug abuse and violence.

At the other end of the scale, Quanesha was a girlie-girl, dressed like she was in a pop video, wore gold, make-up and made sure she was the possession of the gang leader, whom, she said, had 'mad swagger'*. He had an obligation not to let himself become a cuckold – she was his and nobody else's.

There are still so many girls we aren't able to reach, that we don't know about or simply won't engage with us. It is estimated that 12,500 girls and young women are closely involved in gangs in the UK, and that a further 12,500 live in fear of them. Most of them are in London. Areas of social deprivation have the highest levels of gangs. A 2008 study uncovered forty different gangs in just one borough of south-east London.[21]

We knew that boys aged fifteen to seventeen were targeting girls between the ages of thirteen and fifteen. We knew some of their nicknames and ages from what the girls told us but not much more than that. These boys were linked to older criminals who were making serious money from drugs and vice, and who saw these girls as a useful commodity. Once they're in, gang life over-rules everything else; the girls start staying out at night; some might go missing from home for three or four days at a time, then a week, then ten days. By this time the older criminals have become involved. They take the girls to parties all over the UK. The young gangs have broken them in, now the older ones put them to work.

Some of these girls are full of themselves to start with. Suddenly their lives are exciting, like in some rap videos, older men are paying attention to them, buying them food, giving them drink and drugs, designer clothes and driving them to parties where they're welcomed like the star of the show – which they are. Even so, burnout comes fast and hard. The physical and psychological stress is impossible for most to cope with for long.

They soon learn that they don't want a drug habit; they don't

---

*In other words he was, relative to anyone else his age in the area, rich and powerful.

want to get drunk every night; most of all, they don't ever want to let themselves be raped ever again.

But there is no escape.

Sometimes a girl is put into a care home. But the gangs know where they are. They wait outside, bombard them with texts and catch them – along with other girls – as they come out.

Girls like Hannah are seen as property and tools, to be used as alibis, decoys, information gatherers or to hold drugs and/or weapons. They are given a choice – do what the gang says or be raped: *their* 'choice', *their* 'decision'. Once the girls know the boys are serious about rape, they don't even have to say it anymore: 'I need you to look after these drugs [If you don't we'll rape you].' The girls see it as a fact of life. It's the only life they know.

Many don't feel like victims. Some adapt and turn their situation into a warped version of popularity and success. They don't see themselves as being passed on from man to man, but as breaking up and going out with new boyfriends. They say they want to go to these parties and sleep with men, they say it's their choice and they're making a living from it, when it's anything but.

All of them are carrying anger. We see the results all the time. Some fight the weaker boys; some fight other girls, or total strangers. For some, the anger bursts out of them at unexpected moments, in a seemingly random manner, even if they don't consider themselves to be victims.

Gang rape was Hannah's first sexual experience. Badly injured, she gave her first police interview from her hospital bed. She wasn't able to tell them much, nor did she want to.

With no evidence and no witness statement worth a damn in court, there was not much the police were prepared or able to do. Life resumed except that now, for Hannah, everything had changed. Until her rape, Hannah had been a good student, not a blemish on her record. After, her schoolwork slipped, then she stopped going to school altogether.

The gang was waiting for Hannah's return from hospital, ready to start exerting pressure but, thanks to Beatrice's presence, they were wary. It's delicate work; the last thing you want is for your intervention to make the girl's life more difficult.

'Can we come in?' Beatrice asked.

Hannah spoke through a yawn. 'Who's your little friend?'

'Natalie. She works with me. I'm just showing her around.'

'Come in if you want.'

We followed Hannah down the hall.

'When did you go to bed?'

'Please, you're not my mum.'

'When?'

'Late, all right. I dunno, it was late, all right?'

'Hannah, it's not good that you're tired going to school. What would have happened if there was no one here to wake you?'

'Yeah, but I knew you was coming. And yous never quit, innit?'

'OK, but you've got to get ready. We're late already. Where's your mum?'

She shrugged. 'At her boyfriend's.'

Hannah's mum had raised her daughter well but didn't always set the best example. And although she'd been there, in tears of horror, sympathy and anger for Hannah after the rape, she didn't want to talk about it anymore. It was, as far as she was concerned, in the past now: you had to get on with things. She too had faced horrible events in her life and that was how she had coped: put it behind you and move on. It's understandable. We're not always mentally equipped to deal with life-changing events, and placing them firmly in the past can allow life to continue.

But Hannah was struggling. She didn't want to talk, which

suited her mum, whose attention was focused on her new boyfriend, but that didn't mean that Hannah was coping or that gently cajoling her into talking wouldn't help. Beatrice was there as an alternative parent, the one who'd perform the tough roles of motherhood – one of which was banging on a door for a half an hour just to see that Hannah was OK; the other being ready and willing to talk about anything under the sun – and without a shred of judgement.

'So what did you do last night?'

'Nothing much.'

'So how come you went to bed so late?'

'Couldn't sleep, so watched TV.'

'When you've finished your GCSEs you can watch as much TV as you like but right now you have got to study. You can stay up late to study if you want.'

'I'm stressed, you know? My head hurts all the time. I can't think with all this shit going on.'

'I know. It isn't easy. But you know I'm here, don't you?'

'I know, innit. I can call or come see you whenever I like. I know. Thanks. But what are you gonna do to stop them? You, my mum, the school, the cops, can't stop them. They're not going anywhere.'

'I can't make them vanish from your life. But I can be here. I'm a text or a phone call away, day or night.'

The threat of self-destruction loomed over Hannah.

Beatrice was in the strongest position to help. Unburdened by state mandates, police policies, she was there to listen without recrimination. She would only offer positive reinforcement; tell Hannah she still, even after everything, had a chance.

Hannah knew it too. But she needed constant reminding. That was why it was so important for Beatrice to bang the door hard and long.

As we walked, Hannah stayed silent and hunched, a frown on her face.

'I feel like there's eyes on me every time I step out.'

'Just one day at a time, sweetheart,' Beatrice said. 'Every day is a victory. Every day you're at school is a step closer to where you need to be.'

Beatrice knew only too well the kind of life that was waiting for Hannah if she succumbed. She would be there, no matter what.

1943

Basil Henriques, chairman of the East London Juvenile Court, says that the teenage girls he encountered in his court were 'attracted to anybody in uniform, particularly a soldier who can afford to give them a good time'.

At this time the youngest prostitutes are based in Stepney in London's East End. It becomes the focus of runaways from outside of London, and for London girls who abandon school.

According to a local doctor: 'We had thought it (the prostitution of children) couldn't happen here ... so it was a lesson to the over-complacent that eternal vigilance is needed to maintain a decent standard of conduct in any State. For the first time, the London authorities have opened a unit of fifty beds for girls under sixteen with venereal disease.'[22]

CHAPTER SEVEN

SUSPICION HOLDS
YOU TIGHT

Nikki arrived with a suitcase at our front door. It contained every-thing she had, including school textbooks.

'Where have you been?' I asked, taking the case and leading the way to the lounge.

'Living rough. Slept on the night buses. Driver let me sleep on one when he locked it up for the night. Spent my last 30p on the loos at the train station to get clean, do my make-up and get a drink of water.'

Nikki had wild, Amy Winehouse-style hair that looked even wilder after her stay on the night bus. With her make-up, adult clothes, figure and nose and lip piercings, she looked much older than fifteen. She was also exhausted and starving.

'How long have you been living rough?'

'Over the weekend.'

'What happened?'

She lifted her top. Red and blue bruises covered her ribs. I could also see her left eye had a lurid yellow bruise, partially hidden under make-up.

It was 9.30 a.m. I called the police. They said they'd be over as soon as they could.

We knew some of Nikki's history. Her biological father had raped her and her younger sister. He was in prison, finally, but her mum really knew how to pick them, these bruises were from Mum's new boyfriend, Phil. Even worse, we suspected Nikki's mum was pimping her. Unfortunately this was all it was: a suspicion.

About a year earlier, Customs officers stopped Nikki from travelling on her own to Cyprus. Unable to explain exactly where she was going, who she'd be staying with and for how long, the officers refused her permission to fly, cancelled her passport and called the police. Nikki's mum said it was all a mistake; that her aunt was supposed to fly with her but hadn't turned up, had got the day wrong. The police saw their nice flat, Nikki's younger sister playing happily and left it at that.

If you're not looking, if you don't ask the right questions, then you won't see what's in front of you.

We also knew that Nikki moved home with her mother and younger sister every few months, each time into a large furnished flat. They had iPads, large TVs and Xboxs, shopping delivered by Ocado, and an account with John Lewis, yet Nikki's mum didn't have a job.

Nikki wouldn't tell us anything more about her home life, except that she didn't want to go back.

If I could, I would have put her in the London Refuge, a short-term shelter for teenagers in trouble, financed by St Christopher's and the NSPCC, as well as a couple of other charities. The London Refuge was run by experienced respite workers and was fully independent of social services. We had an excellent relationship with them and could book kids in the same day. They'd be able to stay in one of the four bedrooms for a week or two, while we researched their lives and worked with social services and the police to make sure they had a chance of a safe life by the time they left.

Unfortunately, thanks to a loss of funding, the London Refuge closed in 2010. It was the last of its kind.[23] Now we often found we had to try to sort out kids who arrived at our door in crisis that same day. We had to call the police and social services and hope they'd have enough time to talk to the family, find an available foster carer, or a care home with a bed.

The police arrived with a social worker at 5.30 p.m., eight hours after I called. This was a girl who'd been beaten up badly enough to run away from home and sleep rough for an entire weekend.

Police officers come in all shapes and sizes, from the blood and guts officer who loves to feel some criminal collar, to the cowboy in the area car who's seen too many buddy cop movies, to the fast-tracked bureaucrats and, the category that these two fell into, cappuccino cops.

They were dressed in designer suits, the woman wore a pencil skirt and heels, so clearly wasn't really ready to chase criminals on foot or to rush to the aid of a colleague in danger. The man held a huge, pint-sized paper coffee cup; his eyes were already so wide he looked like some crazed drug addict – and he could neither stand nor sit still.

We took our seats in a counselling room. Nikki was asleep in the lounge.

Female officer: We've been to visit Nikki's mum. She's filed a missing persons report and she wants Nikki to come home.

Male officer: And we don't see any reason why she shouldn't go home.

Me: But she's been beaten up by a grown man.

Female officer: Well, he does have an awfully big bite mark on his hand.

Me: But he is an adult. Nikki is thirteen. She's covered in bruises.

Male officer: Mum says he's only there on weekends. It's a week-day.

Female officer: We think she should go back.

Social worker: The situation's not perfect but we don't have a better option right now. Besides, Nikki's mum has said she's prepared to engage with us.

Me: (getting desperate) Until they move home. If we send her back there, then can you guarantee her safety?

Female officer: (sighing as if talking to a child) Well, can you really guarantee anyone's safety?

As a charity, in these sorts of situations, we were completely dependent on social care. If the child wasn't half dead and bleeding from knife wounds, and if the mum wanted them home and the police and social services were prepared to let them go, there was nothing we could do.

As much as I wanted to, I couldn't blame the cappuccino cops. They had untold cases on their files, they just wanted to solve the problem as fast as possible so they could get back to the case of the four-year-old who'd been raped by his uncle.

Ditto for social services. I knew what it was like working in child protection in central London, running from one case to another, hoping to snatch a piece of your own life at the end of the working night, which is, no doubt, suffering in all sorts of ways from the 'bloody job'.

So with two bodies too busy and the third powerless to help, we talked to Nikki.

She would go home. We would be in touch and we were always here for her if need be. Social services would come and visit. And that was all.

She took it well.

'Thank you for sorting this out,' she told me as she left.

I watched her head towards the high street with the social worker; straight back into the situation that had made her desperate enough to come here for help.

1948

It is revealed that children of both sexes have been trafficked for sex through unregulated private adoption agencies for almost thirty years. Some were 'adopted' dozens of times. The fitness of the adopters and their home were not questioned. Thousands were passed from their parents to complete strangers, often in exchange for money. Tens of thousands of children were adopted during this period.

The 1948 Children Act outlaws the adoption of female children by single men. It does not outlaw the adoption of male children by single men.

Children's charities cite many examples of single men purchasing boys of all ages for sex. Dozens of cases are reported:

A mother who handed her thirteen-year-old daughter over to a young married man who then left town. She was found by an NSPCC inspector in a 'common lodging house ... where she had been for a fortnight with a young man, twenty-four years of age (not the one to which the girl was originally given).'

A ten-year-old girl was adopted by an unmarried couple. They slept with the girl in the same bed. She gave birth to the man's baby. Authorities later found the baby's body buried in the back garden.[24]

The law is not amended.

CHAPTER EIGHT

THE SONG OF THE SOCIAL WORKER

Anne was one of my favourite social workers. She was in her early forties and had developed an extremely gloomy worldview that was sometimes so extreme I wasn't always sure if she was being serious.

This line of work could darken your mindset after a while, but I think Anne tended towards morbidity long before she signed up. I could only guess that her doom-and-gloom outlook was her way of coping with the disaster scenarios that unfolded in front of her each day. Nevertheless, she took grim realism to the next level, even for our profession.

She had the build of a decathlete, always wore a dark jumper and trousers, black trainers (social workers always need to be ready to run for their lives, she said) and carried a large black bag slung over her shoulder. Not many people, male or female, would be prepared to take Anne on, physically or verbally.

Anne was on her lunch break and decided to stop by to update me on a couple of cases and to let me know that Nikki's return home had gone well. We grabbed a quick cuppa and sandwich in the lounge.

Anne had taken over Nikki's case after the other social worker quit.

'She married the Holy Grail,' Anne explained.

'Rich husband?'

'Banker. She now does charity work, gratis.'

'So how are things with Nikki?'

'No sign of the father and the mother at least made all the right noises.'

'Did you believe her?'

'That she made the right noises is the best I could have hoped for. As for believing her? Well I wouldn't call her a liar to her face, for the moment at least. Nikki's definitely on the edge in terms of being taken into care, as far as I'm concerned.'

'You will keep me updated, won't you?'

'I shall. Your project is a dim light amongst the darkness and confusion of modern day social care. It seems half my cases these days are CSE [child sexual exploitation] related, and so I appreciate the help and effort and – sorry hang on.'

Her mobile had started to ring.

'Hello. Yes. So he's not coming in then. Right. Thanks. Bye.' She threw the phone back in her bag.

'Bad news?'

'Can't remember the last time I answered the phone and it was good news. There's a pair of fresh files waiting for me on my desk. My manager is off for the day. No discussion. Deal with it. Damn. I had planned to spend today writing a report and two core assessments.'

'How's your caseload?'

'Well, the maximum officially recommendation is fifteen. My actual caseload is, right now, forty. If we were going to bring that down to the level recommended by Lord Laming we'd need about another fifty experienced social workers. You haven't got any hiding in here, have you?'

I smiled.

Lord Laming had made the case for a minimum number of caseloads in his 2003 inquiry into the death of Victoria Climbié. He also recommended that, when allocating cases, managers must ensure social workers are clear what has been allocated and what action is required. According to Anne, these recommendations haven't, in the ten years since they were made, met reality.

'We deal with what we're given,' Anne said. 'You know what it's like. No amount of training can prepare you for the real world. It all goes out the window and you fight as best you can to get the work done. All of us already work evenings and at weekends to meet deadlines for court and child protection processes. We've stopped moaning to one another and work in grim silence, saving our strength for arguments. None of us mention the B-word*.

'I have two fantasies. I dream of walking out of the door, going home, packing a bag, taxi to the airport and vanish. The other is a variation on this where I win the lottery and I fly somewhere exotic. Instead I have conversations with my boss where he tells me I'm not closing enough cases quickly enough. For example:

'"*Manager*: You've had this Robinson case for weeks. It's too long. Why haven't you closed it yet?"

'"*Me*: Not all cases take the same amount of time. Some are tougher than others and they have to be seen through."

'"*Manager*: But there are new cases coming in every day. If you can't take any of these cases, then someone else has to take the slack. It's not fair and you're letting this happen too often."

'"*Me*: Don't judge me on my speed, using a handful of difficult cases. Look at my work overall. Look at the results."

'"*Manager*: You know it doesn't work that way. There are numbers, requirements we have to meet."

'"*Me*: Can I ask you a question?"

'"*Manager*: Of course."

'"*Me*: What about all the cases I put away under your time limit? There've been at least seven cases I can think of that I've

*burnout

closed in a fraction of the time, compared to this one, and with good outcomes. I've saved the department several weeks' time. How about we take that time into consideration when dealing with the more difficult cases?"

'"*Manager*: This meeting is over."

'I hate my boss and I don't hate my boss. He has to allocate the cases that come in and I hate him for it. But if he doesn't, then we end up being punished for having poor performance scores. Scores shouldn't matter but kids don't count, numbers do. Bad numbers mean we're not working hard or well enough. Even worse, bad numbers leads to visits by inspectors. And once they start inspecting you never get any work done – and they sack "underperforming workers", whatever the hell that means. Most social workers I know leave after two years, after they get the B-word. I've been here three and a half.'

Anne listed main reasons for leaving, in no particular order:

1. Increasing caseloads of increasingly horrible and depressing cases.
2. The associated sense of overwhelming helplessness.
3. Way too much admin carried out during unpaid overtime on antique, unwieldy operating systems.
4. That never-ending feeling of dread that you've missed something (because you have, it's impossible not to) coupled with the stress of trying not to hurry cases and people that cannot move at the pace you want them to.

'I have heard tell of some authorities – I am sure they are mythical – who have such things as protected caseloads and – heavens above – overtime is paid if someone goes above their allocated amount. As I said, I am not sure whether they actually exist.

'Anyway, somehow in the middle of all this, we're trying to

ensure effective care planning for children. Talking of which, have you read the serious case review on Khyra Ishaq?'

I hadn't read it, yet. The report, into how various agencies missed chances to save a seven-year-old girl from being starved to death by her mother and stepfather, had just been published.

'Do you know how many cases Khyra's social worker had at the time?'

'No.'

'Fifty.'[25]

'Good God.'

'Yes. And the press let this fact slide on by. They stuck to the party line: social services are to blame. And I suppose we are, but only because we're not bloody superhuman.'

All too often, when the press publishes stories about social workers who have messed up, sometimes with terrible consequences for a child, blogs and comments from the public flood in. They unite under Facebook groups in the name of hatred and call for the social worker to be hanged by the neck, or urge them to commit suicide.

What would you say if you personally knew that social worker being lambasted in the press? That she saved you from violence, neglect or rape when you were a child? That she had fought to make your case heard? That she had found you a placement with a loving foster family? That she was the first person to listen to your mum and worked with her to help her overcome her heroin addiction and keep the family together? That she challenged the police over charging your mum for something she did when she was high, so that you could stay with her? That she fought to keep your family together when the teacher, police, solicitors all thought otherwise?

For everyone out there, whether you hate or love social workers, if something happens to you or your family, they come running to help.

Every social worker I've known has had the noblest of intentions (and every social worker certainly starts out that way) and has done his or her absolute best, making difficult decisions, sometimes in the face of lies, misinformation or lack of information – all the while carrying with them the nagging fear that something may have been missed, ready to become terror the moment it becomes reality.

The harsh reality doesn't match their noble intentions.

'My husband knows better than to ask me what my day was like,' Anne said. 'Besides, I couldn't do that to him. Why should he have to deal with the trauma my job brings? But although I don't talk about it, I can't forget it. It's made worse precisely by the fact that I care so much. The emotional and mental cost is too high. I'm just a hamster on a wheel. Try and imagine dealing with forty different families, all with varying needs and differing approaches to cooperation. Try and remember their names, not to mention the names of friends and relations. My husband's solution is for me to leave my job.'

Nearly every author of every serious case review says that the caseload of the social workers involved was 'excessive'. But they know the harsh reality won't allow them to be reduced. The Social Work Task Force was set up to undertake a comprehensive review of front-line social work practice and to make recommendations for improvement and reform of the whole profession, across adult and children's services. They decided against a national limit for caseloads, arguing that employers should be responsible for capping them according to the complexity of cases.

'So that's my working life. It is what it is. But I'm still frightened that one of these cases is going to leap out and bite me and it'll be me in the newspapers, with people demanding my head on a platter.'

1952

A report into a Manchester remand home for 126 girls aged fourteen to sixteen is published.

Six of the girls were pregnant and sixty-four were suspected of being involved in 'immoral behaviour'.

'Many pick up or are picked by men in the streets of Manchester and then go to houses which are being used as brothels. Many are initiated by older women, perhaps between twenty and thirty, who have degenerated into prostitutes. There are usually about one or two a year who have been definitely procured by some woman – in some cases the girl's own mother – who owns the house in conjunction with a man and they come to court, the man for living on the immoral earnings of the woman and both for keeping a house for immoral purposes. Many houses are known to the police, or suspected by them and the girls are found actually with men during raids on the premises.'[26]

CHAPTER NINE

WHAT I THINK AND FEEL

Anne saw us as a useful resource and sometimes brought us cases, one of whom was Janine, a fifteen-year-old girl in foster care. Janine had lived with neglect and abuse for years and didn't like to talk about her feelings, but her school counsellor called to say that Janine had had a breakthrough of sorts, and had disclosed some disturbing new information.

There'd been a couple of verbal questionnaire forms, freshly photocopied and lying in two piles in his office. Janine had arrived early for her meeting and, while she was waiting, something had made her fill them out and leave them behind. When the counsellor arrived, he found the forms and no sign of Janine. She'd once been a top student and it was clear there was nothing wrong with her writing skills.

The first form involved finishing simple sentences, e.g., 'What I like best is—'. There are no right or wrong answers; it's used to help teenagers express their thoughts and feelings, giving the therapist some insight into the anxieties of the young person they're trying to help.

Janine had described how she liked 'smoking weed', how she hated her 'boyfriend's mates' and how grown-ups didn't understand her, or bother trying to. She wrote that her mother 'wished I'd never been born,' while she imagined her teachers thought 'I am a waste of space' and that other children in her class thought she was a 'slut'.

Janine described how her father, who was separated from her mother, showed no interest in her life, while her mother just made her feel 'angry and unloved'. Her siblings, who were doing comparatively well at school and in life in general, made her 'feel ashamed'. She had no friends in which to confide.

She usually 'ran away' when her mother tried to get her involved in family activities, and similarly ignored her teachers' efforts to get her involved in schoolwork – she 'ignored' homework and was 'frightened' of her textbooks. Janine ran away to be by herself but when she was alone she did not know what to do, which made her even more frightened for her future.

In the second questionnaire, which examined feelings, Janine described her fear of her 'boyfriends' mates', how she 'had' to do whatever her boyfriend wanted and that 'smoking weed' helped deal with her fear and anxiety, but only when she was 'high'. The rest of the time she remained frightened and sad about the way her life had turned out, accompanied by the constant dread of a bleak future. She said she was lonely, cried all the time and had nothing to live for.

Finally Janine wrote how angry and upset she felt after 'five of my boyfriends' mates had sex with me'.

When Anne caught up with Janine at her foster carer's and showed her the forms, Janine broke down.

She didn't know how to tell anyone, she said. She didn't think it would do any good anyway but her head hurt so much, she was so lost, confused and frightened that she thought she was about to go mad. She didn't even want to drink and smoke weed but the more wasted she got, the less she thought about her life, her situation and the future.

'The counsellor asks me all these stupid little questions. How am I feeling? How can I answer that when I don't know? It just suddenly started to come out when I started filling in those forms.'

Her answers had been short, powerful and true.

When Anne was ready to leave, Janine's foster carer, a middle-aged woman in her fifties, followed her to the pavement.

'Can I have a quick word?'

'Of course, what is it?'

'I walked into the bathroom when Janine was in the shower the other day.'

Here we go, Anne thought. If she's seen injuries on top of this, that's the rest of the day gone.

'She had tattoos.'

'That's it?' Anne replied, relieved. 'That's what you're worried about? Tattoos? You know how many teenagers have tattoos these days?'

'Um. Well, there were lots of them. And these aren't like any normal tattoos I've seen anywhere before.'

'How do you mean?'

'They're um, very ... sexual.'

'Sexual? In what way?'

'Erm. There's a large picture of a devil masturbating, it covers the whole thigh and his, its, er ... member is huge; it reaches around to—'

'I get the idea. So there were others?'

'Yes, I couldn't see them all clearly but on her stomach, back, legs.'

'Were there any fresh ones?'

'Well, the devil one wasn't finished; hadn't been coloured in. The others were. They all looked very expertly done.'

'OK, thanks for telling me.'

'There's something else. My mother is in hospital with a terminal illness and I'm not sure ...'

She broke off.

Anne nodded.

'I'm so sorry to hear that. I think, in light of today's revelations, I need to reassess Janine and get her out of London, to a secure care home, or at least a care home that's a long way from London, nowhere near a train station and with crap phone reception.'

Anne was ready to discuss Janine's case, among others, at the mid-morning inter-agency meeting but there were no-shows from the police and the Crown Prosecution Service, which was fairly typical. They had just as many cases, and statistics-based performance reviews besides. The last thing they wanted to deal with was a multi-agency meeting, a mass collision of paperwork and agendas – and yet it's the lack of multi-agency work that's criticised in serious case reviews.

After the (non) multi-agency meeting Anne set the wheels in motion to get Janine moved to a care home a long way from London and prepared a report to fax to the police so they could start investigating the rape. Then she turned to the deep pile of Section 47s. There were so many she could barely look at them. She sat, paralysed for a few moments by the sheer volume. One section at a time, she told herself.

Then, an urgent call.

The police had been called to a domestic. A fourteen-year-old girl who assaulted her father disclosed to a police officer that he'd sexually abused her. The officers had arrested the father and he was at the station undergoing forensic tests, including penile swabs, undressing on a large white sheet, putting on a white paper suit (aka a 'rape suit').

Father–daughter rapes can be hard to prove. The law accepts the possibility of DNA transference as a result of the fact that they're living together. Sandra, the daughter, was with the police's child protection team, about to undergo a memorandum interview. In the meantime Anne needed to find a foster carer. Sandra had a history of bunking off, turning up for classes in dirty clothes and occasionally smelling of alcohol. She'd been in trouble for fighting with other pupils and for shouting at her teachers. All classic signs of the consequences of abuse.

Anne grabbed her bag and was out the door, texting her husband a familiar message as she walked.

<Don't wait up>

The S47s owned the night.

1959

The Street Offences Act 1959 and the Sexual Offences Act 1956 are made into law.

Intercourse with a girl under thirteen years of age: maximum penalty life imprisonment.

Sex with a girl between thirteen and sixteen years: maximum penalty two years.

Loitering in a public place to sell sex: maximum penalty two years.

Encouraging the prostitution of a girl under sixteen: maximum penalty two years.

The Acts fail to distinguish the ages at which a young woman may be charged with offences of loitering and soliciting.

So, women legally unable to consent to sex were prosecuted for attempting to sell it.

The Act leads to the organisation of child prostitution in the 1960s, through cafés, clubs and massage parlours.[27]

CHAPTER TEN

THE PLACEMENT

I was in the lounge with fifteen-year-old Sandra. Mediterranean skin, bone thin, large brown eyes, full lips, small nose and high cheekbones. Tight black jeans, white T-shirt, brown jacket.

Sandra was here to confess.

Another runaway, this time from her foster parents. Another one of Anne's cases.

With fostering, a child is offered, and then it's up to you. It's always a heart-fluttering moment, listening to the details, knowing that a scared and/or angry child is waiting to learn their fate and that they could be with you in just a few hours.

Debbie said yes straightaway. She was forty, married to Jim, a senior civil servant. They had a son, Will, sixteen, and Emma, fifteen, and lived in a large home in Stroud Green, North London.

Sandra was their second placement.

It was Will's birthday and dinner plans were abandoned. He didn't mind. He knew that his mum had wanted to be a foster parent since she was a little girl. An unusual ambition for one so young, but Debbie's dad had been raised by foster parents who'd taught him to reward society when it had been kind to him, something he passed on to his daughter.

Debbie was calm, empathetic and perceptive. She knew there was no A, B, C guide to being a great foster parent; everyone's different and brings their own set of skills to childcare and some kids are easier to get on with than others.

To start with, Sandra was quiet and polite. Debbie knew this would change. For the moment, Sandra was just grateful to be in a calm environment, where money was not a worry, where she was far removed from threats of violence, fear and sleepless nights.

There would come a time when she'd be ready to test the boundaries of this new world, and any psychological trauma would emerge in 'difficult' behaviour. Debbie looked forward to it. The sooner problems emerged, the sooner they could be dealt with and, hopefully, healing could begin.

When a young stranger is granted instant access to a family's inner sanctum, the family dynamic changes. At dinner that first night family conversation had a slightly muted quality. They discussed the usual subjects – school, work, family and TV shows – but not quite in the usual way.

It grew a little awkward at times. There was little common ground. Will and Emma were both near the top of their classes while Sandra hadn't been to school for almost a year. The kids were reluctant to quiz Sandra about her friends, family and school, as the answers would not be straightforward. These topics would have to be dealt with in Sandra's own time.

At least she ate everything on her plate.

When Jim got up to do the dishes, Sandra's mouth fell open in amazement.

When Debbie asked why, Sandra replied: 'My dad never does the washing up.'

Debbie saw from Sandra's expression that she'd forgotten for a moment that her dad was the reason she was here.

Quick change of subject. Debbie suggested the kids take Bernard, the bear-sized family dog for its evening walk.

Once Jim had finished the washing up, they sat with Sandra. Jim and Debbie chatted about their lives – everything from Jim's job, their kids, how Jim proposed to Debbie, to how long they'd been married, so Sandra could get a feel for who they were.

They told Sandra that they would always be there for her. That she could tell them anything. That she should be honest and they would repay that honesty with faith; that they would stand by her 100 per cent no matter what.

Sandra nodded, said nothing. Debbie had a suspicion then, a mother's intuition perhaps, that she still didn't know Sandra's full story.

Two weeks in, they met Sandra's boyfriend, seventeen-year-old Matt, tanned, thin and good-looking. Debbie had already found out that Sandra had a boyfriend. Sandra talked on her phone a lot. Whenever it buzzed she dashed to be alone but Debbie had overheard enough to realise there was a boy in her life.

From that day, something changed.

Walks with Bernard, who Sandra had grown to love and to whom she fed extra biscuits whenever she thought no one was looking, came to an end. Sandra helped herself to Debbie's make-up, started skipping school and smoking, and Debbie caught Sandra on her mobile in the small hours.

Sandra always remained quiet and polite, however, and as soon as Debbie brought up any of the above, she didn't shout or deny, just apologised.

Then Jim overheard her planning to get fake ID so she could go clubbing. He thought it was quite normal for a teenager. He was the same when he was her age. Besides, the law said they couldn't lock her in her room or take away her phone, so all they could do was to keep talking to her, advise her what they thought was best and stay patient when she decided to ignore them.

Jim said there was a limit to what they were able to achieve. They had to accept that. Debbie told him this was easy to say, much harder to do, especially, Debbie thought, as they'd made such little progress. Sandra still barely talked.

Will and Emma got on fine with Sandra, Debbie said, only because they exchanged a couple of words at a time. Sandra made it easy for them. They'd got used to her and were carrying on with their lives without interruption.

'And what,' Jim asked, 'is so bad about that?'

'You know what I mean. Something's not right, I just know it. I feel like we're being used.'

'Well, we are foster parents.'

'Something's wrong. All this silence is driving me mad.'

One month in.

Taxis stared picking Sandra up, to take her to Matt's, she said. A week after the first taxi they started coming every other night. Then Sandra didn't come home.

They called her mobile. She answered and told them she'd be home in the morning.

She arrived sporting a dragged-through-a-bush-backwards look, wearing new jewellery, different clothes and smelling of alcohol and cigarettes.

Debbie tried to talk to her but still Sandra said nothing. Debbie called the cab company and asked where they were taking her. The telephonist checked on his computer and told her the cabs were taking Sandra to three different addresses over thirty miles away.

Then she got a phone call from Anne. Anne told her that she'd just had a meeting with the police. Sandra's boyfriend was one of a group of men under investigation for the sexual exploitation of children.

Debbie started to feel light-headed. That man had been in the same house as her teenage daughter.

Anne said they hadn't known until the police had got in touch.

It was a huge operation, they said, and there was nothing they could do in the meantime to stop her from seeing Matt.

Sandra did not think she was being exploited, would not give evidence nor would she help them in other ways.

Legally Debbie and Jim could not prevent Sandra from leaving the house. A parent would have a better chance, but obviously they could not send Sandra home as her father was under investigation.

Debbie said she couldn't get her head around this. Anne said she would look for another family, further away.

That wasn't what she meant, Debbie said. She didn't want to let Sandra down. But at the same time she felt so helpless. Debbie struggled with the idea that she couldn't stop her.

'Every night Sandra is with you,' Anne said, 'is a night we know she's safe and secure. That's better than where she was before and the best we can hope for right now.'

'All we can do is keep trying to make her part of this family,' Jim said afterwards. 'Perhaps if we do that she'll want to stop.'

They watched as the taxis came and went. Debbie, one of life's great carers, worried so much that she stopped sleeping. She struggled to understand that Sandra was, over her own free will, going to work for a pimp, and yet there was nothing anyone could do to stop her.

Two months in. It was almost Christmas.

Anne gave Sandra our details. Said she should look after her sexual health and that we were the people to talk to.

She came.

And she talked. I think it had something to do with the fact that she could leave whenever she wanted, physically stop the conversation and exit the building.

Matt wasn't her boyfriend. She was going out with Naddy, a real man, she said. Naddy was a Rastafarian who pimped her out to clients to keep him in cash and weed. He paid for the taxis, clothes, cigarettes, cheap jewellery and gave her cash so she could buy her own make-up. Naddy told her he was glad she was with a kind foster family; it made things very easy for him.

It was a few days before Christmas when Sandra arrived at our door, in a bad way. We sat in the lounge; I asked her what happened.

She started to cry.

'You don't have to go, you do realise that, don't you? If you ask, there are people who can help.'

'I'm sorry,' she said, 'I'm so, so sorry.'

'About what?'

'I don't want to go anymore. The last time it . . .'

'What?'

'It was really awful. Oh God, I feel so bad. I lied. I lied to every-one. I'm so scared. I made a terrible mistake. I want to put it all back the way it was but I can't, how can I?'

She was weeping now. In between sobs she blurted it out, the truth that had been weighing on her.

'My father didn't do anything. He never touched me. He thought Matt was my boyfriend, didn't like him and wanted to put a stop to it. Naddy told me to say Dad raped me. He said I'd go into care then we could see each other all the time. Dad would be questioned, there would be no evidence and they would let him go, but by then it would be too late, I'd be in care, then we'd have all the freedom we wanted. I didn't know that I was going to have to do what Naddy made me do.'

Her father returned, but to a very different world, one in which his daughter had betrayed him for another man. He had lost his job, his friends. They could not believe that his daughter would make up something like that.

And Sandra couldn't go home now, not after what had happened. She couldn't be left where Naddy could get to her, either. Sandra was placed in a care home, far away from London.

Debbie hadn't wanted to let Sandra go. She wanted to keep her promise: that no matter what they would stand by her. Jim told her it was not her fault; there was nothing she could have done differently. They hadn't known the full story. Nevertheless, a sense of shame lingered, a belief that she'd failed her charge. She was heartbroken.

Jim tried to reassure his wife.

'Try not to worry. Sandra is in a care home now, she'll be safe there.'

PART II

1969

The *People* newspaper publishes an investigation entitled 'Schoolgirls on the Game' and claims that under-aged girls, dressed to look older, were commonly involved in prostitution in 'almost every city in Britain'. One girl was fifteen and still at school. She picked up her first client, a forty-year-old man, when she was thirteen after her friends said 'they were doing it'.

'They thought I was chicken because I had no experience. So I went with the man to prove I was their equal.'

Once caught, those under seventeen could be sent to a children's home but as the article said: 'Too often at such institutions the not-so-intelligent young girls are influenced by the old hands and there is no saving them.'[28]

CHAPTER ELEVEN

SARAH'S NEW LIFE

A new flat. Her own. Her first proper home. Shame it was in such a shithole of an estate.

No curtains over the windows, worn and pitted concrete floor and a boiler older than she was that made more noise than the Tardis. Nevertheless, this flat was the peak of a long ascent from the land of drug addiction.

Sarah looked out over the estate: four blocks, six flats high, arranged diagonally to one another. She wondered, as she did every day, why, as she was once a crack addict, had the council put her here? Drugs of every kind are all around in the real world, they'd said at the drop-in, so you have to be able to cope.

The flat wasn't much but everything worked and it was dry and warm. Equipped with a small grant, she'd bought sofa, small TV, wardrobe and bed; pots, pans and plates; fridge, food and bedding, all from a charitable depot that helped people like her.

That done, she sat in it, alone. Eighteen, bored, depressed and lonely. The TV told her that another, alternative reality existed but she didn't know how she was going to make the leap from here to there.

'Militant' Sylvia (so-called for her socialist leanings and for lending her considerable weight to anti-government protests every week) was a forty-something ex-casualty nurse who now ran the drop-in. She explained that Sarah was not alone. They were all alienated. Society had cast us aside, she said, and didn't want us back.

'I think you've got a warped sense of self-worth,' Sylvia, herself a former addict, clean twenty years (although now addicted to biscuits), told her. 'You're frightened that people will laugh at what you say, and that what you say and think isn't worth sharing. You're scared that people only love you for your looks.'

Sarah knew she needed new friends. None of the old ones. They were all still out there, still using, if they were still alive.

She washed her face, lit a roll-up and put on the kettle. She opened the fridge. No milk. Nothing at all, in fact.

Even though she knew exactly what was in it, she checked her purse: £9.97. A week till benefit day. Poverty was no fun. She was too young to get any benefits worth having; too young, underqualified and unskilled to get anything more than a minimum wage job, not enough to live on.

She made a mental shopping list:

White Pasta (that turns from rock to rubber after fifteen mins of boiling).
Cheese (a bargain-basement block shot full of preservatives, that tastes nothing like cheese).
White Bread (when you roll it up you can bounce it off the wall).
Margarine (all the slippery, oily trans-fats required for an early death).
UHT Milk (white water that tasted of Pritt Stick).

Eating healthily was beyond her means.

She pulled on some clothes, emptied the kitchen bin and opened the front door. It was 11 a.m. She went to put her rubbish in the chute and discovered a human turd on the floor.

'Fucking junkies. Fucking shithole.'

She didn't like the coffin-sized lifts, so took the stairs, trying not to breathe too much. The caretaker tried but there was no beating the urine. It only took one junkie who'd been shooting up in the temple-like peace and quiet of the sixth floor stairwell in the small hours to stagger into a corner and take a swaying leak. It trickled and dripped down through the night; dry by dawn, and the smell remained for ever.

Sarah was on level six. The dealers were on five and four. Five for grass, four for the hard stuff. It was a mild sunny day but Sarah went with her hoodie up.

Sarah was beautiful. And that had always been a problem.

At school, when boys' eyes had started to slide in her direction, she'd shyly smiled at the occasional comments. After all, it was supposed to be flattery, wasn't it? She was desired and that felt good.

The many and varied propositions eventually grew tiresome. Sarah did not know how to play along, so said nothing and avoided their hungry eyes.

One boy, Kev, pursued her for months, but his dream grew ever more distant, for while Sarah grew tall and shapely Kev remained short and became spottier. He did everything he could think of to impress and romance: gifts, promise of the time of her life. Sarah got so used to saying no she couldn't have said yes if she wanted to.

Finally, after she rejected his declaration of love on Valentine's Day, Kev lost his temper.

'Why do you do this to me?' he demanded. 'After all I've done for you. I've bought you presents, told you how beautiful you are. I'll do anything you want.'

Sarah snapped. 'What am I supposed to do? Give in to you just because you think you're trying extra hard? Just because you want me?'

Kev became her worst enemy. He spread rumours and insults.

She heard herself referred to as a dry, cold-hearted bitch, especially when she didn't respond to whistles, the occasional bark and comments about her bottom, breasts and legs.

She found refuge with older boys. Her looks made it easy. They liked having Sarah around and they made her haters shut up. She was protected. They treated her like an adult, shared their drinks, then their drugs, skunk then coke, which she took and then, after a while, they demanded sex in return.

Sarah knew all about drugs. Both of her parents were heavily into coke and skunk, although her mother had always warned her against them. She didn't want to give the older boys her body. But she wanted – no – *needed* the coke, so she stole from her parents – and ended up taking the lot.

With her mother's urging her father beat her – you DO NOT touch Mum and Dad's stash.

Sarah left home, threw herself into the drug-dealing crowd and let her beauty take her to the top, to Tray, the biggest and most psychopathic of the dealers. She was swept up in the same raid that saw Tray put away on multiple counts (including torture) and, as her parents neither wanted her nor cared about her, Sarah was taken into care.

She lived with other girls who, she knew, bitched about her behind her back, because she was so beautiful. It was her beauty that had made her so alone and she hardly talked to anyone.

Levels two and three were exclusive to the over-sixty-fives and were secured with proper entry systems. There was no getting through those doors. They kept intruders out, but the old folk were marooned. The estate was on a large patch of open grassland. There was a large, open car park and a row of shops across the road, beyond the public loos.

For an old person, that was a serious trek, like crossing a desert where gangs of bandits lay in wait in the dunes, preying on the pension-heavy caravans of the elderly. One old woman had encountered a delirious crack-head in the corridor. He sexually assaulted her. She hadn't left the building since.

Returning with her shopping, Sarah spotted two sawn-off Coke can bottoms, the centre burned black where they'd cooked up. Three hypodermics lay in a cluster by a tree just outside her block, one with its point uncapped. They hadn't been there when she left.

It was 12 p.m.

Sarah's mouth watered at the memory of the taste of crack, the delicious high that obliterated the meaningless of life, that solved all the problems Sylvia said the government couldn't: social isolation, fear and dread of an empty future.

Sarah didn't have money. She didn't need it. She had her beauty. Currency that was good anywhere.

She wasn't the kind to only do a small rock here or there each day. She was the three-day solo binge, no food, sleep, ten grams per twenty-four hours, kind of girl. There was nothing social about her addiction. She lost everything before – including herself, her weight, her hair and clear skin.

Crack gave her a high but she had never felt so low than when she was using. When she stopped she'd never felt better. But still the drug called. It felt good to be wanted. She knew it would feel good to give in, let it take you and stop living.

The cans and needles were signs that the first fix of the day was complete. Now the addicts were out on the town again, doing whatever needed to be done to raise the money for the next life-solving hit: shoplifting, burglary or selling their bodies. Repeat in the evening and then late at night. Wee in the corridor, poo in the privacy of the rubbish room and then to bed, ready to do it all again the following day.

A teenager in a red baseball cap, T-shirt and tracksuit bottoms was on the stairwell as Sarah climbed, puffing. He was rolling a joint from the grass he'd just scored, a quality test and one for the road at the same time.

He checked her out. She pretended to ignore him.

Through the red fire door and into the corridor, just wide enough for one with a shopping bag. Her door was of unpainted MDF, the concrete around the frame was cracked and broken; the previous tenant had been 'evicted' by the police. The door didn't fit properly and Sarah had to kick it while holding the key turned all the way to the right.

She made tea, lit a roll-up and looked out of the window, to the east. A view of crowded rooftops, a motorway full of cars. A town shrouded in haze in the distance.

'Fucking Rochdale.'

Her case was closed. Tray was gone for life. She'd chucked her SIM cards, forgotten names and the 3 a.m. numbers, the ones she could call when she was really desperate.

She was on her own. Alone. Lonely. Depressed. She'd have to do something, otherwise she'd go mad.

1976

A man is convicted and sentenced to six years in prison for actual bodily harm against a fifteen-year-old girl, having unlawful intercourse with her and for living on her immoral earnings. The girl had been in the care of a children's home when she met the man and began to work as a prostitute, giving him all of her earnings.

In court, she said: 'He invited me to his home and was nice to me. He told me he wanted money to buy a car and asked me to help him. I agreed.'

She earned at least £100 a week, working every evening and weekends, for a total of five months. She continued working despite being cautioned under the Street Offences Act and despite social services being informed.

The girl told the court: 'I lied to the police to protect him as much as possible. I don't know why he had such a hold on me. He would be nice but he was horrible when he was angry.'

A local paper also quoted the girl as saying: 'Another time I left a note saying I wasn't going to work for him anymore but he came and found me at the corner of my road and told me if I ever stopped working for him he would run me over with his car.'

Two other girls from the same children's home, both aged fourteen, were also working as prostitutes. The *Daily Telegraph* reports that one of them, arrested for soliciting, was three months pregnant.

More cases of care-home children selling their bodies on the streets emerge.

A local paper interviews a policewoman: '... she had seen many thirteen- fourteen- and fifteen-year-olds on the streets of Manchester, trying to undercut the older girls by only charging 50p instead of the usual £5.'[29]

CHAPTER TWELVE

THE PCSO GOES FOR A WALK

Alan the Police Community Support Officer, forty-seven, rotund, sharp-eyed, close-cropped grey-white hair, had a regular beat. Every day he made the same bet with himself: how many burned cans, foils, pipes and needles would he find? How many runners and addicts would he pass?

Starting at the clock tower, he spotted the ten-year-old white kid on a mountain bike, one of the YIvA's* runners, talking to a black teenager.

He walked east, past the clock tower, took the next side street and walked south, towards a new-build estate. A small crossroads. Each corner heavily salted with cigarette ends. A couple of balls of foil. Unpeeling them, Alan saw they were black in the middle. He sniffed and nodded. It was a crack and smack dealers' drop-off zone with four escape routes should the local plod bother to show their tired faces.

One needle halfway up the long alley in front of the temple. Balls of foil in the alley behind the dealer's house: one, two, three. Lad with cap pulled down low, dirty grey jogging bottoms, on his mobile, sitting on the wall between trees and bushes outside the Sally Army.

He nodded hello to two old addicts who knew the score. Their fix, freshly bought and already consumed, meant they were free to beam happily back at him.

*Young Invisible Army

Another one outside the Drapers Arms.

The two black men waiting to score in a car by the tower blocks stared back at him with contempt.

In a bush in a new pedestrianised estate a hundred metres from the tower block was a needle.

In front of the tower block: three hypodermics in a cluster by a tree, one with its point uncapped.

For the seventh time, he dug out his blue gloves, carefully picked the needles up and dropped them into the sewer.

Alan looked up. He knew drugs of every kind were being sold in there. And he saw the girls coming and going, all times of day and night. They usually gave him the finger, swore, laughed hysterically and ran.

Alan was a former army sergeant who'd barked orders with so much enthusiasm that he'd developed vocal chord paralysis, which made shouting impossible. Honourably discharged, Alan thought he might try the police. He was too old for the regulars but, if he liked, he could join as a PCSO. It had to be better than sitting behind a desk getting soft.

He tried to tell the 'real' cops but they didn't do anything. They didn't know, didn't want to know, they just let it roll. Alan wondered, as he did every day, just what was the point of this job?

1976

A deputy director of a regional social services department is quoted as saying: 'Many of them [child prostitutes] want somebody to care about them. The hardened pro knows very well the client doesn't care at all but the young girl is likely to be looking for affection.'[30]

CHAPTER THIRTEEN

THE CUCKOO MEN

Name: Ben
Age: fifty
Profession: outreach worker

We parked the transit on the edge of the estate. This was the Magic Bus, my very own local outreach group. Even though I was fifty and looked like a not-so-hairy version of Hagrid, but with worse teeth, I got on with most kids. They had a chance to inform us about what was happening in their lives and on the estate while having a sandwich, soup and/or cuppa and digestive, or if they were extra lucky, yours truly's very own bolognaise sauce with a buttered white crusty roll.

This estate was home to some of the most troubled souls in the north-west of England and was one of eleven estates in the area that had been struck off the council's regeneration list a few months earlier (in other words, abandon hope all ye who live here). Industry was still in decline. Youth unemployment was up. Hope was down.

'All right, Ben?'

It was Andy. I like Andy. He's a drugs runner. He's ten years old.

'Not bad, Andy, yourself? What's been happening? Still working for Fat Bob?'

'Yeah.'

Andy sleeps with his mobile tied to the bedpost, so it dangles down over his head. He won't miss it when it rings in the small hours. A typical night for Andy begins when the phone rings. It's 2 a.m. Andy sleeps through it. It rings again and this time he answers. A voice tells him what he needs, tells him to hurry.

Andy gets up. He's sleeping with his clothes on and just has to put on his Reeboks. He checks on his mum. She's not there. Sleeping on the pub sofa again. He sighs, stops trying to be quiet, grabs his keys and goes out into the hall.

The stash is in the meter cupboard, not even in the flat. Fat Bob made him a special lock. Andy checks up and down the corridor. Small hands move fast and he leaves with the coke in a plastic bag down his pants.

Andy is a member of the Young Invisible Army (YIvA), the tens and under who work as runners and lookouts in return for a tiny bit of blow or a few quid. Has been for almost six months now. He can't be questioned, jailed or arrested, so he holds the stash and delivers it as and when Fat Bob runs dry. His motivation for not getting caught is payment and securing a place in the RIvA, the Real Invisible Army – more money and more responsibility.

He's on the first floor, so jogs down the stairs and out through the heavy automatic door. Andy is a fast runner. The cold air does the last bit of wakening and he's running quickly alongside his block.

He's got a fob for the other door. The little light goes green, the door buzzes, clicks and swings open on auto and he's in, takes the lift to the fifth. He knows better than to take the stairs. Never know who you might meet coming down – or what you might step in.

Exit the lift, turn right, through the swing door and stops by the middle flat. The bitter smell hits. Andy doesn't like it. He says he won't ever touch drugs. He taps and stands back, making sure they can see him through the eye-hole.

It opens.

A fat teenager is standing there. Red tracksuit. Spliff on.

'Delivery.'

'Hand it over.'

Andy doesn't move.

'And?'

'Payment.'

'Fuck me. Come in and hand it over.'

Andy rummages in his pants and hands it over.

'Bob!' the fat teenager shouts. 'Squirt wants paying.'

'In here.'

Andy walks into a bedroom. There's a guy in his mid-twenties. Fag on, squinty eyes, chain and tracksuit. Fat Bob, long-term local dealer, in and out of prison. Just out and back to work like it was nothing.

He gives Andy £10 and Andy runs home again.

On weekends, he might do this five times a night. Andy is understandably coy, but I imagine he's amassed a large roll of notes by now. Andy strikes me as a boy with a plan.

Andy's mum was an alcoholic and on her own. She worked in a pub cash in hand and all the drinks she could persuade the punters to buy her. She was a good woman who loved her son but Andy knew there was a limit and he needed to look out for himself. He was street smart, heard and saw everything and understood it too. And as I was the only one who listened to him, Andy told me everything.

'It's going all right,' Andy said. 'But there's a new crack house.'

'Which block?'

'Hartford. On six.'

Greg and Tel showed up next, on a motor scooter, stolen for sure. Greg was short for fourteen, had thin lips, half-closed eyes. He was quiet and always starving. He was one of those types that makes you think he might lose it one day and machine-gun a bus full of nuns, only for people to say, 'He was such a quiet man.'

Tel was thirteen and overweight, rude and destructive. He rustled up a huge green gob of spit, launched it into space and watched it land with a splat.

I watched with disgust.

'Surprised that thing don't spout legs.'

Tel laughed.

I looked at it then back at him. 'Looks like one of those face suckers from *Alien*.'

'Love that film.'

Tel was another teen who'd released himself from the burden of a free education. He slotted in with the rest of the ghetto kids, although even they barely tolerated him. Tel tried too hard to impress, to act the fool, to be the estate jester.

They all smoked weed. I'm sure most of them didn't like it that much but it was the done thing. For them, smoking weed, drinking alcohol and breaking the law passed for maturity. As did random sex, not that many of them got any.

What they saw going on around them, they copied. They kept their tiny stashes hidden in lampposts, beneath hoardings and under bushes. They scattered whenever they saw the law, even though they would have had to have blown spliff smoke right up a bored police officer's nose to inspire an arrest.

'So the new crack house causing much trouble, is it?'

'Dunno,' Andy said, screwing up his face. 'Not really. Just lots of people coming and going.'

'How many people, do you reckon?'

Andy shrugged. 'Not been watching it that close. Maybe ten an hour?'

'It's a girl's flat,' Greg added suddenly. 'She's all right. I think they took it from her.'

'Really? All right, you say?'

Greg nodded. 'Yeah. Not like a junkie or nothing. Normal. Good-looking too.'

'I seen her,' Andy said. 'Some bad shit happening, I reckon. I seen them hit her in the face, take her away with them and one of 'em was walking behind and he hit her in the back of the head when he thought she were walking too slow.'

'How many?'

'Three of them. Two black one white.'

'Blokes?'

'Yeah.'

'You see them around here before?'

'A bit. Been hanging out in a car near the towers.'

Tel interjected. 'They stabbed this bloke on the high road the other day.'

He proceeded to act out the stabbing and was rolling on the floor gurgling manically when Alan the PSCO rolled up behind him.

'All right, Tel?' he said.

Tel leapt to his feet, a look of embarrassed terror on his face. Alan wasn't bound to the same confidentiality I promised all who spoke to me. The three lads grabbed their food and wandered away.

'All right, Alan, what's the score today?'

'So far, I've got seventeen balls of foil, seven needles, six cans for cooking and a prossie in a pear tree.'

'That's more balls than usual.'

'Indeed it is.'

'Heard about the new crack house, then?'

Drugs are insidious. They creep into young people's lives. To start with, they're fun. First-time users are surprised – especially if it's crack.

'Well this isn't as bad as they tell us on TV,' they think. 'I feel great. I can handle this, it must be only idiots who become proper junkies.'

But they don't see it, the drug is taking them over, becoming them, brainwashing them into believing that what's happening to them is not really happening to them. I was a junkie, too. Heroin. I crossed every line I drew. I said I'd never use needles, never rob from a mate, never beg and never share a needle. All of them crossed.

I watched heroin take my sister, suck flesh from her bones, emptying her insides. The drug killed her at twenty-six. Her body wasn't strong enough to take it anymore. She just took her usual dose, the gear was cut with a little less junk than usual and when she nodded out her heart stopped. Dead in a shooting gallery at the end of a walled-in alley, hidden behind a door of corrugated iron. Covered in rat bites. She looked like an old woman.

I got into heroin first. My sister had followed me. I see her face every day. I see her laughing, before the drugs, I see her crying when she needed drugs and I see her hollow face after she died.

I owe her her life.

All I could do was save mine, so I stopped it the methadone way. Amounts reduced each week. Weaning me off. By the time I got down to my final week of doses I was dreading the roasting, the sickness that comes with total meth withdrawal. I'd already been fairly sick, skin formicating with non-existent bugs in the night.

When I went to collect my last dose they told me they'd been giving me green water for the last two weeks.

The man behind the counter looked me in the eye and smiled. 'You're clean.'

I literally did not know what to say. I was pissed off by the con but at the same time I was so overwhelmed by the fact that I was sober, I couldn't speak. I couldn't remember the last time I'd not taken any chemical to get me through the day.

I'd never been so scared. Somehow I held myself together, re-schooled and became a community outreach worker, funded through a combination of donations and small council grants.

Now I work with young vulnerable people, drug addicts and prostitutes. I do what I can to help kids affected by drugs, which isn't a huge amount, but is definitely better than nothing. My work brings me into close contact with Police Community Support Officers like Alan, who agrees he's a wasted resource.

PCSOs spend their days patrolling town centres. They talk to the street sweepers who tell them where they find needles, the postmen who know which houses and flats are being used to sell crack, local people who know exactly what the thieves are steal-ing every day. Yet the 'real' cops don't want this intelligence. They'd rather sit outside drug dens in unmarked cars looking like Bodie and Doyle, right under the eyes of the lookouts.*

It's all a bit hopeless anyway. There is no drug squad as such. If you have a drug squad then you have a drug problem and nobody wants a drug problem on their patch, so they look the other way until something really bad happens and they're forced into action. Crack houses on council estates are low priority. Close one and another one opens to fill its place. Until we do something about why people are fuelling the demand for drugs, we won't solve the drug problem.

Along with Militant Sylvia at the drop-in, Alan and I shared a free and frank exchange of information. He was a wise old boy but

---

*Unmarked police cars often have sequential number plates making them extremely easy to spot. I kid you not; this is 100 per cent true. Ask any dealer worth his salt and he'll rattle off the local plod's unmarked registra-tion numbers before you can say 'Get your trousers on, you're nicked!'

struggled to engage with youth, fault of the uniform more than anything. I helped him with that. In return he told me what he knew was happening on the streets.

The more intel we had, the more we were able to understand and engage with the kids who wanted or needed help. Somehow, between us, we liked to think we made a small difference.

1976

An independent inquiry is set up to investigate the cases of three teenage girls living in care homes who were coerced into prostitution. One of the girls' mothers states that her daughter 'became a prostitute because she went into care. Other girls at the home told me later that [she] was soliciting, kept running away and the social workers seemed powerless to stop her.'

The assistant general secretary for the British Association of Social Workers stated that it was: 'impossible – and undesirable – to monitor girls in care every minute of the day ... Many girls in care are sexually active, and in their own time it is likely they will make undesirable contacts. This could lead them to prostitute themselves for money. This situation will be true of children in the care of local authorities all over.'[31]

CHAPTER FOURTEEN

AT THE DROP-IN

The drop-in wasn't working for Sarah. Situated in a small side street, it offered free tea, biscuits, advice and a chance for addicts to come and share their stories in what Sylvia described as 'a positive environment'.

It was in an old sweetshop. There was room for three sofas around a small coffee table, a desk with computer to one side, facing the wall, and a tiny back room for private one-to-ones with Sylvia.

Sarah had been given the address by her social worker and came because she simply had nothing else to do – and for the free quality tea and biscuits. She'd been sitting silently, listening to people talk about things she neither knew, cared about, nor understood.

'There's so much wrong with the world, it ain't true.'

The speaker was a young alcoholic male with large green eyes, lank, curly hair, and skinny build. His face carried a look of permanent bewilderment, like the earth was an alien planet. Behind his wide, worried eyes, however, he was engaged in a terrible struggle against the urge to walk out, head to the offie and buy six cans of Tennent's Super, his one-time mental eject button. Sylvia told him every visit to the drop-in was a victory.

A tall woman with green highlights and a husky voice, sitting on the third sofa, nodded in agreement. She'd told Sarah she got into the Nineties' rave scene and had emerged twenty years later

with a set of scars and no memory of the stories that were supposed
to go with them.

She carried a diary that told her what she was supposed to be
doing each day. She couldn't ever remember writing anything
down. 'It's as though someone else is writing life's instructions for
me, and I have to obey,' she said. 'Weird as hell, innit?'

Sarah didn't know why she came to listen to other addicts repeat
clichés they'd heard on TV shows. It was as if they knew them to be
true and they were something addicts were supposed to say but,
Sarah thought, none of them really believed them – but then at the
same time they didn't know what they really wanted to say or feel.
They were as confused and as lost as she was.

Life just didn't make sense sober.

'I mean, there's no jobs are there?' the man continued. 'Then
there's the isolation, the sense of hopelessness of it all. What
choice do we have?'

Sarah sipped her tea and shrugged.

A young man entered with an open Coke can in his right hand
and took the seat next to her. He was black, knife scars on his
cheeks.

'All right? Name's Lawrence.'

'Sarah.'

'How's it going?'

She shrugged.

'Been here long?'

'Nah.'

'Where you from?'

'London.'

'Which part?'

'West.'

'Lambeth.'

'OK.'

'Don't talk much, do you?'

Sarah shrugged.

'That's cool. Each to their own.'

Lawrence was struggling, she could tell. He didn't want the gangsta life he'd tried to leave before but he also didn't want what he'd got now: a life on benefits in a small town where the only jobs he had a shot at were the ones he'd spent all his life swearing he'd avoid.

Sarah was of the same mind.

Lawrence took a swig of Coke and then looked at the man with the lank hair.

'How you doing, Eric?'

'You know, one day at a time.'

'We got to stick together, isn't it?'

'Other people's love keeps you alive.'

I don't have that, Sarah thought. I need a reason to live.

She got up. There was a phone at the back they could use. She called her mum. She wasn't supposed to but she couldn't help it.

'Mum, it's me.'

'What the fuck do you want?'

'To let you know I'm OK.'

'You don't have any fucking idea of the mess you left behind, do you? The police came here after you left and nicked Jim. Fucking personal* was all he fucking had but they're treating it like he was Cocky Warren or summink. All because you couldn't handle—'

'Mum, I'm sorry. I didn't know. I had nothing to do with that—'

'Sorry don't fucking help us now, does it? Bit late for that, innit? Stabbed in the back by my own daughter.'

Sarah hung up.

Two men came in. Alcoholics. Both were carrying fishing rods

*personal: for personal use only

and both were only a little larger than dwarf size. Father and son. Bad, old school blue and green tattoos, old leather and denim. They smelled fermented and looked shifty.

The door to the back office flew open and Sylvia burst through, as though onto a stage.

'Off fishing then, boys?' she boomed, towering over them.

''S'right,' the father said.

'Just the two of you then?'

''S'right.'

'Very well, here's your bait money. Have fun. Don't forget you promised to show me the catch of the day.'

''S'right.'

She turned to Sarah. 'Bless them. Silent when sober, dangerously talkative when drunk. Still, they've been on the wagon for a couple of months now. I like to offer them something to do, so they don't drink but I never know if they're going to blow the bait money on Tennent's Super and sit by the canal with their rods in the water, getting, well, talkative.'

'Right, well, I'm off now.'

'Come back tomorrow, OK?'

Turn right out of the door and carry on another hundred yards, up an alleyway, behind a makeshift door, inside a courtyard that was nothing more really than the bottom of a steel fire escape, was a shooting gallery. Lying around the rubbish and needles were skeletal, vampiric Polish men, who made their fix money selling stolen charity clothes to second-hand wholesalers. You really didn't want to go that way. Jack the Ripper would have thought twice.

Sarah turned left.

1978

The *Sunday Times* reports that prostitution among schoolgirls is increasing due to marital breakdown, family instability and increased sexual activity. They estimate that the number of cases has doubled in five years, and were backed up by the head of Scotland Yard's juvenile affairs bureau. The article cited the example of the case of a fourteen-year-old girl who had run away from home and was found by police working in a massage parlour.

The article concludes: 'Until we understand why girls feel the need to run away – from home or from these residential homes ... underage prostitution seems set to increase.'

The *Sunday Times* states that there are two ways in which young girls became prostitutes, one in which older men groomed or coerced them and another in which girls were influenced by peer pressure. The peer pressure method was most common among girls sent to a children's home or approved school, where older children influenced them.[32]

CHAPTER FIFTEEN

TURNING RIGHT

Elton had stayed for the weekend. Sarah met him at a party. She had found out about the party thanks to memory-loss girl; someone had written the time, date and address in her diary. Sarah memorised the address and had walked past takeaways and garages, smoking a roll-up and telling herself she wouldn't go in. She was just going to have a look, to pass the time.

She found it. She walked up and down the street for half an hour. Then she went in.

Men talked to her. Asked for her number, gave her their numbers. They asked what she did for a living. A model, surely. Had she thought about modelling? Lots of money in it. She sat on the sofa, held a drink, vodka, in her hand, but didn't sip. She knew what would happen if she did.

'Hi.'

She looked up. Tall, well built, black. Older. Small silver ring on little finger. T-shirt, jeans, boots. Seemed sober.

'I'm Elton.'

'Sarah.'

'How you doing?'

'All right.'

'Cool. I'll see you later. I got to say hi to some people.' He walked away.

Sarah watched him talk to other girls. He made them laugh. He wasn't being sleazy. Then he talked to some friends. They smoked a joint. He glanced at Sarah every now and then. He knew she was watching him.

She was sitting with people she didn't know. She wasn't listening to any of them. The music was loud but not so loud that she couldn't hear.

Elton came back.

'Come with me.'

'Why?'

'Because I want you to.'

'What for?'

He smiled, took her hand and led her outside.

They smoked cigarettes and talked for twenty minutes. About nothing much but everything at the same time. She knew then.

Elton put down his drink, looked at her in the eye, put his hands either side of her waist. She didn't resist. He kissed her, gently. Their hands moved, gently, then they drew closer, tighter. It felt right.

Sarah let herself go. She felt herself dropping away.

They had sex.

And then they binged. The moment Sarah saw the little packet, long-forgotten synaptic connections clicked happily back into life. She let the thrill spread, did nothing to stop it.

Elton was from Manchester. He was an outreach worker of sorts. He worked for a tight crew that had started to overstep clearly defined boundaries. He was looking for markets to exploit. They needed a base. Elton was Bad News.

The following weekend, Elton stayed until Tuesday.

Then he asked if a mate could stay. They stayed the weekend.

Elton stayed the week. Then Elton asked if his mate's mate could stay.

They never left. These guys were serious. Hard. They moved with purpose, ferocity. They were older.

Sarah was trapped. Sarah's binge never stopped. They threw her bags like they were sweets.

They all had her.

Then they stopped throwing her bags. They waited until she asked. Elton knew he had her attention. He held up a bag. Sarah's eyes locked on. Elton closed his fist over the bag, spoke.

'Look at me.'

Sarah obeyed.

'You see this man?'

He was standing behind Elton. Asian. Smart suit, looked like a successful businessman.

'This is my mate Vinnie. You're going to fuck him. Then you can have your fix. You have to earn it now. You understand?'

Sarah did.

'Then you're going to help him find more girls and bring them to wherever the fuck he wants. Then you come back here when you're done. Understand?'

Sarah did.

Elton held up a mobile phone.

'This is yours now. Only Vinnie and me have the number. You do not give it to anyone else. If you fail to answer it any time of day or night, I'll come looking for you. You do not want that to happen. Lose it and you're dead. Understand?'

Sarah nodded.

'This is a place of business now. You do not say shit to no one. You do, I'll kill you. And then I'll find out where you're from and I'll rape and kill your family. Understand?'

'Won't say anything.'

'You can't ever say anything. Not now, not ever. Ever. Understand?'

Sarah, crying, trembling, withdrawing, knew what point she

had reached and why. She knew what she'd done. She said yes. She needed the bag more than ever now.

Elton opened his fist.

There's a line you tell yourself you'll never cross. You might go so far but you won't go *that* low. But you do.

1984

The Criminal Law Committee states that the criminal law should not intervene in the private lives of citizens or seek to enforce any particular pattern of sexual behaviour further than is necessary 'to preserve public order and decency to protect their citizens from what is offensive or injurious and to provide sufficient safeguards against exploitation and corruption of others'.[33]

In other words, in the eyes of the law, the privacy of individuals is considered more important than protecting children and young people, the mentally ill and others considered to be vulnerable or weak.

The same year, the government reduces benefit levels for under-twenty-fives. Benefit penalties are introduced for those who abandon or refuse youth training schemes. Housing benefits are reduced. Obtaining hostel payments is made more difficult. As a result young people's entitlement to welfare benefits is determined by age rather than need or financial commitments. Youth homelessness, poverty and prostitution increases.[34]

CHAPTER SIXTEEN

NOWHERE GIRLS

The nightmare: Nikki, sixteen, tall, wild dark hair, perfect nose, was in bed. She was splayed, handcuffed at the wrists, tied at the ankles. Phil, shaven, tattooed, was screaming, screaming, screaming at her. She didn't know what she had done. Terrified, she screamed back at him.

Balled into fists, his hands pounded and cracked her ribs. As Nikki cried, coughed and tried to draw air to scream, Phil punched her in the head, snapping it across the pillow.

The room spun.

When she came to there was no sign of Phil.

She cried. It was over. He'd gone. She'd survive. Now she had to find a way to get free and she would run away. This time she would never return.

But he *was* there. Just out of view. He took a step forward. He was holding a pair of pliers. He straddled her on the bed, knees either side of her hips and put the jaws over the edge of the ring in her belly button.

'This first. Then the nose, lips and ears.'

She begged him, no.

He pulled.

Nikki woke up sweating, the covers all twisted, pillow wet. She sat up, clutching her stomach, feeling sick and looked around her.

A bedroom, ten feet by fifteen, windows at either end. A single bed, cupboard, bedside table, clothes on a green, rough carpet; rings, make-up and hair dye on the small chest of drawers.

Her room was in a large Edwardian building surrounded by teenage litter – everything from lager cans, cigarette butts and fast-food wrappings to discarded hoodies and broken shopping trolleys. There were thirteen other residents, each living in single rooms, shared bathrooms and kitchens. The corridors were strip-lit, smelling of fresh paint, with posters about drugs and sexual diseases on the walls, alongside pictures of happy, smiling teenagers of all nations, all getting along.

The other children were violent, sexually malevolent or just plain loud. Even with her headphones, drum and bass over-whelmed Nikki's Amy Winehouse. The workers inhabited an office surrounded by overstuffed cabinets. They seemed to Nikki to be more interested in these cabinets than in her.

She ran away from the first home. When the police caught up with her they asked her why and she told them she hated the place. A week later she was moved after Josh, a sixteen-year-old psycho, attacked her with a fire extinguisher. He'd been taken away.

Now she was alone again, hundreds of miles away from home, in the care of the State, and she had nothing. Nikki had been used to having money. At least in her old life sometimes she had money, sometimes she didn't; sometimes she earned it, sometimes her mum gave it to her.

The people at this home were OK but Nikki saw no reason to talk to them, nor they to her, no more than they had to. She wouldn't say it but she was scared of the other residents. She was in some weird no-man's-land, physically and mentally.

After Customs had stopped Nikki on her way to Cyprus, they confiscated and cancelled her passport. Now Nikki's mum had left the country with her sister, on her way to a 'job', leaving her with

Phil. The sadistic bastard had no control over his urges. A neigh-bour had called the police.

After she got out of hospital, Nikki spent a short time with a foster carer before she was told she was going to stay in a care home, and that the safest place for her would be away from London. A long way away. Somewhere in the north-west.

So here she was, 'in care', whatever that meant, facing depres-sion, self-hatred and fear on her own. No one to talk to.

Sometimes she slept all day; sometimes she lay awake all night. She was so lonely. She missed her sister. She missed her mum. If she hadn't been so stupid before they would be together now. She only wanted peace and security.

Her phone vibrates.

It's Sarah.

Nikki ignores it.

Sarah came up to Nikki when she left the home for the first time. She had told her how things worked in this town. How girls like them got on. Nikki said she was from London. Sarah said they could be friends; they could do this together. Make it a business. Make sure they got what they wanted, what they needed.

There were a lot more men for very little money. They were poor, badly dressed, they didn't know how to party; they were old, rough and violent. They all seemed to know one another and arrived in groups.

Her phone rings again and again.

Nikki picks up.

'Please come.'

'No.'

'Please.'

'Why?'

'I need you there.'

'No, you don't.'

'I do, really. Really do.'

'Why?'

'Because I need *you*.'

'But it's always the same. I'm sick of them.'

'It'll be good this time, promise. And we'll get lots of money.'

'It won't. And we won't.'

'Just for a couple of hours. If you hate it you can leave after we get there.'

'I'm not going.'

'I'll wait for you. In case you change your mind.'

'Whatever.'

Ten minutes later Nikki got up, got dressed and went to put on her make-up. There was hardly any left. No money for any more.

She looked out of the window. Light grey clouds hung over brown rooftops packed together in narrow roads. It looked still, dead.

She'd heard there was more. Mum said if you did it with enough of them, then eventually one would fall in love with you. Maybe this was how she would find The One.

This was all she knew. It certainly wasn't going to happen in the care home.

She left her room.

The carers were in the office.

'I'm going out.'

'Where?'

'Walk.'

She went. They didn't try to stop her. Couldn't. Attempting to stop her physically would be assault.

*

She walks slowly past takeaways, minicab companies, pound shops. It's cold. A sign on the building says it's a hotel. The paint is peeling. It has a peculiar smell, damp and rotten.

Nikki is tired and wants to smoke but the party is already in full swing. Sarah is there. And another girl she hasn't seen before.

Nikki has a bad feeling but Vinnie has her by the arm. He's smiling. More men are arriving. He takes her into another room. Bed with mattress, metal frame, rough carpet, sink, toilet, filthy shower, high and small window with bars across. It smells so bad she wants to retch.

Vinnie leaves her with the supermarket vodka.

Men come in, one at a time.

She quickly loses count. She is sick. She is sick over the bed while one of them is on her. Still they come.

She tries to drink to block the pain but it doesn't stop.

The men are cruel. They say awful things and hurt her on purpose.

When the last one comes in Nikki is curled up in a corner of the room. Blood and vomit covers the bed. She tells him she can't. He doesn't listen. He is fat, old, sweaty. He pulls her up, throws her onto the bed and starts to beat her, over and over. She can hear someone screaming. It's her. Her ears fill with hissing, humming, feels the repeated shock of something pounding her, stops feeling any pain. The last thing she sees is the door opening.

1990

A report, 'Not Much Juvenile Justice', is published. The author states: 'Many defended their "men" (pimps) and social workers didn't always see what was going on as abuse. These young girls had found a solution and were happy with it. Why go back to a care system that couldn't care for them?'[35]

The report argues that poverty is forcing vulnerable young people into the arms of pimps and into prostitution, which provides them with money and a place to live. Worst affected are runaways – either from home or from care.

CHAPTER SEVENTEEN

FEET ON THE STAIRS

Janine did not know how long she had been away from her care home.

This house was derelict, more or less. There was no running water, nowhere to wash. The door was locked. Every so often she heard the front door bang and another man would enter the room. In between, Janine slept and waited.

She screamed to be let out only once. She didn't do that again when the man, a taxi driver called Zev, came in and hit her. He made her beg for drinking water, made sure she knew exactly what she was. The tattoos, he said, what kind of woman has tattoos like that? Only a whore and a slut, a woman who likes to suffer.

The tattoos had been done by Janine's former 'boyfriend', a man her mum and dad – a pair of heroin addicts who barely acknowledged her existence – did not know about. Neglected, Janine skipped school, changed clothes and walked the streets.

She stopped at the tattoo parlour and looked in the window. Fascinated, she went inside. A man, in his twenties, arms covered in ornate tattoos, was inside, yelling at someone on the phone. She flipped through a book of his work.

He hung up the phone.

'Do you want one?'

'Maybe. How much?'

'How old are you?'

'Eighteen.'

'Sure you are.'

'You need some help?'

'You want a job?'

'Uh-huh.'

'Got some stuff that needs cleaning. In back. Tools and things. I'll show you how. Then you do it. Then we'll see.'

In the back room was a large red barber's chair, a butler sink, and a lot of equipment. The tools were soaked in water and bleach, then run through an ultrasonic cleaner, followed by another soak solution, then sealed in sterile bags and placed in a large pot to sterilise them some more.

The man, whose name was Mark, said he cleaned his tools better than a hospital cleaned its surgical instruments. It looked complicated but Janine had a good memory and once you knew each step it was straightforward.

Mark was on the phone, yelling, when Janine finished.

'I'm done.'

'Hang on, I'll call you back. No, I'll call you back, dumbfuck. Christ, people are such idiots ... Are you an idiot?' he said to her.

'Nope.'

'We'll see. How about five quid an hour? You can come by and work as many hours as you can after school.'

'Don't sound like much.'

'Cash in hand and a generous staff discount.'

'OK.'

He was kind to her. They grew close. She got tattoos. Small to start, a brightly coloured butterfly on her shoulder blade. Mark praised Janine's skin, said it made the colours jump out. His friends, who hung out in the back room most nights praised her too; they had a laugh, shared booze with her, weed, treated her like an adult. They called her their club mascot.

When they were alone, Mark said he was an artist and wanted to make Janine into his masterpiece, to be the crowning glory, and to photograph her for his book. He'd been waiting years to find the right body to tattoo. For best results the canvas – the skin – needed to be young.

Janine would be a joy to work on, he said, stroking her skin.

She agreed.

The tattoos grew bigger. The designs more explicit.

At home, Janine argued with her parents. The school had written to them several times. Grades were down. Attendance was bad.

Mark passed Janine joints and alcohol until she was semi-conscious and then he worked through the night.

He wanted to have her. He told her she was beautiful, that her skin was beautiful. They kissed one night, then again another night.

Then he raped her.

Then his friends had their turn.

One morning she woke up with the outline of the devil's tattoo.

She didn't go back.

Janine had only been in the care home a few days when an older girl approached her in the street. She complimented Janine on her dress, asked Janine where she got it. They started talking.

Sarah told her how it was. That Janine was in a shit situation but there was a way to independence. There were these men she knew. They were mature, smart, polite, had money and they wanted to hang out with beautiful girls like them. Sarah was beautiful. Sarah told Janine she was more beautiful than her. Janine liked Sarah. Janine told Sarah about Mark and his friends.

Great, she'd already had sex, so she knew what she was doing, right?

Did she want some weed? They could go to her flat. There were men with gear there.

They made Janine feel welcome, shared their gear. There was one guy, Elton, handsome, who raped her. She liked the look of shock on his face when he saw the tattoos.

Then Elton said she had to go with a friend of his, Vinnie. Vinnie drove a nice car. Made a change from motorbikes. Vinnie didn't have sex with her but there were plenty of others at his party.

Now this. Life had been bad before. But that was nothing compared to this.

Janine was hungry. They'd barely fed her. Her clothes hung loose. She was so tired. Too tired to resist, too tired to kill herself.

Still they kept coming, a never-ending parade of fathers, brothers, grandfathers, uncles. None of them were put off by her condition.

She was asleep when Zev came in, slapped her awake, half-carried her down the stairs.

She arrived back at the care home, dirty, clothes hanging from her, starving, patches of blood on her clothes.

They asked her where she'd been. She knew they knew. It was up to her, they said, if she wanted to go out and get wasted. She could stay or go. It was her choice.

Janine said nothing and went to bed.

Outside, the men waited.

It was only Sandra and Gloria's second night in the care home. They went with Sarah in a taxi to an empty house.

The men had grown confident. It was so easy with the care home girls they didn't have to bother with much of a 'seduction', just bring them, use them and send them back. Nobody cared. No one would believe them. No one would even listen.

They had vodka. Gloria asked if they had any weed. The men made some calls. They said they had new 'bitches'. The house was dark. They drank. More men arrived.

One of the men told them not to resist. There was no chance of escape.

The girls begged to be left alone. Sandra didn't know what to do. Do what they wanted so that it would be over quickly and they would leave her alone or cry, or resist, in the hope it would put them off?

It made no difference. The men, more than a dozen, raped them. Watching each other, encouraging each other, insulting the girls.

They left them alone in one of the rooms. Sandra and Gloria thought about jumping out of the window but they didn't know the way back to the home. The men would soon outrun them and they might kill them.

One of the men came into the room. Said he was going to take them back tomorrow. He threatened them. He said they would be shot if they didn't do what they were told. They would find their families and hurt them. There was nothing they could do.

They were raped again.

The following morning the men put them in a taxi and dropped them close to the care home. When a staff member asked them where they'd been, they said they couldn't remember.

The men waited for them every day. They spent more time out of the care home than in, staying in flats all over the north-west, above restaurants, kebab shops.

The care home knew. Nothing was done.

1991

An official inquiry is launched by Bradford Council to find out why pimps were able to pick up girls each evening from three care homes and take them to men in houses, flats and guest houses, where they were sold for sex. The pimps returned the girls each morning. All the men were of Pakistani heritage.[36]

CHAPTER EIGHTEEN

BODY BEHIND THE BIN

Ben

I found her next to a wheelie bin behind the new-build block of flats across from the town centre early on a Monday morning. Since I got clean I discovered I was an early riser. Liked getting out early for paper and fags. Maybe a drive, walk the dog. Today I'd decided to walk the estate and check out the weekend drug detritus. Thanks to Alan, I knew this spot had become a favourite among users.

She asked me where she was.

I told her.

She coughed, sat up. She was a mess. Her head hurt. Blood in her mass of wild hair, red bruises on her knees. She must have fallen here. Maybe she was thrown.

'You should go to hospital.'

'If you try to make me suck your dick I'll bite it off.'

'I'm not going to do that.'

'I swear. If you even fucking touch me I swear I'll bite it right off.'

'I won't. What's your name?'

'Why do you care?'

'I'm trying to help you.'

'I don't need your help.'

'What's your name?'

She touched her face. 'This is fucked.'

'I'll call an ambulance.'

'If there's an ambulance, there's feds and after the feds come social services. They got me into this fucking mess.'

'Then we should go to casualty.'

'I ain't going to no fucking hospital neither.'

'You need a doctor.'

'I ain't seeing one.'

She stood, staggered, moaned and sat back down.

'Why not?'

'Because.'

'Police looking for you?'

'No. Do I look like a criminal?'

'Yeah, actually, you do.'

Slight smile.

'Fuck off.'

'So where have you run away from?'

'Why do you think I've run away?'

'Come on.'

'None of your business.'

I offered my hand to help her up.

'Come on.'

'What for?'

'To get cleaned up.'

'Where?'

'There's a twenty-four-hour shop on the other side of the car park and a drive-in Maccy-D's. I'll get some things. You can clean up in the public bogs just opposite. When you see a mirror you might change your mind about hospital.'

'What time is it?'

'Six-thirty. In the morning.'

'Fuck. What day is it?'

'Monday.'

'Fuck.'

She made to get up, stared at me, still suspicious.

'You look homeless.'

'I'm married with two kids and a badly trained dog with a weak bladder. Between them all they run me ragged.'

'Put your hand away. I ain't touching you.'

She stood, swayed. Tall, thin. Maybe sixteen. Underneath the clothes, make-up and attitude, she was scared.

'Can you walk?'

She took a step and winced.

'Yeah. Ow.'

'Sure?'

'Yeah.'

I beckoned her forward.

'Come on then.'

'You try to fuck me you'll be sorry.'

'I won't. What's your name?'

'Nikki.'

She followed me, moving slowly. There were other wounds I couldn't see. She stared at the ground as she walked, hands holding her ribs, wincing.

The shop was three minutes' walk. It took fifteen.

I bought antiseptic, cotton balls, painkillers, water and hand soap.

'Why are you doing this?'

'Because you need help.'

She went into the loo. The streets were still deserted. The occasional car hauled past. Dawn turned the tower blocks pale yellow.

I went into Maccy-D's and came out with two breakfasts.

She emerged fifteen minutes later. The dried blood was gone; her hair was wet, traces of make-up still remained. Beneath her injuries, the swelling, the anger and pain, I could see the little girl. Sad, lonely and beaten.

'You take anything last night?'

Her eyelids were tweaking. Pupils letting in too much light.

'What's it to you?'

'Just wondered.'

'Nah. Lots of vodka. Head's killing.'

We found a bench on the estate's grassy knoll. She sat two feet from me. I put the breakfast next to her. She took a McMuffin, had a king-size bite, took a handful of fries, chewed, swallowed. Swigged orange juice.

She'd finished before I'd had three bites.

She looked down every now and again. Her expression told me she was remembering something unpleasant.

The town was still quiet. Grey but you could already tell it would be a warm spring day. A couple of cars passed by. Some people went in and out of the shop.

Moments of peace. That's all she got. This was one of them. Always tempered by the feeling that they would soon end and that dark things lay ahead, waiting patiently for her arrival.

'I haven't eaten like that in a long time,' Nikki said. 'There's a lot of things I haven't done for a while now. I haven't been somewhere I can lock a door and feel safe. If I could lock a door then I'd know no one could fuck with me and that would feel really fucking good.'

'You in a care home?'

'Yeah.'

'You going to go back?'

'I don't want to but what else can I do?'

'You going to see the people who did that to you again?'

'No fucking way.'

'Is there someone you can call? Someone you trust?'

She looked across the car park, thinking.

'Yeah, maybe. My mobile's out of credit. You got a phone I can have a lend of?'

1997

The new Labour government publishes guidelines about the involvement of children in prostitution: '... children do not voluntarily enter prostitution: they are coerced, enticed or are utterly desperate. It is not a free economic or moral choice.' The guidance describes men who pay for sex with children or juveniles as child abusers who are breaking the law.[37]

Three quarters of sixteen- and seventeen-year-olds not in education are unemployed or without an income. Homelessness amongst the young is reported to have increased.[38]

CHAPTER NINETEEN

METAMORPHOSIS

Before Vinnie, there was Ali.

Ali told Paula, fifteen, thin, blonde, glasses and braces, that her parents were just an ordinary husband and wife, doing the same simple jobs, day in, day out. They had no real knowledge of the world beyond this, what was possible. Ali said he could show Paula a better world with a bright and exciting future.

Paula previously understood that, according to her parents, an education was the route to an exciting life. She'd stuck with school, even though she'd reached that age where she wanted to rebel, drink, smoke and be with her friends and dream of glamorous futures.

The town offered little for a rebellious teen to do, however, except to hang out in small clusters in parks, shopping centres and the streets, sharing a cigarette or occasionally trying a little alcohol.

Then Ali appeared. He was older, handsome. He had money for booze and cigarettes. He said they could come with him and party, if they wanted. He introduced them to more handsome young men. They were older, polite and generous with their time and money.

Paula wanted to see them again.

Next time, when she saw them waiting in a car, she was pleased and jumped in without question. Her mum and dad owned a faded old hatchback that smelled of dog; this car gleamed and smelled of leather.

The men liked to hang out, drink, smoke, have a laugh and enjoy life. They had money, power, places to be, new cars, flats and pubs. They always dropped Paula within walking distance of home, always on time, so her parents would never know.

Paula hid the smell of smoke and booze by jumping in the shower and brushing her teeth as soon as she came in, or if she was too tired by calling goodnight from the upstairs hallway while they watched *CSI*.

Her new friends smoked grass. She tried it, liked it and sometimes, when she'd been drinking too, fell asleep in their car on the drive home.

Months passed. Ali and his friends were always pleased to see her, treated her like a lady, as if they were all Prince Charmings competing for her hand.

They took her to a house. Vinnie was there. Older, smarter, richer and powerful. Handsome, always in a suit, respected by the others. Paula was amazed when Vinnie showed an interest in her, always taking the time to talk, to listen to what she had to say.

Vinnie has a party, invites Paula. He has a kick-ass stereo. The music is uplifting; heavy beats with guitar and a chorus of chanting voices. Paula smokes, drinks, laughs, takes a pill, everyone is her friend; everyone is beautiful. The music gets louder, they have to scream to make themselves heard, so they stop talking and everyone dances, dances, dances.

It is the greatest feeling Paula has ever had. She is totally alive, so happy, every part of her sings and vibrates with the music. She is so lucky, she thinks, so lucky to have met these people. They rescued her, filled her drab life with light and colour. She loves her new friends. Most of all, she loves Vinnie. He wears gold. Buys designer. He makes things happen. Friends come to him with problems and he makes the problems go away.

Vinnie bought the house with overseas money. His family doesn't know about it. This 'secret' house is on the other side of town, where no one minds much what happens. His family live next door to one another in two houses in a good part of town. His wife and children in one house, his wife's mother and father next door. Vinnie's mother and father are back in Pakistan. He gives to several charities and helps the young men in his community who want to get into business.

Vinnie plans ahead. He has a lot of money hidden away. Should he ever decide to leave his family, and he is not planning to, but if he ever needs to, he can. Should he ever need to set up in a foreign country, he can. It is his money. He wants no one else to have any of it, least of all the taxman.

Vinnie likes young girls. He arranges for them to come here. He has them first. Then he puts them to work. They make him money, not as much as his other businesses, but they are part of a larger picture, a package. They also give him power over the men who want them. If the girls fall apart, or become too damaged, he discards them.

Every time he sees her, Vinnie tells Paula she's beautiful. He tells Paula that their relationship must remain secret. Her parents would not understand. His parents would not understand. It's a race thing. It has nothing to do with age. People fall in love at any age, it's not as if we can control it, is it?

It's like Romeo and Juliet, Paula thinks. She can't believe her friends are talking about going out with classmates when she is seeing these men, when Vinnie, a grown man with money, property and power, loves her. She feels sorry for her friends' sad little lives.

Vinnie wants to talk to Paula alone, upstairs. She runs up the steps happily; worry only hits her once they enter a bedroom and are alone. Music thuds against the floor.

Vinnie tells Paula she is pretty.

Something is wrong.

He strokes her cheek.

Something is wrong.

Paula says she wants to go.

Vinnie asks her to stay.

Paula says she wants to go back to the party. She turns to leave the room.

Vinnie grabs her, pulls her back. She falls, lands on the bed. Vinnie tears her clothes, tearing apart, tearing down. She twists away but he is more than double her weight and he is on top. His legs on hers. Arms over her head, held by one of his hands. She screams. He hits her. She screams. He tells her to shut up. Cutting, tearing. Paula wails in agony.

Afterwards, Paula cleaned up, washed the blood out and away. She hid everything. There was no way anyone should find out. She'd be in so much trouble. She was so ashamed. Every time she left her home, school, men were everywhere, waiting to bring her back again. There was nowhere she could go, no escape. No one to tell.

She belonged to Vinnie now.

They're all out there, thousands of girls, numbed by drugs and alcohol and passed around, shared for sex. They once dreamed of Prince Charming. Instead, usually after weeks and months of grooming, taxi drivers, burger flippers and kebab cutters queue up to rape them.

They give the girls vodka, cash and clothes. It's either give in or resist and be hurt and have it done to you anyway.

Paula had sex with several men at a time, several times a week, at kebab shops, flats and houses and in cars and taxis. Vodka was necessary. If she drank enough it hurt less. Her number was passed around. From friend to friend, to friends, all sharing. Vinnie made sure she always answered.

He made Paula look into his eyes.

'You do what I say and you tell no one. If you call the police or talk to anyone, I will find you and then I'll kill you. And then I'll find your family and I'll rape your mother, your sister and kill your father.'

He stared at her. 'Understand?'

The men knew each other. Some were from the same village back home. Some shared houses in the town. Some faces she grew to recognise.

It was a business, systematic and orchestrated, an unrelenting machine. Vinnie had a colour-coded book with names, numbers, tallies and girls, so he knew who owed him what and for whom.

He sold Paula cheaply, £10, £20 a time, going for high volume – lots of customers added up. For such a price they all owed him favours in return – they were in this together, their little secret.

Other girls had Vinnie's phones too. There was no way out. Paula gave in to what she saw as her fate. She grew angry and became violent with friends and family and at school. She started running away from home and from school and staying out all night.

Vinnie drove Paula and other girls to Manchester, to men who wanted fresh meat because they were tired of the same. Those girls were driven back to Paula's home town.

Lots of taxis arrived. Lots of men. They were excited at the thought of new girls. There was no choice. Drink hard, drink fast and please God let them be quick.

They turned nasty the moment she refused. Paula had just wanted a break. But the next man didn't want to listen. He had paid for his slot. There were more than twenty waiting. Time was limited. She had many to get through. He put his hands around her neck, called her a white bitch and slammed her against the wall.

Other girls told Paula this had been going on for years and years. Dozens and dozens of girls. Several times a week. The same men, over and over, men who kept pictures of wives and children in their wallets; they were even on display in little silver frames at some of the addresses. None of them knew what their husbands and fathers liked to do to little girls.

She was taken to a room above a kebab shop and laid on a bare mattress. Raped by grandfathers. Given money. Told to keep her mouth shut. Raped by three men in a hotel. Paula cried herself to sleep. Woke up with tummy ache. She went to the doctor who passed her on to a sexual health advisor. After receiving advice about contraception, Paula went home.

She was raped again. The pain got worse. She went to an outreach centre. They helped her get into emergency accommodation.

Two uniformed police officers came. She told them what had happened to her. They wanted to know why she went back after the first time. Paula could not explain. The police officers shared a look. They were sorry for her but if she could not answer this question, if she was not prepared to help herself, then there was nothing they could do.

The pain got worse. Paula went to A&E.

Vinnie, who had eyes everywhere, found her.

His friends took her to the secret house, threw her into a room, locked the door. When Vinnie came in and marched towards her, Paula curled up in fear. He started to hit her. Paula tried to escape and he grabbed her by the hair, pulling, pulling, pulling her back until she thought her neck would snap.

Paula knew no one would be looking for her. Everyone would think she'd just run away again, like normal. No one knew where she was.

Paula's parents, David and June, middle class, middle-aged, middle-management careers, mortgage nearly repaid, had known for months that their daughter was being sexually exploited by a group of Asian men.

Paula started coming home with gifts – perfume, jewellery and mobile phones – and refused to explain where she got them. She'd bounce in and say: 'Do you like my new ring/gold chain/jacket/perfume?'

They'd ask her where she'd got them and when she wouldn't tell them they grounded her. She turned violent, pushing her mother before running out of the house, yelling that they couldn't stop her.

Paula stopped doing her homework, and was suspended twice for fighting at school. Then she started throwing away her uniform, running off to god-knows-where. The school told the parents that they had to do something about their daughter's behaviour, otherwise she could end up being excluded.

But the school knew about the gangs of young Asian men who were grooming young girls. They knew that some of those men had relatives in the school. They knew but said nothing. The problem was too big, too complex.

Four months later, June and David did not know their own daughter anymore. Paula stayed out nights and came home filthy and covered in bruises. They reported her missing and tried to lock her in her room but she broke the lock to get out.

They called the police more than a hundred times and would wait up all night, then go to work the next morning, after the police brought her home. The police picked Paula up from lay-bys, bus stations and car parks. Very often she would be insensible, drugged with heroin, her mouth open, her eyes elsewhere.

June and David were fined after police found Paula lying drunk, with cannabis in her pockets, in a railway station waiting room. The police wouldn't help them. The school wouldn't help them. They seemed to think Paula's behaviour was June and David's fault. June and David started to wonder if Paula's transformation was something to do with them; was there something they could have done differently?

Then she vanished for three nights in a row. David went looking for her.

Vinnie let go of Paula's hair. There was a commotion outside. He left the room.

The front door crashed open. Paula could hear shouting. It was her dad. He'd found the address by calling one of the men on her phone and asking where Paula was. The man thought he wanted to have sex and gave him the address.

The police arrived.

Paula was bruised, screaming. Several Asian men were inside the house. Other girls were there. The police saw a white man beating an Asian man in the hall. They restrained the white man, who fought against them.

'These fucking Pakis have raped my daughter!'

'Calm down!'

'Get your hands off me! She's upstairs. These Pakis are raping her. Let me go! I don't understand! Why aren't you doing anything about this? Why won't you do anything?'

'If you don't stop struggling we're going to have to arrest you.'

The Asian men were calm, expressed confusion at the man's ranting. The man he'd attacked had a bloody nose.

Yes, his daughter was here, they said. She was fine, unharmed and upstairs. She was here with two of her friends who were watching TV in the lounge.

Paula appeared on the stairs.

'Dad? What are you doing?'

'He says you've been raped,' one of the officers said.

'That's ridiculous!'

'She doesn't know what she's saying! Those fucking Pakis have threatened her, threatened my family! Let me go!'

'He just kicked the door in and started hitting me,' the man with the bloody nose said.

Paula's father fought to get free. The police arrested him for racial harassment and assault. Then they left, leaving the men at the house with the other two girls.

A week later two police officers found Paula lying on the tarmac. She was semi-conscious. It was after midnight. She had been thrown from a car. They took her to A&E to get cleaned up and have stitches put in, and then brought her home.

The police were prepared to fine David and June. David made them look at Paula's phone. There were hundreds of explicit texts. He said if they didn't do something this time, he would go to the papers.

Hours later, June and David were talking to two city detectives, one of whom said that their case was not unique. There were others, lots of others.

1999

Community Care magazine (read by everyone in social care) publishes an article explaining how young girls involved in prostitution may 'defend her man to the hilt' and 'social workers don't always see it [prostitution] as abuse'. They are not usually 'nice, polite children. They tend to be scruffy and have attitude problems' and are, therefore, seen by some social workers to be at fault.[39]

CHAPTER TWENTY

SHOCK

Natalie

My phone woke me. I reached out from under the duvet and grabbed it.

'Natalie?'

'Who is this?'

'It's Nikki.'

I sat up.

'What is it? What's happened?'

Nikki told me how she'd been kidnapped and raped by dozens of men on repeated nights, that several other girls were involved, that at least one older girl had been helping the men to get girls, and that hundreds of men were involved in what seemed to be an organised operation.

'Does anyone at the care home know about this?'

'The people at the care home know about it but aren't bothered. The police know too but they haven't done anything.'

'Is there someone with you?'

'Some geezer called Ben. It's his phone.'

'Can I talk to him?'

She passed the phone.

'Who is this?'

'My name's Ben, I'm an outreach worker, usually drugs and alcohol. I found Nikki this morning, unconscious behind a wheelie bin.'

'Is she OK?'

'Well, she's very clear about not taking my advice and going to a hospital, but she'll live.'

'Do you have somewhere you can take her, for the moment?'

'I can't take her home. There's the drop-in for now, I suppose.'

'Right, do that, stay with her. I'm going to make some calls.'

At 9 a.m. I called the local authority where Nikki's care home was based.

'We have no record of anyone by that name on our system.'

'That's impossible!'

'If Nikki's in a private care home, then we won't necessarily know about it. They're under no obligation to inform the council.'

'But the local authority—'

'The local authority where they're from doesn't always tell us that they've put a child in care on our patch. There's no system of reporting for this situation. We only find out when someone like you calls us.'

'You mean other people have called? About similar situations?'

'That's all I can tell you, sorry. I can try and arrange for someone from social services to see her but your best bet is to call the police, and take it from there.'

I called Anne.

'Anne, how is it possible that a vulnerable child can be put into care and no one from the new authority knows they even exist, let alone that they are in their care?'

'What's going on?'

I told her about Nikki.

'No doubt whoever signed the papers for Nikki didn't know or think to call the local authority. Probably thought the care home would do it.'

'How many other children have we sent to this part of the world?'

'Dozens, I'm sure.'

My heart pounded. I felt sick and dizzy. I tried to imagine what that experience must have been like for Nikki – to be sent somewhere for her own safety, only to fall prey to monsters worse than the ones we had sworn to protect her from. I imagined myself being put into a situation where I could be raped. My stomach heaved.

How many other children had suffered similarly? How the hell could this have happened?

Ben

Nikki refused to let me call the police. It was a view I would have sympathised with in my younger days. You just didn't trust the cops.

'I tell you what,' I said, as a sleepy-eyed Sylvia made tea, 'how about I call my mate Alan?'

'Is he a cop?'

'Not exactly.'

'What does that mean?'

'He's a PCSO but it's his day off today.'

'What good would that do?'

'He might be able to advise. Alan's one of the good guys, trust me.'

Alan showed up a few minutes later.

'I knew *something* was going on,' he said. 'All those girls coming out of that block but I never realised how bad the situation was.' He turned to Nikki. 'You ever been in that tower block up the road?'

Nikki nodded.

'You've got to tell the police.'

'No!'

'It's the only way you're going to sort this out.'

'Alan's right,' Sylvia said. 'If you don't you'll have to go back to the care home. And if you complain then they'll move you to another care home where those men can find you and it will carry on. You need to realise that you're the victim here. We want to help you, and the police will too.'

'Let me call someone I know in the CID,' Alan said, 'a detective who's really on the ball.'

'That'd be great, Alan, thanks,' I said. 'What do you say, Nikki?'

'I feel like it's my only choice.'

Half an hour later, two grim-faced detectives in grey suits arrived. Sylvia loaded them with tea and biscuits and I told them what I knew. Nikki told them what had happened to her the previous night.

'Would you be prepared to come down to the station and give us a statement?'

Nikki stayed silent.

'We've been after Vinnie and these other men for a while now. We need witnesses. If you could give us a statement, Nikki, it would be a huge step forward for us. You can bring one of your friends with you, if you like.'

'What's going to happen to me?' Nikki asked.

'We'll make sure you're safe.'

At that moment the door opened. Eric, the long-haired recovering alcoholic, was standing there, wide-eyed. We all turned to look at him.

He stopped, blinked. 'Um. I'll just come back later, shall I?'

Sylvia walked quickly across the room and, ushering Eric out, said: 'Sorry, love, we're a bit busy right now, I'll be here in an hour, OK? Remember, every day is a victory!'

I turned back to the detective.

'So you've known this has been going on?'

'Yes.'

'And you haven't done anything to stop it?'

The detective's face flushed red but he stayed calm. 'There are only three of us in the county assigned to these sorts of crimes. We need witnesses like Nikki to come forward. What do you say, Nikki? You think you can help us?'

All of us, two reformed misfits, an ex-army sergeant and two detectives looked at this bruised and beaten little girl.

After a long moment, Nikki nodded.

2003

Police in Blackpool state that fourteen-year-old Charlene Downes, a victim of sexual exploitation, has most likely been murdered, even though they haven't been able to find her body.

Surveillance led to the arrest of two men, both later cleared after 'grave doubts' were raised about the integrity of the police's evidence. The men were each paid £250,000 in compensation and a detective was forced to resign for failing to properly transcribe surveillance audio.[40]

CHAPTER TWENTY-ONE

MAKING GOOD

It was mid-morning. Sarah was in her flat. The flat. Not hers anymore. Everyone was sleeping. Elton was out. God knows where. Maybe Manchester. She fucking hoped so.

Sarah was beyond help. If she told the council what had happened, they'd evict her and Elton would kill her.

Same for social services. And if she told the police, and they believed her, then they might raid the flat to try to get Elton, but he employed twenty-four-hour watchers. The moment a police boot touched the stairs, any evidence of drug dealing would disappear down the toilet. The stash was kept in the cistern for this purpose.

They might arrest her and then she'd find herself in a youth offender institution, or if she were *really* lucky in the sort of bedsit where they accepted people who weren't accepted anywhere else, which was somewhere Elton's people would easily find her.

Everything she'd done was her fault. Her choice. She had gone way past her breaking point. She'd been vomiting blood. Having some serious back pain. Crack, which Sarah once thought was her saviour, had now shown its true self. Since day one, it had been eating her from the inside.

Still, when she was straight she wanted to be high. But again, when she was high, she wanted to be straight. She couldn't stop. Not as long as she was in this situation. Sarah wondered whether she'd ever really had fun on the drug. She'd only lost things since she started. She'd used it to console herself about her shitty life but it was the very thing that was making her life so shitty.

She wasn't living. She might carry on like this for another ten years. If that was likely then, she thought, it would be better to kill herself now. But there was still something in her that made her feel bad enough to want to, desperately want to, try to put some things right.

So many girls. Girls like her. She'd tricked and betrayed them all.

The flat was locked from the inside. She needed the key.

She went into the kitchen. Behind the fridge, inside a small hole chiselled into the wall, was a spare key to the mortise lock.

She moved the fridge. It wasn't easy. She'd lost a lot of weight and was weak. Every sound was like an explosion to her.

Nobody came.

She took the key and pushed the rattling fridge back into place.

She walked down the hall to the front door. Her hands shook. She put the key in the lock, turned it, opened the door and stepped into the empty hall.

No one there. No watcher at the end of the corridor.

If they come out now, she thought, or if Elton appears in the hall, then they'll know I'm trying to escape and they'll kill me.

If they want to kill her, she thought, then fuck it, let them.

She looked down the corridor. She pulled the door to, walked back down the hall and went into the bathroom. She reached into the cistern, found what she was looking for. She opened the package carefully, took enough for one last hit, closed it again, leaving it just the way it was.

She turned, left the bathroom, walked down the hall, opened the front door, stepped out and closed it quietly behind her. She took the stairs, and ran, ran, ran, out of the door, across the knoll.

Escaping.

When Sarah turned up at the drop-in, Sylvia just knew.

'Can we talk in private?'

They went to the tiny back room and sat either side of a small desk covered with papers and a dusty old PC monitor.

Sarah told her everything, from when she met Elton to running away.

'I want to talk to Nikki. She's in a care home. I want to speak to her. You could find her.'

'Why?'

'To say sorry. It was my fault. She got really badly hurt.'

'Why?'

'I was the one who made her come.'

'But the men who hurt her are to blame.'

'It was my fault.'

'There's no way you can see her.'

'Please. I'll say I'm family.'

'That won't work. She's been to the police.'

Sylvia told Sarah what had happened the other morning.

'What's going to happen to her?'

'I don't know.'

'She was badly hurt.'

'She was but I think she will recover.'

'What will happen to her?'

'They'll put her in another care home a long way from here.'

'She deserves better than that.'

'I'm sorry.'

'They just dump us all in together, don't they?'

'They do.'

'We deserve better than this.'

'Yes, you do.'

'I have to talk to her.'

'I'm sorry.'

Sarah began to cry.

Sylvia moved around the desk, sat next to Sarah and put a huge arm around her shoulders. Sarah sobbed, twisted towards Sylvia, hugged her, head on her chest, and sobbed.

'I'm sorry. I'm sorry. I'm sorry.'

Eventually, she pulled away.

'Do you want to say it?'

'What?'

'Tell me what you would tell her.'

'Pretend?'

'As if she were here with us now. Get it out in the open.'

Sarah thought for a while, then spoke.

'I don't know how I ended up like this. I suppose I came from a bad home. Mum and Dad beat me, threw me out. You know it, right; that's your story too. I used to wake up every day, in pain, hungry. I used to wake up with the hope that an answer would come. I used to think the answer was love. Then I thought it was money. Then I thought it was something else. Then I thought it was drugs. Then I didn't care anymore. Each day I try not to remember what happened the night before.

'I didn't wake up this way. I didn't wake up and become someone who hurt people. I wanted to be a good person, someone who helped; someone with some kind of reason to be alive. In some way I thought I was helping you. And the others. In reality I knew there was no hope, we had no chance. Our bodies are all we've got and we might as well face up to it because nothing better's out there for us.

'And you were so nice. You were the nicest person I ever met.

I took what was left of your shitty life and wasted it. I don't know why. I don't know why I've done what I've done. I don't know why but I'm sorry, I'm so, so sorry.'

She started to cry again.

She stopped a few minutes later.

'Feeling better?'

'I don't know.'

'I think you are, but you don't know it yet. I also think you need to do what's right. I think you're ready to do what's right.'

Sarah nodded.

2003

Papers report that Victoria 'Vicky' Agoglia, fifteen, a white girl who absconded from her privately run Rochdale children's home twenty-one times in two months, died of a heroin overdose after being used for sex by older men who paid her in alcohol, coke and heroin.

Vicky, who had ambitions of becoming a model, had previously reported being raped. She was in the care of Manchester Social Services, who had placed her in a care home run by a company called Green Corns.[41]

CHAPTER TWENTY-TWO

THE RAID

Ben

'Ever Ready' Eddie was a new, fresh-faced, bright-eyed and yet-to-be-disillusioned detective sergeant who had, much to everyone's surprise, been tasked to deal, as fast as possible, with the town's growing trade in crack and heroin. The names of new arrivals, especially new arrivals like Eddie who liked to make an impression by raiding the addresses of long-established drug dealers, spread fast in the criminal community.

I first heard of Eddie from Andy the runner. A short while later I got a call from the man himself and he asked me to give him an insider's view of the local scene. Half my age, tall, dark-haired, wonky nose, rugby fan, completely free of any obvious cynicism, he'd been told to do something about the big city gangs in places like Manchester moving into smaller towns across the north-west.

'We've been thrown a bit of cash to try to do something about it,' he said.

Here was a man who thought he could actually make a difference. I liked him.

'From a policing point of view, the best way of dealing with drug dealing is straightforward hard graft. We stay on top of the crack dealers by raiding their bases and close them as soon as a new house opens for business. We chase them out of town. Then they go somewhere else and become someone else's problem.

'Then that area needs to employ the same method. Eventually the dealers will run out of places to go and will have to find something else to do to make money. In the meantime we've solved half the town's problems. I have a dream where the streets are clean and these troubled young people turn their attention to other things and stop being eaten alive by drugs.'

He was planning to raid Sarah's flat/Elton's crack den.

Sarah told the police everything. She had nothing to lose. She told them where the stash was, where they kept the money, who was likely to be inside, where the watchers watched, when new drugs arrived and how the door was locked.

There was no so-called 'New York latch', named after dealers in the United States who bolt one end of a thick iron bar to the middle of the front door and wedge the other end into the floor at a forty-five degree angle. No amount of battering would get you inside if one of those was in place. Fortunately, the fact they were on the fifth floor meant these guys thought they would see the fuzz coming from a long way off.

'We're going in on Saturday night, hopefully when they have most of the stash inside.'

'Runners bring them small stashes from another location,' I warned, 'and top them up through the night, so you might charge in and find nothing, or just a small amount.'

'Not Elton. This is still his only base in the area. Sarah's seen some large packages go in the bathroom. Besides, at least fifty per cent of this is disruption. We go in, move them out, and hit them again as soon as they open somewhere else in town.'

'Also, there's the matter of the police number plates.'

'Yeah, I know about that. I'm going to use my own car. It's twelve years old and looks it. It'll fit right in.'

'They'll still see you coming a mile off.'

He held up a bunch of keys.

'Not if we're neighbours they won't.'

Saturday night and, next door to Elton's flat, in what had been until the previous week an empty property, a room full of officers were quietly tooling up.

Eddie, unshaven, unwashed and in his worst rummage-sale clothes, had 'moved in' a few days earlier, carrying in body armour, batons, the Enforcer (the 30-kilogram battering ram) and assorted bits and pieces in suitcases and boxes.

Another five officers then snuck inside during the small hours of Friday night and spent the following day waiting quietly, watching DVDs, until Saturday evening arrived. This was when Elton was expected to be in full business mode, dealing with the weekend crowd, as well as his usual 24/7 customers.

Eddie gave the pre-raid briefing while reggae beats pounded against the wall next to him.

'We're going to have to be fast,' he said. 'Securing the flat safely is our goal. Surprise is everything. They're not expecting trouble and the only thing keeping us out is a puny latch. Jez will carry the Enforcer just in case, but Clive will lead – his size-elevens should do the job.'

Clive was about the same size and build as the Incredible Hulk.

'We're going into a small hallway so, Clive, there will be no space once you're through. If someone is in front of you, pick them up and run with them dead ahead into the lounge. I will be right behind and peel off into the bathroom, going for the stash.

'Next man behind me the first bedroom, man after that second bedroom. Lots of fucking noise right? We scream police so no one inside panics and has a pop, thinking we're the rival gang from downstairs, OK?

'Intel says no muscle, no guns but there might be knives, so eyes open. Anyone sees a weapon or encounters resistance just scream for backup.'

Eddie radioed the unlucky officers who'd spent the day in the back of a rusty Transit trying not to move and peeing in plastic bottles. They were the catchers and would stand under the windows, just in case anything evidential came flying out of the windows.

The team moved to the front door.

Eddie turned the latch, heart pounding as adrenalin surged. This was always a thrilling moment – on the verge of the unknown, not knowing what will be waiting on the other side; thoughts of people with weapons, being outnumbered, fighting, falling to the floor with needles all around . . .

'Ready?' Eddie whispered. 'On my count. One, two—'

Clive's boot sent the door flying, breaking the lock. The huge officer charged through. Finding nothing in his way, he ended up in the kitchen. Eddie, right behind, turned the corner into the hall, first left into the bathroom. Nothing in the cistern.

The other cops piled into their assigned rooms and came up with two teenagers in the master bedroom, one in a red tracksuit who flicked his one and only spliff out the open window as they entered the room, and another sitting next to the stereo with a huge grin on his face.

One of the officers yanked the plug, cutting the music, as Eddie came in, looking severely pissed off.

'Word spreads fast round here, don't it, Eddie?' the grinning teen said.

2004

Two separate research studies estimate that more than 70 per cent of adult street prostitutes were once in the care of social services.[42]

The British National Party wins a council seat in Keighley in West Yorkshire. They seize on a campaign of a local mother whose daughter was one of several who had been abused by Asian Muslim men. During the trial, one of the accused told the jury: 'You white people train them in sex and drinking, so when they come to us they are fully trained.'[43]

CHAPTER TWENTY-THREE

IN CARE, IN DANGER

Nikki had been pimped by her own mother.

Sandra had been groomed, had lied to her foster parents and lied about her father raping her.

Janine, her body vandalised, had been raped by bikers.

Gloria, a crack addict, had sold her body for her fix.

Considered too vulnerable, their problems too difficult to overcome, they had been sent away, somewhere safe, away from their problems, for their own protection.

Except it had been anything but. These children had ended up suffering more than if they'd remained in London and had been left traumatised beyond most people's reckoning. What was the point of handing them over to care homes only for them to run away and then to be raped countless times?

How on earth could this be allowed to happen?

Every year the UK spends £2.8 billion on 65,000 children in care. Over £1 billion of this is spent on 5,000 children who live in children's homes. This works out at about £200,000 per child per annum.[44]

Children's homes are a last resort, used when a child, more usually a teenager, is at risk from their parents or from someone in their immediate environment, from whom their parents are unable to protect them. If fostering either fails or is considered too risky, the care home is the next best option.

Of the 1,800 children's homes in England, three quarters (76 per cent) are run by the private sector, very often housing just one or two particularly troubled children, sometimes charging taxpayers more than £250,000 a year per child.[45]

For example, Castlecare, which runs forty children's homes from its headquarters near Leeds, was bought by Baird Capital Partners Europe for £9 million in 2004. The company has expanded by buying two smaller childcare companies, Quantum Care and Sovereign Care, for £1 million and £1.3 million respectively. In 2009, Castlecare charged annual fees of £378,000 for a place at one children's home.[46]

Simon Havers, the chief executive of Baird, told *The Times*: 'the young people in Castlecare homes receive first-class care from experienced, specialist staff . . . Castlecare provides care to young people with exceptionally challenging behaviour. Fees reflect the high level of specialist support that the individual young people need.'[47]

When *The Times* looked at the companies behind children's care homes, they found one private equity fund had made a return of more than 500 per cent in just six years. Is it morally right for venture capitalists to profit from children who've been abused and neglected?

In recent years, wealthy global investors have snapped up small care homes and fostering services across the UK. Many care homes are clustered in the north-west, in areas where houses tend to be much cheaper and wages lower than average. Popular areas include Rochdale, Blackpool and many areas in the West Midlands, but also the southern coastal towns of Margate in Kent, and Worthing in West Sussex. Houses can be bought and set up as care homes without planning permission or permission from the local authority.

Ofsted, the government's standards watchdog, must be

informed so they can carry out inspections, but they have no say in their setting up and they are not allowed by law to inform the police or councils of their existence.

If there are six people or less staying in a home (the national average for private care homes for children is 4.1)[48] then it can be simply registered as a family home. It won't qualify as a 'house in multiple occupation', which needs planning permission and notification. Interpretation of the regulations varies from council to council but often councils and communities do not know about the existence of a new children's home.

Amazingly, even when the local authorities are aware of a new children's home, they are not allowed legally to pass on the details to the police. The police might only get to know of its existence when they are called to a house because something has gone wrong – a child has run away, for example.

According to the Association of Chief Police Officers (ACPO), even host authorities are not being notified of children being placed in their area by the placing authorities. They only find out when the child causes enough trouble to come to the attention of the police. So, even the council in which they are receiving care does not know they are there.[49]

These children couldn't be more alone.

But it gets worse.

The police have access to the sex offenders' register. They also know the locations of specialised hostels and halfway houses for sex offenders and newly released prisoners. But care home companies are not required to check this with the police before they buy and convert a house into a care home.

Some police services have produced 'heat-maps' that show large concentrations of children's care homes (the ones they know about) are practically next door to sex offenders' hostels, people out of prison on licence and various halfway houses. They tend to end up in the same neighbourhoods, thanks to the cheap housing.

Thanet North MP Sir Roger Gale said that on one road in Margate, children in care were living 'cheek by jowl' with fifteen registered sex offenders.[50] The location of these homes also means that (in 2011) 45 per cent of children in care were sent outside their home authorities. That's 22,000 children.[51]

Almost 8,000 were placed over twenty miles away from their home authority's boundary. One local authority actually managed to place every single child in its care outside its boundary.[52]

Sometimes there may be a good reason to move them away from home – for their own safety perhaps, but this remains rare. Evidence clearly supports the logic that the further children are from their family and friends the more likely they are to run away (usually to try to see them).

So vulnerable children are being sent hundreds of miles away from home and are deposited in houses from which they feel compelled to run away, only to escape into streets filled with sex offenders. It seems as though some privately run care homes are unintentionally providing perverts with a constant supply of vulnerable children. Hardly a world safer than the one these children have left.

The Association of Chief Police Officers reported in 2012 that 'a number of children's homes have, following Ofsted inspection, been given a "good" or "outstanding" rating, yet the homes have children repeatedly going missing. In these cases there is no consultation with [the] police or LSCB (Local Safeguarding Children Board) in that grading.'

ACPO gave the following example: 'West Mercia Police informed Ofsted of a private care home in Shropshire that had reported a child missing on thirty-nine occasions between 6 June and 25 October 2011 and had made over a hundred reports in total in that same period ... Ofsted subsequently supported a good award for that home. The child in question has continued to go missing from the home and 130 missing reports have been made in relation to her.'[53]

Detective Inspector Phil Shakesheff, of West Mercia Police, provided another: 'A recent case was in Telford, and it was two privately run care homes owned by the same person ... they had about four children in each home, next door to each other. They telephoned the police over 900 times, created 300 missing person reports, and that home got a good Ofsted report.'[54] Ofsted's Deputy Chief Inspector John Goldup said: 'In its inspections of children's homes, Ofsted regards the issue of missing children as one of the main indicators of the quality of care.'[55]

One of the most startling facts about care homes is the number of children who run away from them. Care home staff are power-less to stop children from leaving. They are not allowed to lock doors to prevent teenagers from meeting their abusers. Physical restraint can be used only 'to prevent injury', the definition of which does not, apparently, include the injuries sustained through sexual exploitation.

Children's homes are required to report any missing incidents to the police, the authority responsible for the child's placement, and the child's parents. The local authority is required to report on whether they have run away for more than twenty-four hours to the Department of Education once a year.

Local authority figures for 2011 reveal that 930 individual chil-dren went missing. By the local authorities' own admission, this data is not accurate. Many authorities do not actually know how many children they have in care because the placing authorities haven't told them.[56] In at least 36 per cent of cases, they were not able to report if a child had gone missing because they did not know they were in their care.

Ask the police the same question, using a twenty-four-hour time frame, and they reply that 5,000 individual children are going missing from care every year.* They'd add that they respond to more than 17,000 incidents.[57]

The police spend 14 per cent of their time looking for missing people.[58] And they'd also like it to be known that searching for them is expensive (most police services are trying to find ways to slash expenditure in line with government cutbacks). The police procedure for finding a missing person includes:

Searching home address of missing person
Searching the area where person was last seen
Checking with local hospitals
Checks on mobile phones and computers used by missing
    person
House-to-house enquiries
Reviewing CCTV footage
Co-ordinating media coverage to raise awareness and appeal for
    sightings
Specialist searches (helicopters, divers or dogs)

Finally, if you ask the ultimate experts, the UK's Missing Persons Bureau, they say that 10,000 individual children went missing from care homes in any given year, with 42,000 incidents in total. This figure relates to all children reported as missing, regardless of whether this was for more or less than twenty-four hours.[59]

DI Philip Shakesheff of West Mercia Police made an excellent

*Although this figure is equal to the entire number of children in care homes at any one time, one must take into account the fact that care homes have a high turnover, so some children stay for a few weeks before being fostered or returning home and are replaced by another child as soon as they leave.

point when he said: 'I am baffled to understand why we are only collecting those individuals who have gone missing for longer than twenty-four hours, because all the evidence suggests that children are likely to come to harm in the first couple of hours as opposed to over twenty-four hours.'

The conclusion can only be that children's homes and local authorities are failing to report all cases of missing children. In fact, they are short by somewhere between 4,000 and 9,000 children. One can only guess why this may be.

Repeatedly running away is often an indicator that something is wrong in a child's life, or that he or she is being hurt or abused. The University of Bedfordshire has researched runaways from care and found that over 50 per cent of all young people using child sexual exploitation services on one day in 2011 were known to have gone missing (25 per cent over ten times), and 22 per cent were in care. The number of children in the UK in care who have been sexually exploited is about 21 per cent.[60]

On top of this, the researchers had 'been informed about children's homes being targeted by perpetrators of child sexual exploitation, with multiple children across extended periods of time being groomed and abused by the same perpetrators . . . These children are particularly vulnerable because they often feel unloved, and frankly they are often unloved, so they are very susceptible to being groomed by men who tell them how much they love them, and give them gifts. It is easy to see how such children can fall into the grip of exploiters . . . The young person can be left feeling deeply conflicted – wanting to escape and yet being drawn to their exploiter.'[61]

Care homes are supposed to replace a failed family home – a staff member is by definition a care-giver, in essence, a substitute parent, there to provide love, attention, understanding and guidance. It's a lack of love and attention that has led many children to end up in care.

The home should be a place of safe refuge, where staff are able to supply plenty of empathy, love and patience. It seems, however, that many care homes use different definitions for the concepts of 'care' and 'home'. They often interpret 'care' as 'control'. Workers are trained to restrain young people rather than talk through their problems. Simon Cottingham from the Children's Society said staff are given training in restraint, but not in listening to young people.

The most common complaint made by young people in care homes is that no one listens to them when they complain. As one teenage girl put it: 'Basically I used to go missing all the time . . . I went to a girl's house and there was like prostitution going on there, and that affected me, I didn't want to be in that environment, and I didn't know till afterwards. I went back and told one of my care workers about what had happened because it disturbed me, and after that they put on my risk levels "suspicion of prostitution", and since then I haven't said anything to them, I haven't told them anything, because I feel like they didn't listen to me then, they didn't listen to the story, they had their suspicions that I was a prostitute. I didn't say anything to them after that. I guess it is the way they perceive things. You say things to them, and in their heads like when they are writing it down on paper, they don't think about the way it affected you. They just saw it as prostitution, they thought "she might be a prostitute", and that's all they wrote down. They never took time to listen to how I felt about it.'[62]

Some staff, not trained in sexual exploitation, exhibit less than desirable attitudes to the children in their care. An inquiry into the attitudes of care home staff found that some professionals saw the children in their care as 'troublesome', 'promiscuous', 'criminals' or 'slags who knew what they were getting themselves into' and had made an active choice to have sex with older men, and that this was acceptable, even when they were under sixteen.[63] This attitude has become institutionalised.

It doesn't help that this attitude is not restricted to care home staff. Some social workers and police officers often view children who run away repeatedly as 'streetwise' and therefore require less attention, when the opposite is true. One young person's social worker said: 'Well, if she won't stay in then that's what will happen to her.' Thanks to these attitudes, signs of continuing or new abuse and exploitation go undetected – causing more damage to children already on the edge, helping their abusers to get exactly what they want.

Local authorities, struggling to impose cutbacks on vital services, are handing over hundreds of millions each year to private care homes, so they can deal with the complex issues of these children who need compassion, patience and attention.

The reasons children give for running away from care homes include:

Unhappy.
Missing their family.
Missing their friends.
Nothing to do.
Feeling held prisoner.
Isolated.
Bullying from carers or fellow residents.
Abuse.
They feel they are in the wrong place (often children are placed where there is a bed, regardless of whether it's the best home).
No one listens to them.

Because they can. The system has taken away all the power
they've ever had, even to make the smallest decision about
their lives. The only way they can take control now is by
running away.

For attention. It may be the wrong kind, but if you're not getting it in the care home then why not go and see someone
who at least wants you to be there?

The councils are clearly not getting their (the public's) money's
worth. Incredibly, the solution care homes come up with when
children run away is to move them – into another care home,
without looking at the reasons why. Some children have been
moved thirty to forty times. This is not uncommon.

By moving a young person with a history of running away, they
are spreading the problem as that person brings their history to
bear on other residents – not to mention the fact that predators
are able to stay in contact with their victims and follow them to
a new care home full of new girls for them to exploit.

The staff are not always well trained. Alison McCausland
MBE, a retired police officer who now helps young people who go
missing from care, said: 'You can have someone looking after a
young person, who the day before their experience may have been
working at a deli counter in Asda.'[64]

Amazingly, there is only one all-female secure care home in the
UK that specialises in helping girls who've been sexually
exploited. Clare Lodge, run by Peterborough City Council, provides 'an intensive and therapeutic environment, including an
in-house psychiatric and psychological provision'.[65] One, in the
whole of the UK. And we know that somewhere between 5,000
and 10,000 children are being sexually exploited in the UK.

For now, even though councils are still paying £200,000 to
£250,000 per child per year, many care homes use inexperienced

workers who are paid little, meaning that staff turnover tends to be high and so agency workers (temps) fill in when necessary. The corporation approach to childcare makes sure certain Ofsted regulations are achieved but the actual care of abused children does not fit well into a financial model that requires profit.

In 2012, shortly before he was sacked (his choice of word) in a reshuffle, Children's Minister Tim Loughton said a new system of measuring how many children go missing each year will be introduced, while more would be done to ensure that children's homes are properly protected and located. He also stated that more will also be done to make sure children are sent to homes closer to where they are from.

Mr Loughton's departure in September 2012 came as a shock as most children's organisations thought he had been doing a good job. He'd spent five years in the post as a shadow minister and two in the coalition government and had worked tirelessly to highlight and improve children's services, arguing that not doing so would be a 'false economy'. After his dismissal, Mr Loughton accused PM David Cameron of 'downgrading' the ministerial team dealing with children and young people. In a tweet, he attacked the decision to merge two children's posts into one: 'V worrying to see that children & young people brief downgraded to just 1 minister at DfE (Department of Education) now and Dept net loss of 2 Minister of State ranks.'[66] This is most worrying because these changes really need to happen overnight.

To sum up, at the moment, children in need of specialist care are removed from their homes and often sent to care homes 200 miles away. Their local authority does not always tell the new authority that a child has been moved into their area. The care home owners have to tell Ofsted about their establishments but Ofsted cannot tell anyone. Care homes can be set up without the council being aware of them and new care homes are not automatically placed on a police database. When a council is aware of the existence of a new care home, it cannot legally tell the police, who manage the sex offenders' register. The homes are often bought in areas where properties are cheap and are therefore in locations close to sex offenders' hostels and people out of prison on licence.

Children are at greater risk of running away while they are in a care home that is under no obligation to stop them from leaving and when they are a long way from friends and family. Care homes cannot monitor children's phone communications.

It seems as though a sexual predator has designed the current childcare system – because at the moment sexual predators are more likely to benefit from it than the children it is supposed to protect.

In fact it is impossible to reach any other conclusion: the current system is perfectly assembled to send children primed for sexual exploitation into the arms of sexual predators. In other words the system has been trafficking the UK's most vulnerable children. Unfortunately, the system is also perfectly assembled to help sexual predators escape justice.

2006

Cerise Fletchman, fifteen, of Afro-Caribbean heritage, dies in a car driven by Suhel Afzal, twenty-six.

Cerise had been reported missing from her privately run Manchester children's home seventy-nine times in the five months before her death and had been identified as a victim of 'sexual exploitation by older males'.

A care worker who saw the girl being collected by Afzal, who was later convicted of causing death by dangerous driving, said he begged her not to leave but had no choice because he had no powers of restraint.[67]

CHAPTER TWENTY-FOUR

WHAT THE CROWN PROSECUTION SERVICE DOESN'T TELL YOU

Natalie

The phone rang.

'The Crown Prosecution Service has decided to charge,' the detective told me. 'This is a real victory.'

'You mean you've tried before?'

'Yes, the CPS doesn't usually go for cases of he-says versus she-says, particularly when the witnesses aren't that reliable. Going to court is hugely expensive.'

Seventeen men had been arrested and interviewed. Seven, including Vinnie, were charged.

Nikki, Janine, Sandra, Gloria and Mika were moved to other care homes a long way out of the area. Paula stayed at home with her parents, who were now being helped by a local charity specialising in helping victims of child sexual exploitation.

Sarah was not charged, neither would she be called as witness. Doing so was not deemed to be in the public interest, according to the CPS. Although she was involved in the conspiracy, she hadn't made any money and had been first groomed and then forced into coercing the girls. As an addict her credibility had been so badly damaged the CPS felt that they could not rely on her in court.

Once she knew the full story, Nikki forgave Sarah, something I think many would have found hard to do. Ben found Sarah a place in a fantastic refuge for adults recovering from drug addiction.

'It was the men that were the monsters,' Nikki said. 'They used Sarah like they used us. I would have ended up in trouble without her anyway. All it would have taken was for me to wander the streets for a while and some bloke would have started chatting me up. I would have gone for it.'

All the other girls agreed to become witnesses. This was a huge commitment.

I stayed in touch with them while we waited for the trial. All of them had trouble sleeping and suffered flashbacks and panic attacks, and their fear about testifying grew as the trial date drew near. It didn't help that the date was changed twice, extending the wait by a week each time.

When I saw the charges the CPS had put to the defendants, I developed some reservations about whether this would all be worth it. They had been charged with 'Intentionally causing or inciting a person under sixteen to engage in sexual activity' (maximum penalty: fourteen years – five years if the offender is under eighteen).

But then the CPS's own guidelines state: 'The age of the defendant will be highly relevant. Even if the defendant is over twenty-four, a prosecution may not be in the public interest if he had reasonable cause for believing that the girl was over sixteen.' Five of the men were under thirty.

CPS charging practice guidelines also state:

Prosecutors may face a situation where:

1. A complainant under sixteen has alleged rape or other forms of non-consensual sexual activity.
2. However, the credibility of the complainant is so inherently poor, or so badly damaged, that he or she cannot be relied upon as a prosecution witness and there is insufficient evidence to proceed on the non-consensual offence; BUT

3. The defendant accepts that intercourse or other forms of sexual activity took place, but claims that the complainant consented. His account therefore amounts to a denial of the complainant's allegations, but an admission of guilt to an offence of Unlawful Sexual Intercourse.

   In these circumstances Prosecutors must decide whether to accept a plea based on the defendant's account, as the prosecution are not in a position to put evidence forward which contradicts the defence's version of events, or to abandon the case entirely.

I called the detective for an explanation.

'According to many CPS lawyers,' he said, 'juries are "easily confused" by long lists of charges. Far better to target criminals with two or three crimes, even better if it can be one – just one thing to think about throughout the trial.'

'But that might not be beneficial to the defendant.'

'Official charging guidelines say it is. Also, we can't trust a jury to be capable of grasping complicated concepts like grooming. If social workers, care homes and police officers have struggled for so long, then juries aren't going to find it any easier to understand the psychology that explains why a girl supports her pimp, or stays with him after he has raped her and sold her to other men.'

'I think most people are able to grasp the concept, as long as it's explained well.'

'According to the CPS, juries tend to see things as "either you did or you didn't" – as does the law.'

So the men were not charged with grooming, specifically the offence of 'meeting a child following sexual grooming', with a maximum sentence of ten years.

'But there's rape, surely. That's a potential life sentence, isn't it?'

'It is but alas, no. Rape is difficult to prove, thanks to the issue of consent and the mistaken age defence.'

So no rape charges.

'And internal trafficking?'

According to the CPS, 'Internal trafficking is characterised by the recruitment, grooming and sexual exploitation of young teenage girls in the UK by organised crime gangs. Investigations may arise in circumstances where a child has gone missing (often, but not limited to, children in local authority care). They may be sexually abused before being taken to other towns and cities where the sexual exploitation (prostitution) continues. Since 2008, the maximum sentence for internal trafficking is fourteen years.'

'The girls have been trafficked from one town to another, from one house, flat, hotel, restaurant to another,' I said.

'No evidence. We have no surveillance, no recordings of intercepted phone calls.'

So no internal trafficking charges.

'So we're left with "Intentionally causing or inciting a person under sixteen to engage in sexual activity"? A crime for which these men are able to put forward a reasonable defence? In other words, these men, who are responsible for the planned execution of hundreds of rapes committed against dozens of girls, have a good chance of escaping a long prison sentence – or any sentence at all.'

'That's for the jury to decide, but our case is strong, although I expect we'll have a battle on our hands. But we will be ready.'

'You might be, but I don't know if the girls will.'

2007

Police in Blackpool state they believe that fifteen-year-old Paige Chivers, a victim of sexual exploitation, has most likely been murdered, even though they haven't been able to find her body.

Police and outreach groups eventually identify sixty Blackpool girls as victims of sexual exploitation – by one gang. All the girls are aged between thirteen and fifteen.[68]

Five years later, in July 2012, an Ofsted report brands children's services in Blackpool 'inadequate'. Inspectors demand immediate action to ensure vulnerable children are made safe.[69]

CHAPTER TWENTY-FIVE

ABUSE BY ANOTHER NAME

It's not unusual for victims to cry in court. Revisiting painful memories of physical suffering, allowing the psychological horror to resurface, is emotionally exhausting. You are there through no fault of your own, yet still you have to suffer – relive the feelings of disgust, shame and embarrassment – while all your torturer has to do is deny, deny, deny.

Imagine then, being a teenager, standing behind a screen in a courtroom full of barristers (not to mention the defence team, the enemy), clerks, security staff, journalists, stenographer and judge, all far older than you and living a life so alien so as to be incomprehensible, and then telling them all, for the record, how the men standing in the dock raped you time and time again. And then listen as those men accuse you of lying, and again as the defence probes your past, attacks your character, questions your integrity – as if you had created this situation simply to spite the accused. The court expects people to break down – and is used to it – but that does not make it any easier.

Paula is tiny. She could pass for much younger. She has short, dark hair; tiny, delicate shoulders; thin, short legs and small feet. As the most credible witness, Paula came in for a particularly hard time. She spent thirteen days under cross-examination. Her abusers knew her too well. They knew how to exploit her, even in court. The barrister preyed on all the same vulnerabilities that Paula's abusers had. They made use of her lack of self-worth. They said she was streetwise when she was not. She was young, vulnerable and so naïve that she had at first been unable to distinguish between abuse and affection – and her experience had left her scarred mentally; she was still struggling with this.

One of the men even managed to contact Paula after he'd been arrested and charged, and persuaded her to change her story. Suddenly, after making detailed and repeated statements to the police about times and places, she said she'd been lying all along. Thankfully, the police were able to talk their best witness back into the investigation.

Then it emerged Paula was pregnant.

The whole case, the future of the seven men in court, including Vinnie, all depended on Paula. Paula still struggled to see herself as a victim. She simply did not know any better, or of any alternative. At first she did not realise that what she'd been through was particularly abnormal or illegal.

Paula was sometimes crass and rude, and she displayed naivety that came across as ignorance, but that didn't make her guilty. She simply didn't value herself and had no expectations of being valued by others. Again, it was all part of what these men had done to her.

The defence exploited this as they constantly challenged Paula's behaviour. They said she claimed to have willingly continued to put herself in 'dangerous situations' and therefore could not be regarded as a victim, but as a willing participant. They suggested she had chosen to be a prostitute. She had not been controlled, they said. If anything, she controlled the situation.

Being sold and used for sex dominated Paula's existence and had defined the person she'd become. Practically any trace of who she'd been before was now gone. How would your fifteen-year-old self cope in the courtroom if you were in her situation?

On one side, the police and the prosecution tell you that you're a victim. That you've been duped, that everything you've believed over the past few years is wrong. You've been used, objectified by evil men who fooled you into loving and then surrendering to them.

On the other, the defence say you asked for it, that you're a prostitute by choice, have a history of theft and deceit, that you manipulated and tempted these good, innocent men to break the law.* They say you have lied, are lying now, to hide your crimes and in the hope of financial compensation.

Paula came to court to face those men again; to face the defence and a jury that had never experienced a victim like her, to support the prosecution who had to put all their faith in Paula's performance, to face a past she herself did not yet understand, all in public (albeit from behind a screen), with journalists noting her every word.

Does that not tell you something? Does it not prove that this child is innocent, good and brave? That she is as good a human being as anyone?

Five girls gave evidence: Nikki, Janine, Sandra, Gloria and Paula. The youngest had been fourteen at the time of the alleged abuse. Paula was fifteen and turned sixteen in the middle of the trial.

For the Prosecution
Sometimes the children were met with looks of disbelief from jury members as they told their stories, sometimes in a matter-of-fact voice, a consequence of rehearsal, of having told their stories over and over again for the police and then for the CPS.

---

*All of the defendants were married. Some had children. They had jobs, paid their taxes, were respected in their community, professed they were religious and therefore bound to be peaceful, law abiding and respectful of women. They did not have criminal records.

The jury listened as Paula described how she stopped going to school after she met the 'older girl' and then how she started staying out overnight. She described going for car rides, drinking, smoking cigarettes then skunk and going to parties. She told them how her relationship with her parents fell apart and then about the first time she 'had sex' with Vinnie (this ridiculous terminology had to be used because the men had not been charged with rape, only with intentionally causing or inciting a person under sixteen to engage in sexual activity).

She described how Vinnie told her that this was how she was going to pay them back for all the treats and good times, by letting men have sex with her in restaurants, fish and chip shops and flats and houses – after they'd paid Vinnie a modest fee, of course. She described how they queued up, sometimes as many as ten at each address.

Paula said that at the time she didn't understand what she had become. Before, Vinnie had made her feel important, loved, attractive and valued. She had had his complete, loving attention. Now, he said, as long as she did what he wanted, then he would still take care of her.

She described how she struggled to believe the police when they told her that Vinnie had taken advantage of her, tricked her into falling in love; that all he wanted was to sell her body, to have sex with her.

Paula said that just as she'd seen the men differently from how they really were, the men saw her as someone different as well. When she understood this, Paula said, she became angry and disgusted.

She also said she was afraid for her family if she informed on Vinnie, how she thought she was stupid, disgusting and worthless and that no one would believe her anyway.

Janine told the jury how she 'had sex' with two men in a flat above a kebab shop, how the men told her to keep it secret, that they were afraid of being seen with white girls because their families wouldn't like it. They paid £60 for Janine that night and all the money went to Vinnie.

Gloria said that her clothes were torn as she tried to push Vinnie away, how he told her there was no point in her struggling as he pulled off her trousers without undoing them, ripping them, how she couldn't breathe once he was on top of her, how she fell into unconsciousness and then how she was later sold to other men about three times a week. She looked at the jury as she told them that she thought this was how life was for girls like her.

Sandra described how she was slapped and called a white bitch, how she was beaten, strangled, kicked and punched and how she'd lost count of the times and places and of the numbers of men that had paid for her.

Nikki told the jury how Vinnie punched her in the stomach so she couldn't breathe or resist and how he then ripped her clothes, how he often said he'd kill her – or one of his mates would – and when she said she didn't believe him he poured petrol over her and threatened to set her on fire.

The Defence's Cross-Examination

The defence told Sandra that she was a compulsive liar; that she had changed her mind before, when she accused her own father of rape. When Sandra said they shouldn't bring up her past they claimed relevance in terms of character. They said she was good at making up stories, at fooling kind-hearted people into believing them and asked her to read the transcript of her police interview where she accused her father of rape to the court.

Sandra tried but broke down, sobbing.

The defence restated the 'fact' that Sandra was a compulsive liar who had lied about the defendants. She had lied when she had accused her father of a terrible crime, and she was lying now.

They spent a lot of time analysing Paula's abuse of her father's credit card as well as her record for shoplifting and thefts from her parents. They told her she was a liar and made a big show of revealing how she had tried to retract her evidence. They said that this was because she knew she was caught out in a lie.

Paula tried to explain that two men had phoned her and asked her to withdraw from the investigation and trial. She described how they pressured her, as well as the control they had over her; anything they wanted her to do, they could make her. When she told the police she was withdrawing her evidence, the detectives guessed what had happened and were able to persuade her to continue.

The defence barrister expressed mock confusion, demanding to know why, if her story was true, did Paula keep texting these men until just before the trial? He said this didn't make sense; if she was scared of them, then surely the last thing she would want to do was get in touch with them again?

Paula couldn't answer.

The barrister insisted, told her to pay attention because this was very important and asked her again – why had she got in touch with her alleged attackers?

Silence.

The defence alleged that Gloria had demanded money from one of the defendants. She had, they said, told the defendant that unless he gave her a thousand pounds she would tell the police that he raped her.

Gloria tried to explain that this idea came from another man who needed lots of money to repay debts. She just did it because he told her to, she said. She didn't think she'd get any of the money.

The barrister asked her if that man was in the courtroom.

He was not.

He asked Gloria if she invented all these crimes to get compensation.

Gloria answered that she did not.

The barrister suggested Gloria was mentally unstable and could not therefore be relied upon to give straight answers.

Gloria denied this.

The barrister told the court that she was seeing a counsellor, a mental health therapist.

Gloria said that was only because of what these men had done to her.

One of the defence barristers attempted to bamboozle Nikki with inconsistencies in her statement, producing sworn affidavits from Vinnie's family stating that he was with his family on the night Nikki claimed he took her to have sex with two clients in a hotel room. He also said that Nikki threatened to accuse the men of rape when they refused to give her alcohol because she was under age.

Nikki became angry and shouted that this was not true.

The barrister continued, stating that although the hotel featured heavily in Nikki's police interviews, she failed to point it out to them when they were driving her around town to look for sites where she'd had sex.

Nikki tried to explain that she was attempting to think of other places at that time. Of course she knew the hotel, she said, that wasn't the point; they were driving around looking for other, harder-to-remember places, to make sure she hadn't left anything out.

The barrister then moved on to the DNA evidence. DNA had been recovered after Nikki made her first statement to the police. He asked Nikki if it matched the DNA of the men on trial.

It did not. Nikki tried to add that other men, who were not in court today, were involved, but the barrister spoke over her by saying he had no further questions.

Nikki was furious. She swore at the barrister and asked him if he had any idea how it felt to be raped, over and over and over again, and not know or understand why, how or what to do about it, because there was no one to tell. And then how it feels when you do tell and no one believes you, to be accused of lying, over and over again.

Janine was forced to admit that she had lied and stolen in the past, while the defendant's record was unblemished. Witnesses testified to his character while she had previously misled police detectives.

The barrister spoke to Janine like a headmaster trying to get through to a wilfully stupid child. He demanded that she concentrate and pay attention. He said she accused his client of selling her body but did not see money change hands. Like the others, he said, Janine demanded alcohol and threatened to make false allegations when they refused. He stated that his client was not her so-called pimp. In a fake attempt at mollification he suggested that she'd had a hard life and this had made her into a hard person, able to hurt people in order to get what she wanted. This was why she lied throughout her life and, he said, throughout the trial.

They had endured, and it hadn't been easy.

'I didn't see the video of my police interview until the trial,' Paula said. 'I thought I looked really stupid. It was nearly a year ago now and I looked and talked so different to how I was in the trial. It made it really hard to focus after seeing that and I think it would have helped to have seen it before.'

Cars kept driving past Paula's home, sounding their horns, attempts at intimidation.

None of the girls expected the cross-examination to be so aggressive, or to be questioned by each of the defendants' barristers. They had been forced to go over the same answers again and again.

'They used long words,' Nikki said. 'Sometimes I didn't get what they were trying to ask; it was all "I put it to you that" and "Is it not the case that".'

'I didn't think they'd call me a liar as much as they did,' Gloria said. 'I was so confused at one point because he'd already asked me and I wasn't sure if he was asking me a different question or not and then the judge leaned over and asked me if I was lying.'

Janine testified by TV link and was horrified to learn that the court could see her on the screen, but she couldn't see them. 'I'd do it from behind a screen if I had to again. I mean, now his family know what I look like. That's scary. Suppose they're all like him? Or they want to get me back 'cause he gets a long sentence.'

Janine broke down several times. She thought the judge was going to make her stop and because of this she put extra pressure on herself to continue.

The CPS lawyers kept checking that the girls were still able to continue. If they thought it was getting too much, they said, they could stop the trial at any time.

On the thirteenth day of her cross-examination, Nikki, in a highly emotional state, accused Vinnie of rape. Vinnie was not on trial for rape and such accusations could not be made, since any news of fresh crimes, for which the men were not on trial, might influence the jury and be prejudicial to the prosecution.

The judge asked to see the CPS and the defence team in his chambers.

Then the defence said that the prosecution had failed to disclose all the evidence to them. The law states that the defence is entitled to see any evidence the prosecution has which might conceivably assist their client's defence. They claimed, correctly as it turned out, that some of the police interview transcripts that according to the defence 'could conceivably expose the girls' unreliability as witnesses' were missing. Disclosure is often argued over in courtrooms up and down the UK and many trials have collapsed because of it.

The judge had no choice but to halt the trial. In the ensuing days, the case collapsed. The girls had had enough. The CPS decided not to pursue a retrial.

The men were freed.

Paula, who had settled back home and was planning to have her baby, later said: 'I was scared and confused to start with. But this whole court thing has helped me. I've been able to talk about what happened to people who believed what I said. They listened. They tried to help and even when I messed things up, they were patient and helped me put it right. So I did it for me and them and so those blokes won't do to other girls what they did to me. Maybe I also did it so that other girls can see it's possible. We have to do this ourselves. No one else can. We're the only ones and we have to stand up and tell our stories.'

Gloria, Sandra, Nikki and Janine continued to live in care, albeit secure care this time, in separate homes, a long way from the north-west of England.

A few weeks later, Sandra returned to her family, under close supervision from social services with additional support from Natalie at Ennett House, a vital refuge where Sandra could go and talk about anything at all in complete confidence.

The same went for Gloria who eventually returned to live with her mother once she'd beaten her crack addiction.

Nikki came back to London and was reunited with her mother and sister when everyone was certain Phil was out of the family picture. Returning her seemed high risk, but with no evidence to support the theory that her mother was pimping Nikki, and because Nikki herself demanded to live with her mother and sister, and thanks to the associated costs of the care home, it was decided to be the best option. Anne was her assigned social worker and again Ennett House was there for her.

When Janine left care she went through a series of foster placements before being placed with a wonderful family and through them she was able to build a relationship with her parents, although she would never go back to live with them. Despite panic attacks and despite finding it nearly impossible to make friends, she did fantastically well at school, and was all set to go to college to study art and design.

It took Sarah many months of therapy, but when she was ready to restart her life, she said she'd decided to train to work in addiction counselling and treatment with young people. Sarah still had a long way to go, but this time, after leaving the treatment centre, she was placed in shared accommodation, which prepared people for life in the 'real world'. She swore she would stick with it.

Although the result of the court case was horrendous for the girls, their battle had not been in vain. People had listened. They had been taken seriously. The police and the CPS were learning. And, in a separate but very similar case that occurred a short time later, an important victory took place.

Yes, it's not unusual for victims to cry in court. However, on 4 November 2010 it was the convicted that wept before the judge. In total, eight men from Rotherham, South Yorkshire, aged twenty to thirty, had been accused of child-sex offences, including rape, against four local girls aged from thirteen to seventeen. Five were convicted. One of the younger girls had sex with all five defendants but had told the court that she thought she was in a 'normal relationship'.

All of the five men's teenage victims were in the care of social services at the time they were groomed and then abused. When the social workers realised what was going on, they removed the girls from their homes and moved them out of South Yorkshire. This led to a police investigation, codenamed Operation Central, which began in 2008.

For the record, the five men were:

Zafran Ramzan, twenty-one, from Rotherham, jailed for nine years after being found guilty of raping a sixteen-year-old girl in her own home, and two counts of sexual activity with a child.

Razwan Razaq, thirty, found guilty of two charges of sexual activity with a child, relating to two different girls. Described as the 'most serious offender', Razaq had a previous conviction for indecently assaulting a girl in his car and had breached a previous sexual offences prevention order. He was jailed for eleven years.

His brother, Umar Razaq, twenty-four, was guilty of one count of sexual activity with a thirteen-year-old girl. He was sentenced to four and a half years.

Both Adil Hussain, twenty, and Mohsin Khan, twenty-one, cousins of Zafran Ramzan, were found guilty of sexual activity with a thirteen-year-old girl and were sentenced to four years.

The jury saw a recording of a police interview with a girl who said she had been assaulted by six of the defendants in the second half of 2008, when she was just thirteen. When questioned by detectives, she said she'd told Razwan Razaq (then twenty-eight) that she was 'fourteen or fifteen' before they had sex.

Barristers representing Razaq insisted that the girl was lying, that she'd told Razaq that she was sixteen and old enough to consent to sex. The girl's denial convinced the jury to convict five of the eight men who stood trial for her abuse.

The men cried as Judge Peter Kelson, QC prepared to sentence them. He said: 'I have to say your weeping cuts no ice with me at all ... The message must go out loud and clear that our society will not tolerate sexual predators preying on children.'[70]

The reason the police were able to take these men to court was thanks to the girls themselves who gave evidence, withstood vigorous cross-examinations and were repeatedly accused of lying. They had led the way; others were following. Cases were at last being brought to court and battles were being won.

Many more were still being lost outside the courtroom, however.

PART III

2008

Eleven council estates in Rochdale (including an estate in Heywood) are dumped from the borough's Neighbourhood Renewal Strategy. Other areas that are dumped include those in which black or ethnic minority communities have settled.

The purpose of the strategy was to narrow the substantial gap in life chances between the 30,000 residents of these areas (30 per cent of the borough's population) and the rest of the borough.

These areas no longer receive the funding that once supported a range of activities for children, young people and adults.[71]

CHAPTER TWENTY-SIX

WHAT HAPPENED IN ROCHDALE

On a hot August night in 2008, in the quiet town of Heywood in Rochdale, a fifteen-year-old girl entered a kebab shop and smashed the glass display cabinet of a drinks fridge. She was arrested and charged with criminal damage. She told the police that the kebab shop cook had abused her.

A CID detective interviewed her about these accusations the following day. They spoke for a total of six hours. The interview was filmed. The girl spoke quietly, telling the officer about the men that had raped her in the kebab shop as well as dozens of other attacks carried out in cars, houses and flats. She told him she had run away from home and moved in with an older girl who had drawn her into the abuse. Other girls had been raped too.

The detective made a show of yawning as the girl spoke, and then expressed disbelief that she would have gone back and let the abuse continue after she had been attacked the first time. The girl gave the detective her underwear as proof. The DNA forensics recovered matched that of fifty-nine-year-old Shabir Ahmed and he was arrested, along with a dozen other men.

Even though the police and Rochdale's Safeguarding Children Board knew the victim was still living with this same older girl, no thought was given to moving the girl to safety. Over the next four months she was abused by up to twenty-one men.

She voluntarily returned to her mother after she fell pregnant.

Social services only became involved when the girl's school noticed the pregnancy and referred her.

It took eleven months for the police to get the case in front of the Crown Prosecution Service (CPS). Despite the DNA evidence, despite the six hours of statements, the CPS lawyer decided that the victim was not credible and that the chances of a successful prosecution were virtually nil.

The police dropped the case, labelling it: 'No Further Action'.[72]

Even after the police were told. Even after they investigated. Even after the case was presented to the CPS. Nothing was done. The girl's abusers were free to continue.

Two years later, the police decided to review the original case and, thanks to a change of leadership, the CPS decided that it was worth pursuing after all.[73]

Forty-seven girls were interviewed and seven testified. All of the girls were white, aged thirteen to fifteen. Fifty-six men were questioned and eleven were put on trial. Nine were convicted. All of them were Asian and aged between twenty-one and fifty-nine years old. Some were married with children.

Shabir Ahmed, fifty-nine, a divorced father of four and former cab and delivery driver, said to be one of the 'ringleaders', told his victims to call him 'Daddy' because he'd tell them off for misbehaving in the takeaway where he raped them.

He told the court that he thought the girls were aged seventeen and eighteen. And, far from being exploited, he said, the girls were entrepreneurs running their own prostitution business. Their 'empire' began in Rochdale before expanding to Leeds, Bradford and Nelson, near Burnley, Ahmed said, adding that one girl (who was actually fifteen) would 'screw the entire Muslim population of Rochdale and Oldham' if she was paid enough.

'They were doing very well,' he added. 'If they wanted to go on

[Alan] Sugar's programme they'd probably win *The Apprentice* . . . It wasn't us victimising them; it was them victimising us.'

Ahmed claimed he was a victim of racism, asking why 'you've only got my kind here'. The police were corrupt, he said, the prosecution barrister was lying and the judge was 'less a judge, more a prosecutor'. The girls were 'police-corrupted' to make up these allegations because 'the police have been tangoing with the press . . . and the Murdochs'. Ahmed's outbursts only served to expose him for the man he was, as did the witnesses that testified against him.

Perhaps the most striking witness was the girl who agreed with him. She met Ahmed when she was just twelve.

'He wouldn't hurt a fly,' she said. 'He didn't do anything wrong to anyone. I trusted him like my dad.' Ahmed, she insisted, was 'one of the nicest people you could ever meet'. The other girls, she said, '. . . didn't get raped. They did it freely, willingly.'

She agreed that pressure had repeatedly been placed on her to have sex with Ahmed, his friends and once, 'for a treat', with his nephew. She was given money and vodka, which, she said, made her feel 'loud and good'. She met strangers in a supermarket car park who took her 'to chill' in flats in Oldham, Bradford and Leeds. 'Different people, different times, different places . . .' And: '[They] pass you round like a ball, like they're all in a massive circle [with a] white girl in the middle.'

One of her friends, she said, was paid to take white girls to one address, and he kept a list on the door so he wouldn't forget who owed him what. These men paid her to 'chill with them', she said.

There were 'thousands of Asians who had links with each other . . . Most you don't even know but you meet them anyway. If I gave a taxi driver my number, give it two weeks [and] then

I'll have about ten Pakis in my phone and then by the next week I'll have a phone book of Pakis in my phone.'

The girl had an abortion when she was thirteen.

For another girl, the crimes began when she was starving hungry and went with an older girl who said she knew 'somewhere we could get food for free'.

Taken into the back room and given vodka, Ahmed said they should go upstairs 'just to talk'. Even though she begged him not to, even though she was crying, Ahmed raped her.

The older girl, who was part of the exploitation, told her that she had a pimp who 'gets paid for us shagging people'. They went together to a flat in Rochdale where half a dozen men were waiting for them.

In her police interview, the girl said: 'We'd be sat here till Christmas' if she told them about every time an Asian man had raped her. She, along with another girl from a care home, was driven from Manchester to a flat in Oldham and, she said, 'All these taxis turned up.' One of the accused admitted that twenty-five men queued up to rape the girls that night.

The first witness, who had come forward two years earlier, wept as she gave evidence. It was only now, she said, four years after the first rape, that she understood that the abuse was not her fault.

Sometimes, she was dropped off at the school gates after a night of abuse, usually by Abdul Aziz, forty-one, a taxi driver who sold her to other men. Even when she became pregnant and moved home to her mother's, her abusers kept phoning her and sometimes parked outside her house.[74]

Ahmed was convicted along with eight others. He was jailed for nineteen years for two counts of rape, aiding and abetting a rape, sexual assault, conspiracy and a count of trafficking within the UK for sexual exploitation.[75] After his conviction, he was put on trial again, this time for a fourteen-year campaign of rape against a girl who was three years old when he first attacked her. The girl was Asian. Ahmed may have attacked her more than 700 times.

She came forward after Ahmed was arrested. The abuse had destroyed any chance of a normal life, she said, and she 'rejected the idea of ever marrying or having a relationship with a man of her choosing'. The prosecution said Ahmed saw her as a 'possession to be used for his own sexual gratification, as and when he chose'. The girl told the court how Ahmed raped her as she sobbed. She added that she thought she'd become pregnant after one of the rapes but had a miscarriage.

'It's all concocted by the police,' was Ahmed's response before adding, to the courtroom in general, 'What are you looking at? You will rot in hell.'

The judge sent him to the cells after another outburst. When he returned to the courtroom to hear the verdict, he smirked as the guilty verdict was read. He was sentenced to twenty-two years in prison. The sentence was concurrent. So, it meant an extra three years in jail, rather than another twenty-two.[76]

Ahmed's co-defendants had brought glowing character references from local community leaders. One of them was a former teacher, while another could recite huge parts of the Koran. They felt they had done nothing wrong. Their defence, like Ahmed's, was that the girls were older and knew what they were doing. They were equally outraged, if less verbose than Ahmed, at finding themselves in court, let alone at being found guilty.

Kabeer Hassan, twenty-five, who had raped one of the girls as a 'birthday treat' courtesy of Ahmed, was sentenced to nine years for rape and three years, concurrently, for conspiracy.

Taxi driver Abdul Aziz, forty-one, a married father of three was convicted of trafficking for sexual exploitation and received a nine-year sentence.

Married father of five Abdul Rauf, forty-three, was also convicted of trafficking a child within the UK for sexual exploitation and received six years. Rauf, who worked as a religious studies teacher at a local mosque, asked a fifteen-year-old victim if she had any younger friends. He also drove some of the girls to be used by other men.

Adil Khan, forty-two, was convicted of trafficking a child within the UK for sexual exploitation and received eight years. Khan, married with one child, made one thirteen-year-old victim pregnant.

Mohammed Sajid, thirty-five, was convicted of one count of rape, sexual activity with a girl under sixteen and trafficking for sexual exploitation. He was sentenced to twelve years and, after serving his time, will be deported to Pakistan.

Mohammed Amin, forty-five, a driver for Eagle Taxis for fourteen years, known as 'Car Zero', was convicted of sexual assault and sentenced to five years.

Hamid Safi, twenty-two, was also convicted of trafficking girls for the purposes of sexual exploitation. He was sentenced to four years and will be deported to Afghanistan at the end of his sentence.

Members of Rochdale council and a solicitor spoke in support of taxi driver Abdul Qayyum, forty-four. Councillor Zulfiqar Ali, a former Mayor of Rochdale, wrote:

I have known Mr Abdul Qayyum since the 1990s when he arrived in Rochdale. He has lived in Rochdale all of this time. All the years he has lived in Rochdale he has always been involved in community activities and always makes time to help others, for example cleaning the neighbourhood, helping out in the local youth club and most importantly he looks after his family. Abdul has a wife and children that live in Rochdale. He has fully adopted the British way of life and

*has made many friends because of this. Abdul is one of those men the
community has really taken to – they are really proud to have him as
part of the wider family. He is hard-working and dedicated.*[77]

Qayyum, whose nickname was 'Tiger', and who gave evidence
through a translator, was found guilty of conspiracy to engage in
sexual activity with a child and was jailed for five years.

Before he was taken down, Shabir Ahmed asked: 'Where are the
white people? You look at your community. Where's school?
Where's social services, where's anybody else? Why doesn't anybody care about them?'

Indeed, hearing what he said and what had happened to these
girls, one wonders how this abuse could have gone unnoticed, as
the then Children's Minster, Tim Loughton, also asked: 'Where
were the support networks which should have protected these
young girls? Where were the people and institutions – from parents to police, friends to core professionals – which should have
provided them with stability and guidance, and stopped them
falling prey to men who lured them with fast food and vodka?'

One of the girls at the heart of the scandal was in the care of
Green Corns Ltd, a subsidiary of Continuum Care and Education
Group, which specialises in 'intense and individual care' for trou-
bled teenagers in single-occupancy children's homes. Essex
County Council paid £250,000 a year in fees to Green Corns Ltd
to look after the teenager.

They had six staff providing twenty-four-hour care for the girl,
the home's only resident. The girl went missing nineteen times in
three months, for up to two weeks at a time. Philip Tomlinson, a
manager at the home, said she sometimes sneaked out without
them knowing and sometimes simply walked out of the house.
Staff tried to follow but 'lost sight of her very quickly'.[78]

We now know what happened when this girl was absent. And so did Green Corns, eventually. The girl, whose records revealed a history of vulnerability to sexual exploitation prior to her arrival in Rochdale, wrote notes to staff asking to be moved. One of them said: 'Asians pick me up. They get me drunk, they give me drugs, they have sex with me and tell me not to tell anyone. I want to move.' This note was passed on to the police.

Ofsted carried out a no-notice inspection of the home following allegations that staffing levels did not meet the minimum requirements at the time of abuse. The results are not publicly available. A previous Ofsted inspection found that the care home employed staff with inadequate qualifications and no training in the prevention of child sexual exploitation.

Despite these concerns, Ofsted found in February 2010 – at the height of the abuse – that staff at the Green Corns home, one of eighteen solo homes run by the company in Rochdale, did 'act appropriately to protect young people from harm'.

British-based 3i sold the home and its parent company for a 'nominal sum' (in the world of finance this usually means £1) shortly before the Rochdale nine were jailed for grooming and sexually abusing teenage girls. The buyer was Advanced Childcare Ltd. This purchase made it the UK's largest provider of specialist children's care and education. Advanced Childcare, which is based in Stockport, less than twenty miles from Rochdale, runs 143 homes employing 400 staff and is owned by GI Partners, a private equity company based in London and California.

3i and other investors paid £26 million in 2004 for Green Corns, which at the time had thirty homes in north-west England and employed 170 staff. They made it clear that their decision to sell was not linked to the Rochdale case or allegations that one of its homes failed to protect its only resident from abuse.[79]

Figures compiled by Radio 4's *The Report* show that in 2011 the top five providers of care homes made a profit of £30 million. *The Report* also said that dealing with missing children from residential homes is estimated to cost police in England £40 million a year (research by Barnardo's suggests this figure might be closer to £80 million).[80]

Steve Heywood, Assistant Chief Constable of Greater Manchester Police, said it had 'learnt an awful lot since 2008 ... It would appear that the [failure] of the earlier investigation led to children being put back in the hands of their abusers. We apologise to any victims who have suffered.'[81]

Nazir Afzal, the new CPS head who overturned the original decision, said: 'I formed the view that [the girl] was entirely credible and that the case needed to go before a jury. I've no difficulty at all in apologising to her. She was let down by the whole system and I suspect we were a part of that. There was a lack of understanding about the way these networks operate. Today it's on the radar of every justice body and every public authority. It wasn't three or four years ago, but it should have been.'[82]

But these networks were 'on the radar' three or four years ago. They had been on the radar of the police, social services, the CPS, parents, and outreach groups for more than twenty years.

2009

Barnardo's reports that although 2,756 children were known to have been sexually exploited in England and Wales in 2009, there were only 89 convictions.) The charity's Turnaround Service reports it is dealing with sixty-eight active cases of child sexual exploitation and twenty-seven referrals of youngsters aged between twelve and seventeen in the Bradford area.[83]

In Keighley, near Bradford, a mother and father tell police and social services that their daughter, Charlotte, is being sexually exploited.

No one is prosecuted. Charlotte continues to go missing for days at a time and takes part in various criminal activities, such as stealing to pay for drugs.

Charlotte's school describes her as a 'model pupil' and a 'kind and caring girl who tries really hard in all her lessons'.[84]

CHAPTER TWENTY-SEVEN

TWENTY YEARS AGO

The seventeen-year-old girl was cold but high; in 'dreamland' she called it. Standing on a street corner in Doncaster's red light district at 10.30 p.m. on the night of 17 December 1993, Fiona Ivison shivered in the Lycra top and miniskirt that her pimp had bought her.[85]

She tried to look experienced, like this was an everyday thing, just like the two older women on the other side of the road. Her pimp, stoned, watched from his car at the end of the street.

Irene Ivison had known the moment she first held Fiona in her arms that she would rather die than see her daughter suffer.

Fiona's first word was 'apple', spoken at eight months. She adored her first school.

One summer holiday, Fiona became Flash Gordon, insisting everyone call her by her hero's name. That winter she made the angel for the family Christmas tree.

When she was eight, mother and daughter were separated on a crowded Underground platform. The train disappeared into the tunnel with Fiona, leaving her mum behind. Fiona smiled when Irene, beside herself, caught up with her at the next station.

Fiona said she wasn't scared at all.

Twenty-six years old, Alan Paul Duffy was already a father of three children. Two were with his wife Karen, whom he'd divorced four years earlier. Now he lived with his girlfriend in Doncaster, and they had a six-month-old baby daughter.

Duffy was unemployed, but that particular December night he had money in his pocket, a £425 community care grant to help furnish their semi-detached house. He cashed the cheque and travelled down to the red-light district.

He approached two women for business and made his way around the corner with one of them. But he couldn't perform, so they stopped and he suggested he try with her friend. But her friend was busy now; he'd have to wait. The woman left him alone, waiting.

Then he saw Fiona. It was 10.50 p.m.

Irene split up with Fiona's dad. Fiona became a teenager. There were fights, but these were overcome, ending in hugs. But there's only so much control and guidance teenagers will take. You can't be there all the time, sitting behind their shoulder, making decisions and sharing advice (not that they'd take it anyway).

The trouble started at school. Kids look for difference and Fiona's vegetarianism was her downfall. Nicknamed 'Veggie Burger', Fiona was bullied. She was sensitive and the bullying hurt her, but once she'd decided on a principle, there was no changing her mind. She still came home with excellent school reports.

Fiona saw the movie *Evita*. She told her mum she would, like Eva Perón, not live to be old.

She was health-conscious, like Michael Jackson, her hero, and despised smoking. She gave her pocket money to street beggars. Passionate about fighting racism, she sought out the company of black people. She said she wanted to make up for all the cruelty they'd suffered.

When she was fourteen, Fiona started hanging out with a man called Elroy, a Rastafarian. He smoked marijuana and had been in trouble with the police. He was also eighteen years older than Fiona. She refused to stop seeing him.

Irene asked to meet Elroy and found him to be an intelligent and thoughtful man. They weren't sleeping together, he said, no need to worry about that, they were just friends.

Tongues wagged. Friends and neighbours dismissed Fiona as a troubled child and avoided her. At school, as word of Fiona's friendship spread, the teasing became bullying and it eventually became so bad that she left for good.

Elroy suddenly disappeared but Fiona replaced him with another Rastafarian, Zebbie, who was in his thirties and moved in the same circles as Elroy. Irene's instinct told her Zebbie was a bad man. He was unable to look her in the eye.

But at the same time Irene was naïve enough to think that no man could possibly find fourteen-year-old Fiona, who looked younger and wore a fixed brace, sexually attractive. Irene did not know it then but Zebbie had convictions for theft and violence. He was also a pimp with a taste for cocaine.

Three years later, she knew. Zebbie had marked her daughter out then. He sensed her vulnerability and knew exactly how to get her – all it would take was time.

Fiona snuck out of the house to go to a concert with Zebbie.

At midnight, Irene phoned the police. They asked her for a description.

'She's five foot four, very slim, about seven and a half stone, with fixed brace and a mass of beautiful thick, dark-brown curls.'

'Try not to worry, she will turn up in the morning,' they said.

She may well turn up in the morning, Irene thought, but after going through God knows what. Only other parents will know what it's like, to wait in fear for your child.

The following morning, with no sign of Fiona, Irene told

Fiona's younger brother and sister that she was missing, making reassurances she didn't believe.

That night, Irene searched Sheffield's most dangerous areas for Fiona. She found Zebbie. Fiona was with him. Fiona said she would have called but she didn't have any money. She had smoked marijuana and, much later, admitted she'd had sex with Zebbie. He'd treated her like a princess, she said. This is how they operate. Nothing comes free; in the end there is always a price.

Irene told the police and asked for their help, but it was too late. That one night was enough for Zebbie. He had taught Fiona about the law.

'I don't have to answer and you can't make me be examined,' she told the police officers, when her mother took her to the station. 'If you do make me have an examination, I can sue you for assault. Those are my rights and I know all about them.'

The Children Act of 1989 gave her the right, at fourteen years of age, to refuse a medical examination. Zebbie had warned her that she would be in trouble if she told the truth. He needn't have worried. In Fiona's eyes this man could do no wrong – the police were racist and picking on Zebbie unnecessarily because he was different, just as the school bullies had picked on her.

Irene could not compete.

The police tried to get Fiona to open up. They offered her cigarettes. She was fourteen. They had already made assumptions about her, that she was a streetwise kid, older than her years, when she was not. It was her inexperience that had landed her in this position.

Irene tried to talk to her daughter, to make her see.

'You've got to let me live my own life,' Fiona said. 'Please don't keep running after me all the time. I will be all right.'

'I only do it because I love you.'

'Don't love me so much then.'

Impossible. Irene scratched the word 'paedophile' on Zebbie's front door.

A friend put Irene in touch with a man who said he could help. He was stocky, bald, tattooed.

'The police won't do anything 'cause he's black,' he said. 'Can you imagine them ignoring the same situation, if a white man in his thirties was with a fourteen-year-old girl? For £200, I'll *make* him leave.'

Irene refused. That was not how things should be done. There was a right way and a wrong way. The right way was to contact social services and the police.

Irene attended a case conference for her daughter with two members of the police child abuse unit and four social workers. She prepared a briefing document for them. They told her there was nothing they could do.

She didn't understand.

This man, who was thirty-three years old with a criminal record, was giving her fourteen-year-old daughter cannabis, and was having sex with her without contraception.

The social worker told Irene they sympathised but that they couldn't do anything unless they had actual physical evidence, or unless Fiona complained.

'But the police brought her back to me from his home in the morning,' Irene said. 'She's told me and she's told her social worker what's happening. She is a child, for God's sake. You have even tried to persuade her to use contraception. What more proof could you possibly need?'

They could not answer. There seemed no sense in putting Fiona on the child protection register, they said, because this was used to protect children abused by their own families.

The only other option was to put Fiona into care, but both police and social services warned: 'Don't put her into care. This is far worse. They can't keep an eye on them and she'll get into all sorts of bad company. She'll be ruined completely if she moves to a children's home.'

On Fiona's sixteenth birthday they went to an Italian restaurant to celebrate and, as her three children laughed together, Irene wondered why it couldn't always be like this.

Fiona moved out of the family home. Elroy had returned and Fiona left Zebbie to move in with him. She was in love with him. She wanted to marry him. They would live together. Irene said there was no way she would finance the relationship. Fiona had chosen a life with Elroy and she would have to stand on her own two feet.

Fiona talked about getting married, the ceremony, the dress and the location. She said that Elroy saved up money from his benefit payments to buy expensive jewellery.

Every weekend Fiona and Irene met at Morrisons for their separate weekly shops. One Saturday, Fiona had a black eye. She said she'd behaved badly and deserved it. Fiona also told her mum she was smoking so much marijuana that she was having panic attacks and heart palpitations.

Irene could not make Fiona understand that Elroy was a lying, drug-peddling woman-beater. Fiona would not listen.

Then, joy of joys, Elroy ended up in prison. Fiona moved home. The power of prison!

But then Fiona started hanging out with Zebbie again. She carried on living at home but often stayed out all night.

One day in December Irene noticed the poker was missing from its usual place by the fireside. She found it under Fiona's bed. Why was she so scared? What did she think could possibly happen to her in the family home?

The following day Irene told Fiona: 'If you don't stop behaving like this I'm going to be identifying you on a cold slab in some hospital morgue somewhere.'

When the other street worker received the tip-off that a client with a thick wad of notes was waiting, she got back to the street as soon as she could. She was too late. She saw Duffy walking away with that new girl who'd been hanging out on the corner.

They were heading towards the town centre.

Duffy couldn't figure this girl out. One minute she sounded posh, the next like she was doing a bad impression of a Rastafarian. They walked quickly away from the red-light district.

They reached the car park at 11.10 p.m. and walked to the top level.

Duffy couldn't perform. Fiona, lying underneath him on the concrete of the top floor of the deserted multistorey, was anxious to get back. It was a long walk.

She told Duffy his time was up. She tried to sit up. Duffy pushed her down, hard, banging her head on the concrete. Fiona screamed. Duffy told her to shut up. A more experienced woman might have obeyed but Fiona, young, terrified, operating on instinct, screamed again.

Duffy put his hand over her mouth and shouted at her to stop.

Where was Zebbie? Wasn't he supposed to be protecting the women who provided his income? He hadn't warned her about leaving the area. He had just provided the dope that kept her docile.

Duffy removed his hand. Fiona, hysterical with fear, started to scream. He told her to stop. She couldn't. Fiona was about as far from help as it was possible to be in a city. He grabbed Fiona by the hair and slammed her head down on the concrete of the car park floor again and again, until she stopped screaming.

Then he put his hands around Fiona's throat and pushed down.

The body of a young girl has been found in a multistorey car park in Doncaster. It is believed to be the body of a young woman aged between fifteen and twenty-two years. She had been badly beaten, and sexually assaulted.

The moment Irene read that paragraph in the paper she knew it was Fiona. She knew again when the police telephoned. They'd never called Irene back all the times she'd reported Fiona missing.

'We're coming to see you,' they said. 'Stay calm.'

There was nothing else she could do. It was 2 a.m. when the two young policemen arrived.

'You don't have to tell me, I know it's my daughter in the car park.'

She confirmed the size and location of a distinctive mole and the police officers nodded. They tried to comfort Irene. The first blow would have left her completely stunned, they said. It had been a quick death. They also said that Fiona had been working as a street prostitute. Now the law said they could do something, when it was too late. They would find the murderer.

Irene was surprised she had, so far, stayed so calm, motionless and quiet. She felt that if the policemen left her alone, she would start screaming and never stop. The worst thing that I could ever imagine happening has happened, she told herself, yet I'm still here. I'm still alive and I'm still breathing. I haven't gone mad. If I can endure this pain, one moment at a time, I will cope.

She called her eighty-six-year-old mother. 'It's Fiona, she's been murdered.' Saying it made it real. Her mother, stoic, came straight over.

Fiona's brother and sister, thirteen and fourteen, were next to be told.

Irene didn't think her youngest daughter was ever going to stop crying. Fiona had told her things about Zebbie. She asked her sister not to tell these things to her mother. She'd done what her big sister had asked.

At the morgue Fiona lay on a dais in the middle of a small room. She was shrouded in white. Only her face was visible. It was bruised and – so, so cold. Irene wanted to warm her up. She surprised the police with her questions. Like the rest of us, she had only seen morgues on television, and in drama.

'Can I uncover her hair? I want to see it one last time.'

The officers looked uncomfortable.

'What is it?'

It had been shaved off for the post-mortem.

Had it been thrown away? Was none of it left? Nothing saved? No lock to treasure?

'I'm sorry.'

Irene bent to tenderly kiss the cold, still, porcelain cheek.

Both Irene's and Fiona's predictions had been fulfilled.

Duffy was arrested on Christmas Eve and confessed. A life sentence awaited him.

On the streets, everywhere Irene turned, there was merriment. People on their way to parties, laughing and singing. Crowds of happy faces. She wanted to scream: 'Stop it! You know what has happened to me? You know what I have been given for Christmas?'

She went to the car park where her daughter had been murdered. Murdered. Her daughter had been murdered. Fiona was gone for ever.

She woke up most nights crying out for Fiona, arms outstretched. She was supposed to save her, to keep her safe, she was her mother and that was what mothers did. But she hadn't. Fiona had been murdered. She was dead.

Irene screamed out in terror: 'I can't stand this anymore. I am mad, I am insane!'

And then, something extraordinary happened.

Irene later wrote: 'In an instant my fear completely evaporated and I was bathed in the most beautiful, loving, warm light. It was as if I was in the presence of a power so good and wonderful that no harm or suffering could touch me. In that light I was loved and safe.'

2010

Ofsted carries out a full inspection of safeguarding services in Leeds. Its report finds them inadequate, with 'weaknesses' in assessments for 'some of the most vulnerable children'.[86]

One month later, sixteen-year-old Chloe jumped from a bridge over the M1. She survived. Chloe had been raped, and had been abused by seven men at one address. She became pregnant. She wanted to keep the baby, get off drugs and to make a new start.

When her pimp found out Chloe was pregnant he raped her, then he 'gave' her to his friends to use for sex. Afterwards, they kicked her in the stomach before taking her to an illegal abortionist.

Her school, a police force, a youth project and the council's social care team all held information about Chloe before she attempted suicide.[87]

CHAPTER TWENTY-EIGHT

A LONELY VOICE

After Fiona's murder, Irene discovered that she was by no means the only one to have lost a daughter this way. For example:

Gail Whitehouse, twenty-three: a mother of two from Wolverhampton, strangled and dumped in bushes in Birmingham's red-light district in 1990.

Sharon Hoare, nineteen: found strangled in her luxury flat in Fulham, West London in 1991. Her mother had not known what her daughter did for a living.

Mandy Duncan, twenty-six: a mother of two, who was working as a prostitute in Ipswich, vanished in 1991. She was never found.

Diane McInally, twenty-three: was found battered to death in Pollok Park, Glasgow in 1991. She was identified by her fingerprints.

Janine Downes, twenty-two: her half-naked body was found in a Shropshire lay-by in 1991. She had three children.

Maria Requena, twenty-six: children found her body parts stuffed into plastic bags in Lowton, near Warrington in 1991.

Natalie Pearman, sixteen: found strangled at a Norwich picnic site in November 1992. She came from a happy family background.

Samo Paull, twenty: found strangled on a Leicestershire roadside in December 1993. She had a baby daughter.

Karen McGregor, twenty-six: her battered and naked body lay undiscovered for days in a Glaswegian car park in 1993.

Dawn Shields, nineteen: found in a shallow grave in the Peak District by a National Trust Warden in May 1994. She was the mother of a one-year-old child.

Julie Finley, twenty-three: found strangled and dumped naked in a field near Skelmersdale, Lancashire in 1994.

Jackie Gallagher, twenty-six: found dead by a roadside in Glasgow in 1996. A man was tried in 2004, but the jury found him not guilty.

Tracey Wylde, twenty-one: found beaten to death in her Glasgow flat in 1997. She had a three-year-old daughter. Despite the thin walls, neighbours said they heard nothing.

Lucy Burchell, sixteen: her body was dumped on waste ground outside a Birmingham nightclub in August 1996.

Looking at these deaths, one could have wondered whether a serial killer was on the loose – women aged between sixteen and twenty-six were suffering strikingly similar ends. But the common thread was not a serial killer: it was the fact that all of these women were involved in prostitution.

For example, sixteen-year-old Lucy Burchell had just passed eight GCSEs. Her parents said she had everything to live for – but they didn't know she'd been working as a prostitute. She would go from school to a children's home with a change of clothes hidden in a carrier bag, before getting changed and setting off for the red-light area, along with one of the girls who was living in the home. Lucy died from a drug overdose after two men, Rungzabe Khan, twenty-five, and Tahir Khan, twenty-six, gave her heroin that was 80 per cent pure.

This discovery ignited something in Irene. She wondered why no research had ever been carried out into what lured girls like these into prostitution. She contacted the families of children who had fallen victim to pimps and who'd been murdered. Far from the usual media picture, these families were decent, caring people who, like Irene, had been left powerless in the face of the pimp's mastery over their children. Without exception, none of them had been helped by the interventions of the police or social services.

She also found that for every sixty women prosecuted for prostitution, only one man was prosecuted for related offences. And Zebbie, the man who pimped Fiona, wasn't one of them. This was despite the fact that laws were in place to tackle pimps: procuring a teenager for the purpose of prostitution, and making a living from immoral earnings, for example.

In Zebbie's case the police said they did not have enough evidence. Witnesses were either unable or too frightened to identify him. So Zebbie carried on making his living from exploiting other girls in the same town – not far from Irene's home.

Zebbie's mother defended her son. She failed to treat Irene's concerns seriously and laughed when Irene came to tell her Fiona was missing. She said: 'I know what these young people are like.'

The reality of what her twenty-six-year-old son was doing with a teenage girl should have been staring her in the face but there is a lack of willingness not only to believe but also to open one's eyes to the blindingly obvious.

Irene never knew the full extent of what was happening until it was too late. Of course, with hindsight, it seemed obvious. Fiona wasn't working, and Irene only gave her a few pounds here and there because she always seemed to be short of cash.

In the last few weeks of her life, when Zebbie had her on the streets, Fiona had earned him £200 a night. Irene didn't know how many Zebbies were out there but she suspected, judging by the number, frequency and spread of similar stories, that there may have been hundreds, if not thousands of men across the UK who were taking advantage of young girls in this way.

And all the police seemed to be able to do was pick up the pieces when these women were murdered. Irene knew that something fundamental needed to change in the way people thought about prostitution. For a start, how could these girls be described as prostitutes? No teenage girl gets up one day and says to herself, 'Do you know what? I think I'll become a prostitute, that sounds like a good choice.' Any girl who worked the streets was not a prostitute. She was a victim of sexual exploitation and needed to be protected, not branded and vilified.

But if people were going to listen to her, let alone believe her, Irene had to answer many questions: What lured young girls into a life of vice?; is a particular type of girl more vulnerable?; how do pimps seduce and control their victims?; legislation exists to stop pimp activity. Why is it not being used?; how many children have contacted outreach agencies?; how many young girls enter prostitution while in the care of a children's home?

Based on her own experience, Irene noticed several things. The community closed in on itself. Fiona was cut off, as were her siblings; as if what had happened to Fiona was catching.

After Fiona was murdered, people approached Irene to express their sorrow. They said it could have been any one of their children, but it was clear they thought it would never happen to their child.

Fiona was often misjudged. She didn't set out to shock anybody by behaving badly. She simply believed in what she was doing and went out with Elroy and Zebbie because she thought she loved them, because she thought they were worth listening to, that society had treated them harshly. It was her trusting nature that was her downfall, not because she was evil.

No child is truly evil. They can be easily led and influenced.

There is much about the world and the motivations of others that they do not understand. We tend to forget this when some newspapers and false stereotypes offer us easy explanations.

Parts of the media placed all the blame on the girls for their own murders. They paid no attention to the pimps who'd lured them into prostitution and then held them prisoner with no hope of escape. In some cases, language was used that implied that the girls were 'slags' and 'tarts', some sort of different species or underclass.

A child cannot legally consent to prostitution, yet the media sensationalise news articles with pictures and terms that heap shame on the child and imply that the child has a choice, categorising them as prostitutes, child prostitutes, teen prostitutes, hookers, sex slaves, or sex workers. The word prostitute (even teen or child prostitute) conjures an image of a woman who knows what she is doing, standing on a street corner with short skirt and low-cut top.

One victim said, 'At fourteen years old, I began to believe that I was a prostitute. I couldn't understand that I was victimised because I believed I must have chosen to be a prostitute. I initially refused to testify because I believed they were now the only people who accepted me. For nearly twenty years I carried a sense of guilt and shame with me, and I can trace it back to one single word: prostitute. [The pimp] might beat you, he might sell you ... but at least he accepts you, society doesn't have a lot of empathy for girls who have been in the life.'[88]

Pimps will tell children that the police won't believe them, that their family will no longer want them, and that nobody will treat them nicely. And, unfortunately, this is often true. This is the reason why many girls, no matter where they're from or what their home life is like, choose to return to their pimps: society has shunned them.

To help child victims understand and overcome what has happened to them, society has to change its language. And the media needs to lead the way. For example:

Ipswich woman arrested for nude photos of teen prostitute

The perpetrator in this article is named 'Ipswich woman' while the victim is labelled 'teen prostitute'.

Alleged pimp, fourteen-year-old prostitute arrested at Holiday Inn

The man is an '*alleged* pimp' while the teenager is, definitively, a 'prostitute'.

Irene found many headlines about her daughter hurtful. For example:

Irene Ivison, the mother of a murdered teenage prostitute . . .
Rookie Hooker Murdered . . .

Irene was one of society's superheroes. After Fiona's murder, she formed CROP: the Coalition for the Removal of Pimping.

She built relationships with several newspapers. She was able to use her 'fame' as the mother of a murdered daughter to get access to the media and draw attention to the phenomenon of grooming of teenage girls by men who exploit them for sex, financial gain – or both.

Irene was once asked: 'Where did Fiona start to go wrong?'

'I refuse to pinpoint any reasons – Fiona is dead because she had the misfortune to meet a pimp.'

She also dealt with accusations of inadequate parenting, a very popular perception of what had 'gone wrong'. 'It is very easy to judge parents in our circumstances. Nobody tried harder than I did. I locked Fiona in her bedroom. I hid her trainers in my car. I attacked him . . . Our daughters do not pimp themselves . . . There but for the grace of God go all your teenage daughters.'[89]

After one TV appearance in 1997 Irene received an extraordinary letter:

> *That night in December when your lovely daughter's life came to such a tragic end, well I was there. I am the lady that also went off with that 'evil man' Duffy. Then I remembered the black guy dropping her off . . . and thinking that he was as bad as the man who took your daughter's life away – they're both to blame.*[90]

Fellow campaigner Fiona Broadfoot said: 'When me and Irene first started, we were so confident that once we actually went public there was no way anybody could ignore it and we really came to earth with a bang and just realised how ignorant people are.'[91]

Trying to persuade TV and radio audiences and newspaper and magazine readers was hard work. Some wouldn't take Fiona seriously and, because her own daughter had been murdered, she was sometimes branded as being over-emotional and a poor judge of reality.

Irene sometimes felt she was being humoured: 'The minute someone knows what happened to my daughter their perception of me changes. It is almost as if they believe that the man who murdered Fiona took away my brains at the same time.'[92]

Irene later learned that Zebbie was involved with another fifteen-year-old. This reinforced her fear that her daughter's death had little impact on anyone else outside of her family. She was unable to persuade South Yorkshire Police to take any action, even though she wrote to the chief constable.

Tired and disheartened, Irene believed that none of the

sensible and obvious points she had been raising were being taken seriously. She became depressed but never stopped, never gave up.

Then Irene developed terminal cancer.

In 2000, as death neared, Irene wrote that she was looking forward to a time when people understood what she was trying to tell them and campaigning was no longer necessary. She worked right up to her last hours of her life. Friends took piles of documents home from hospital after she died.

Irene Ivison struggled to be heard in a society that seems to have far too many other things to worry about, that didn't think what was happening to these young women across the UK was an important enough issue. There remains a serious and terrifying lack of interest in these men who groom and exploit young women.

Even worse, as we are about to see, are those who were supposed to care, knew there was a problem, knew everything that Irene did, and did nothing. Twenty years after Fiona's murder, teenage girls are still paying the price.

2010

The *Telegraph* reports on 8 January:

'A judge spared a former Household Cavalry soldier after saying that the thirteen-year-old schoolgirl he had sex with "made all the running".

'Nigel Thomson was seduced at the Royal Military Academy in Sandhurst by the teenager after befriending her at the RMA stables. The forty-one-year-old former private then took her back to his room where the couple had sexual intercourse.'

The judge, Mary Mowat, said the girl had 'done most of the running' in the encounter and had acted 'precociously'.

Thomson was given a suspended sentence.[93]

CHAPTER TWENTY-NINE

A PRAYER FOR
LAURA WILSON

It was 10 p.m. on a blustery, unsettled October evening in 2010. The towpath was deserted, save for a petite seventeen-year-old girl with shoulder-length dark hair. Rotherham's Meadowhall Shopping Centre loomed over the canal. It was dark, isolated and cold. Not the best place for a late-night meeting.

Laura Wilson was waiting for her former boyfriend: seventeen-year-old Ashtiaq Asghar. Her heart was full of hope for reconciliation. A few months earlier, a friend of Asghar's, an older married man, twenty-year-old Ishaq Hussain, had sex with Laura and she fell pregnant. She decided to have the child. Hussain refused all responsibility. When Asghar found out, he dumped Laura.[94]

She lived with her mother and three siblings in Ferham Park, a small group of streets on the edge of Rotherham. Laura, who had some learning difficulties, struggled to cope with motherhood. Margaret, Laura's mum, had so far done most of the work bringing up Laura's four-month-old baby.

But Margaret wasn't superhuman. She couldn't do that and keep up with her wayward daughter. Laura hadn't finished school, and although she'd enjoyed college placements and work experience in a hair and beauty salon she often skipped work.

Laura also avoided meetings with social workers and family support workers. She didn't know how to answer their questions, nor did she understand what they wanted from her. Laura was confused and overwhelmed by her responsibilities, and frightened about the future.

And then Asghar's text arrived, asking Laura to meet him, to come alone.

Maybe he would come back to her and they would raise the baby together. They'd been inseparable ever since they'd met outside the school gate, until Ishaq slept with her. Maybe Asghar would help her talk to Ishaq, maybe convince him to provide financial support for her son. She'd even shaved her baby's head, as per Muslim tradition.

Laura's mobile rang. It was her mother, asking where she was, adding that it was about time she came home. She said she wouldn't be long and hung up.

Asghar was coming.

The Last Time They Saw Her

The First Social Worker: Laura Wilson was removed from the Child Protection Register in 2005, a few weeks before her twelfth birthday, at the first review of her case, despite the fact that an assessment had not been completed and evidence that she was becoming sexually active and putting herself at risk of sexual exploitation from older men.[95]

Rotherham Council's Youth Offending Team: In July 2007, thirteen-year-old Laura got into trouble at school for assaulting a fellow pupil. She was excluded and the police gave her a final warning. Then it was over to Rotherham Council's Youth Offending Team. A multi-agency team coordinated by the local authority and overseen by the Youth Justice Board, Youth Offending Teams are supposed to deal with young offenders, essentially oversee punishments and help children like Laura with counselling and rehabilitation. Laura did not attend or comply with the programme but in the three months (July to September 2007) they were involved with Laura, the Youth Offending Team did nothing. They explained later that this was because Laura had 'learning difficulties'.[96]

Jeremy Kyle: When she was thirteen, Laura appeared on ITV1's *The Jeremy Kyle Show*. The topic was about children who were out of control. A million viewers watched as Laura's older sister warned: 'Your attitude is going to get you into real big danger.'[97]

The school: In January 2008 Laura's teacher said she was concerned about Laura's sexualised behaviour, especially towards boys who, Laura said, 'dressed cool'. She was also drinking and smoking. Laura's mother told her teachers that Laura was becoming violent at home. The school contacted social services.[98]

Risky Business: In 2000, shortly before her death, Irene Ivison had applied for funding to create a partnership between CROP and Risky Business in Rotherham, a youth service project working with young women affected by issues of exploitation. The plan was to establish patterns in the behaviour of pimps, provide specialised foster placements, and greater awareness, as well as establish multi-agency interventions to protect young women at risk. The week after Irene passed away, the funding was granted.

Laura reported an incident to Risky Business in spring 2010. Three Asian males entered a house where Laura was with a friend and a much older adult – whom Laura described as 'a pervert' – someone she and her friends went to 'hang out, smoke and drink alcohol' with. The men threatened Laura's friend with an air pistol, and fired the gun randomly into the room; they then threatened Laura about telling the police anything. Risky Business tried to get Laura to talk to the police but she refused.[99]

As a result of this, on 21 April 2010 the manager of Risky Business met with social services' locality manager and the head of Young People's Services. The manager kept her notes of this meeting. Although it was agreed that social care would continue with regards to Laura's unborn baby, there was disagreement over the level of risk from sexual exploitation, with social services feeling there were no concerns, while Risky Business believed Laura was still at risk. A compromise was reached in that social services would not allocate a social worker to deal with this particular issue but would refer Laura via the pregnancy social worker for Risky Business to provide support, if necessary.

This was never done.[100]

By the spring of 2010 Risky Business had been reduced to one manager and two full-time staff, which slowed their ability to reach children like Laura, who were slipping through the net of social services. That they were able to have an impact at all was thanks to their enthusiasm and experience, and they were able to collect and collate a wide range of data on young women at risk.

They knew Laura was having sex with adults and many of the key indicators that she was being groomed for sexual exploitation were apparent in Laura's case. They knew she was 'taken into a car with men who encouraged her to drink alcohol'. They reported an incident in the takeaway, which took place when Laura was thirteen.[101]

For the next four years, they watched as Laura and others were 'passed around' by men in their twenties and thirties, who used her for sex and who treated her worse than a prostitute.

Social Worker 5: In September 2009 Risky Business informed social services that Laura was believed to be at risk of sexual exploitation due to associating with men who were named on a referral regarding another girl.

It had been precisely one year since social services had had any contact with Laura. Two days before they were due to visit, a social worker recorded a change of address for Laura and her family. It is still not clear how this information reached social services. The new address took Laura outside their geographical remit. Even though she'd moved outside their area, a social worker did try to maintain contact. Eventually, two weeks after the referral, Social Worker 5 arrived at the new address to find that Laura's family didn't live there.

The team manager decided to tell Risky Business that no further action would be taken unless Laura was re-referred with the correct address. Risky Business did not receive this notification. One week later social services closed the case with the comment that the family were not at the address.[102]

The teenage pregnancy midwife: The teenage pregnancy midwife contacted Children's Social Care Services in November 2009, to inform them that sixteen-year-old Laura (who had been identified as at risk from sexual grooming) was ten weeks pregnant.

No action was taken.[103]

On 19 May 2010, the midwife reported her concerns about Laura's ability to cope and social life to Children's Social Care Services.

No action was taken.[104]

The hospital midwife: On 23 June 2010 sixteen-year-old Laura gave birth to a healthy daughter. The following day the hospital midwife said she was worried about Laura's ability to care for a child. She suggested Laura stay in hospital for a few days, so she could make a more detailed assessment and help Laura prepare for life at home with her baby. Laura's family support worker told the hospital midwife and Laura's mum that she had 'no concerns' regarding Laura and her child. Laura asked to leave and the mid-wife admitted that she could not make her stay. Laura and her baby were discharged.[105]

The health visitor: On 27 July 2010 the family's health visitor called social services and spoke to the family support worker. She had several concerns. She hadn't seen Laura handle her daughter and she suspected that her mother was raising her. Margaret told the health visitor she was concerned about Laura's nights out and the people she was mixing with.[106]

The family support worker: She visited Laura at home on 26 August 2010. Laura told her everything was going well. Her manager said they should close Laura's case because all the work recommended on the initial assessment had been completed and there were no further concerns relating to sexual exploitation.

The family support worker never found out the identity of Laura's baby's father and so he was not assessed. Other people knew who he was – there were a number of issues known to social services associated with the father.

The only time the support worker saw both Laura and her mother between the completion of the initial assessment and the birth of Laura's daughter was on 11 May 2010. They spoke about grooming and exploitation but Laura did not understand that the girls were victims.

In all, the family support worker saw Laura on five occasions; twice in March 2010 when she undertook the initial assessment, once more before the birth of her daughter, the day after they returned home from hospital and on 26 August 2010 when Laura assured her all was well.

The following day, Laura's case was closed.[107]

The police: Even though she was just seventeen, Laura's police file was thick. The first entry dated back to October 2006 when Laura, who was then thirteen, was reported missing by her mother. At two minutes past midnight, Margaret was still on the phone to the police when Laura walked through the front door. The police left it at that.

The police were called again in December, this time by Laura. Her mother had refused to allow Laura to leave the house. It was 9 p.m. Margaret was worried about the people Laura was hanging out with. She'd already reported one incident, when Laura had been in a local takeaway where men had given Laura and a friend alcohol and then asked what they were going to give them in return. Margaret told both police and social services, asking them to do something about these men. The police made an appointment for Laura to come to the station. Laura had had poor attendance at school and had missed just about every appointment ever made for her.

She didn't show up.

The police made another appointment.

She didn't show up.

The incident was closed.

When she was fourteen, Laura was reprimanded for shoplifting. A few months later, in June 2007, Margaret called the police at 1.50 a.m. to report Laura missing. Laura returned at 2.17 a.m., before the police had arrived, and so they did not visit the family home. The following month Laura attacked a fellow pupil at her school.

Then, in November 2008, Laura called the police to say she and her mother were under attack from her father. After this came a burglary and a series of attacks on the home by vandals – a broken fence then a smashed window.

One night in July 2009 Margaret was woken at 5 a.m. by

screaming coming from downstairs. She found Laura in the living room with two teenage friends and a thirty-two-year-old man. Laura had screamed when the man burned her stomach with a lighter. She also said he'd kept touching her.

By the time the police arrived the man had left, along with Laura's friends. Laura changed her story several times as they questioned her. She told the police she'd burned herself, the result of self-harming, something she'd often done in the past. She told the officers the man was a family friend for whom she babysat. He hadn't hurt her in any way.

No further action was taken.

On 20 January 2010, Laura's name was one of eighteen that cropped up in a strategy meeting resulting from Operation Czar, an investigation into the sexual exploitation of children by older men.

Local charity Risky Business reported the incident with the air pistol to the police. Laura refused to provide any evidence about this. A police officer spoke to Laura and her mother at the family home in February 2010 with regard to the possibility that she was being sexually exploited. The officer asked if Laura had anything she'd like to discuss. Laura's response was: 'I don't do any of that. I can take care of myself.'

Consideration of Laura's possible involvement as a potential victim within the remit of Operation Czar ended.

On 20 September 2010, Laura's mother called the police to say that Laura was attempting to leave the family home with her daughter and that if they did so, they would be at risk from older men.

When the police arrived, Laura was packing her things. She'd had a massive row with her mother, she said, and now her mother was refusing to hand over her baby. Margaret told the police that Laura wasn't able to take care of the baby.

Laura said she was leaving despite what her mother thought. The officers could not force her to stay and although they tried they could not persuade her to remain in the family home. Laura said she was going to stay with a friend. Laura promised she would not see the men her mother had referred to and left.

All the officers could do was complete a Gen 118A Concern for a Child form, which was shared with the Public Protection Unit and sent to social services.[108]

Social Worker 7: Two days after Laura left home, on 22 September 2010, her seventh social worker met Margaret and Laura at Margaret's home and they signed a 'Contract of Expectations'. Laura agreed to leave her daughter with her mother whenever she went out. The social worker also had a long discussion with Laura about sexual exploitation. She felt that she had to phrase things carefully to try to ensure that Laura had understood her. The social worker then went on annual leave.[109]

The college: Laura had tried to study hairdressing and beauty at college and although she made progress, working one day a week in a salon, and got on with her teacher, in September 2010 the college's designated safeguarding manager contacted social services, expressing her worry that Laura and her baby had left home and were potentially in danger.[110]

The father of her child: Twenty-one-year-old Ishaq Hussain was married and wanted nothing to do with Laura or their baby. Laura decided to take action. In October 2010, she travelled the short distance to his parents' house and 'shamed' Hussain and her ex-boyfriend Asghar by informing their families of her sexual history with both men. Asghar's mother was furious. She hit Laura with a shoe, said her son would never have a baby with a white girl and called her 'a dirty white bitch', adding that she should learn to keep her legs closed.[111]

The man Laura loved: That October evening by the canal, Asghar took out a knife with a ten-inch blade and stabbed Laura repeatedly. Laura fell into the canal. Still conscious, she fought to get to the side. Asghar stabbed down with the point of his knife into the crown of Laura's head, forcing her below the surface.[112]

2010

An English Defence League (EDL) protest turns violent in Bradford after sixty to seventy thugs confront and throw missiles at police, recalling the race riots of 2001 that tore the city apart.[113]

The EDL, formed in 2009, describe themselves as a non-racist, non-political organisation whose aim is to stage peaceful protests 'against Islamic extremism and its influence on British life'.

Some supporters have been exposed as violent racists. Their website states they are protesting against 'organised Muslim rape'.[114]

CHAPTER THIRTY

THE SECRET REPORTS

Laura's body was found two days later. Detective Superintendent Nick Mason said it was the worst murder he'd seen.

Asghar and Hussain stood trial for Laura's murder in May 2011 at Sheffield Crown Court. It emerged that Asghar had discussed Laura with Hussain and had decided on an extreme measure to silence her. He had sent Hussain a text:

<I'm gonna send that kuffar* bitch straight to hell>

He also talked of buying a gun and 'making some beans on toast', in other words, spilling blood.[115] Asghar, by then eighteen, pleaded guilty.

Lord Justice Davis ordered that Asghar should not be considered for release for seventeen and a half years. The judge also told Asghar that he treated white girls as 'sexual targets' and not like human beings.

Simon Csoka, the barrister defending Hussain, held exactly the same opinion of his own client. Hussain, he said, was 'an unfaithful philanderer whose attitude to women ... absolutely stinks ... but although he's guilty of many things, he's not guilty of murder'.

Hussain was 'in a completely loveless arranged marriage which had never been consummated', to a wife 'he thought of

*non-Muslim

as a sister'. That, Csoka said, was why Hussain seduced so many women, including Laura. Hussain was not on trial for the exploitation of Laura or any other young woman; however, he was on trial for murder. And of that, he was not guilty.[116]

Laura was one of eighteen vulnerable girls who had been discussed during one of Operation Czar's police strategy meetings.[117] Yet it was four months after this before social services became involved, in January 2010, after sixteen-year-old Laura had already become pregnant. Even then, Laura was considered 'low priority'. Social services later admitted that discussions about Laura were 'brief and vague'.[118]

The support worker assigned to Laura's case by social services was inexperienced, barely qualified, and given insufficient support. She was one of two workers assigned to the eighteen girls. Funding was in place. The money was there. Rotherham Social Services simply couldn't find enough staff.[119]

Detectives from Operation Czar were unable to persuade victims to become witnesses. Many, like Laura, did not think they were being exploited. Most were frightened; families had been threatened. Others were intimidated by the thought of going to court. Witnesses over the age of thirteen have to give evidence and face cross-examination.

No one was prosecuted.[120]

It only takes one night to change a child's life for ever. Obviously, the longer and more time a predator gets to spend with a child, the harder it becomes for parents to get their children back.

If the school, the police, the Youth Offending Team and Margaret's mother could have stepped in, together, when Laura went missing in October 2006, and when her school was already concerned about her sexual behaviour, then her life may have turned out differently.

Rotherham's Safeguarding Children Board, which coordinates agency work, launched a serious case review after Laura's death. When the report was complete, most of its findings were not published. All that was available was a heavily redacted executive summary.

Alan Hazell, the board's chairman, said: 'Laura's situation was complex, which made it difficult for agencies to engage with her, but there were times when agencies may have worked differently or more effectively.' He said that her death was the result of 'a boyfriend from a relationship who callously murdered his girlfriend'. And: 'at no stage did we have any evidence that Laura was involved in child sexual exploitation'.[121]

One might wonder whether he had read his own report.

The Times newspaper got hold of an un-redacted copy of the report and went to the high court to fight a gagging injunction to report those parts that had not been made public. With support from the then Education Secretary, Michael Gove, *The Times* won. Black lines had appeared on 61 out of the report's 144 pages. The reason, the board said, was to protect the 'privacy and welfare' of the dead girl's baby, and to protect other members of her family.

The board had redacted the fact that Laura had been identified as one of the eighteen girls in Rotherham who were suspected of being sexually abused by 'Asian men'. Incredibly, the report also said that Laura might have been groomed and used for sex since she was just eleven years old. Included in the review's executive summary was the phrase: 'There is evidence from [Laura's] behaviour that she did get involved in sexual exploitation.'

Also redacted was Laura's history of her experiences of various safeguarding agencies from when she was eleven to fifteen, including meetings that discussed child sexual exploitation.

The report identified fifteen agencies that had been involved with Laura. There had been 'numerous missed opportunities' to protect a child who had become 'almost invisible'. When Laura was ten years old, a close girlfriend was 'thought to have become involved in sexual exploitation ... with particular reference to Asian men being involved'.

Nearly all the agencies had an unrealistic optimism about Laura's cooperation. New information was missed or ignored, as was the family history. Legal experts were not used. Records were not kept.

Laura was not seen by any agency (apart from Risky Business) as the highly vulnerable child she was. If people had spent more time with her, rather than accepting her answers and statements at face value, then the fact that she was unable to grasp issues or remember more than a small fraction of what she had been told would have become clear.

On those occasions support services saw Laura, she simply did not understand what they were trying to achieve (which, it could be argued from looking at the report, was to try to end their involvement with Laura by closing her case).

The report's author, Professor Pat Cantrill from the Department of Health, said that care professionals in Rotherham needed 'improved knowledge of sexual exploitation and grooming, including a better understanding of perpetrators'.

Something Irene Ivison and CROP had been trying to achieve fourteen years earlier.

Professor Cantrill also wrote that it 'only needed one person' to raise their voice for Laura's case to have been taken seriously.

Something else Irene Ivison and CROP had been trying to do. And Risky Business had been doing everything but shouting through the council's doors with a megaphone.

After all, to do nothing is to conspire with the abuser.

To date, no one has been punished, dismissed or penalised for failing Laura Wilson. But this was not the only report that had been kept secret from the public. At the end of September 2012 *The Times* reported on 200 confidential police reports and intelligence files about the commercial sexual exploitation and extensive use of English children for sex.[122] They included:

Report of Home Office-funded Rotherham research project, 2002

'In two cases, police officers responded to missing person reports but left the young women with the suspected abuser, concluding she was safe. When the parents attempted to intervene, they were threatened with arrest and charged for breach of the peace.

'One young woman (aged fifteen) was arrested after being found with an offensive weapon. Despite the presence of a group of men in the house and drugs having been given to the young woman, none of the men present was questioned.

'One young woman had an association with a man 20 years her senior. After having been missing for over a week, she was found in his car under the influence of drugs. Sexual intercourse had taken place. She was fourteen. The man was arrested for possession of drugs.'

Sexual Exploitation, Drug Use and Drug Dealing, South Yorkshire Police, August 2003

'One twelve-year-old girl described being taken to a hotel by some men, and watching while her fourteen-year-old sister had sex with them. One young girl was doused in petrol as a threat against reporting sexual offences. Some Asian men have been reported driving around Kimberworth, picking young girls up. Men from Bradford, Sheffield and Chesterfield are involved.

'Girls in Leeds also know the main perpetrators. They start grooming girls as young as twelve and are pimping them by age thirteen or fourteen. Rape, multiple rapes and gang rape are often part of the grooming process. They have been operating for years. People in the community are too frightened to speak out. They do not talk about them within their own cultural community.'

Lessons Learned Review – Operation Central Report to Rotherham Local Safeguarding Children Board, 2010

'(One of the victims), aged thirteen, was found by the police at 3 a.m. on Monday 7 October 2008 in a semi-derelict house alone with a large group of adult males. She was drunk, the result of having been supplied with vodka for disinhibiting purposes, and there was evidence that her clothing had been disrupted. She alone was arrested for a public order offence, appeared before the Youth Court and received a Referral Order. It is recommended that her case is referred as a potential miscarriage of justice to the Criminal Case Review Commission.'

South Yorkshire Police: Child Sexual Exploitation – A Strategic Problem Profile Report by Force Intelligence Bureau, South Yorkshire Police, 2010

'Some networks have younger, "good-looking" males who will always make the initial contact. These groomers will develop a relationship with victims, who will see the offender as an older boyfriend. He will work to isolate a girl from her friends and family. He may introduce drugs, alcohol or violence into the relationship and once the girl is dependent on the predator he will coerce her to have sex with his friends.

'A common pattern seen is that the victim's mobile numbers will be passed around. Victims ... are often threatened with or subjected to violence if they do not allow the exploitation to continue. In South Yorkshire, one offender attended a victim's home address and told her parents that he was going to "shag the arse off" their fifteen-year-old daughter and if they did not bring her out he would burn it down and take their youngest daughter with him.'

Report of Home Office-funded Rotherham research project, 2002

'Girls in Leeds also know the main perpetrators. They start grooming girls as young as twelve and are pimping them by age thirteen or fourteen. Rape, multiple rapes and gang rape are often part of the grooming process. They have been operating for years. People in the community are too frightened to speak out. They do not talk about them within their own cultural community.'

This same report criticised police for 'in all cases' treating young victims 'as deviant and promiscuous' while 'the men they were found with were never questioned or investigated'.

These reports revealed that organised groups of men who groomed, pimped and trafficked girls across the country were identified by police and social services but never prosecuted. As far back as 1996, a social services investigation found that girls were being coerced into 'child prostitution' by a small group of men who regularly collected them from residential care homes. Up to seventy girls were said to be involved. These findings led to a Home Office-funded research project on the 'detection, investigation and prosecution of offenders involved in sexual exploitation in Rotherham'.

In 2001, a headmaster of a Rotherham secondary school wrote to parents: 'Shocking facts are beginning to emerge regarding the systematic sexual exploitation of thirteen- to sixteen-year-old girls in our care.'

The never-published Home Office project featured the experiences of ten white British girls. It reported that: 'The men linked to the majority of the girls were members of one Asian family' and that takeaway shops were used as bases for abuse while taxis were used to pick girls up from 'outside schools, bus and train stations, residential homes and homeless projects'. The men were mostly of Pakistani heritage, but Kosovans and Iraqi Kurds were also working in organised gangs in Rotherham.

Despite repeated reports handed over to police and social services from Risky Business, nothing was done. One report stated: 'The view expressed by some police officers was that if the young people were not prepared to help themselves by giving evidence then no further action would be contemplated against their abusers.'

A few miles away, in Sheffield in 2007, South Yorkshire Police arrested a group of Iraqi men aged twenty to forty-five who had been going after girls in residential care, the youngest of whom was twelve. Thanks to the bravery of witnesses and an understanding of child sexual exploitation, the prosecution was successful.

According to an internal police report: 'The offenders were well organised. Girls were approached and groomed by the men, coming to think of them as boyfriends ... Once relationships were cemented, the situation changed. The offenders used violence to control the girls, who were then trafficked around the country, forced to have sex with other Iraqi men and used as prostitutes.'

South Yorkshire Police produced a report in late 2010 called 'Child Sexual Exploitation – A Strategic Problem Profile', which stated that while up to 300 children were actively being sexually exploited in the county, only three officers had been allocated to the problem. Two of those had other duties, which took up 50 per cent of their time, and one was part-time.

Joyce Thacker, Rotherham's director of children's services, speaking in late 2012, said Ofsted had praised 'good collaborative working' between police and the council. Some 'work with individuals did not lead to court cases for a variety of reasons' but in many respects Rotherham's services were 'well ahead' of other regions.[123]

The authority's cabinet member for children's services, Paul Lakin, accepted that support for 'a small number of vulnerable young people has not always reached the high standards we always look to provide'. He went on: 'Improvements have been made. Sexual predators come from different sections of the community and are criminals who need to be brought to justice regardless of their background.'[124]

Under Section 18 of the Children Act 2004, the director of Children's Services has responsibility for ensuring that the local authority meets their specific duties to organise and plan services and to safeguard and promote the welfare of children.

They knew there was a problem. And they failed in their duty to protect children, and to do something about it. Instead, they tried to hide the facts behind Laura Wilson's case, claiming they had to do it to protect other members of her family.[125]

Laura Wilson was born the year Fiona Ivison was murdered. Nothing had changed in seventeen years.

2011

Number of reported cases of girls under sixteen raped in England and Wales between 2004 and 2005: 3,980.[126]

Number of reported cases of girls under sixteen raped in England and Wales between 2010 and 2011: 5,115.

That's an increase of 22 per cent in just six years.

Only one in fifteen assailants in reported cases (a total of 303) was found guilty.

Forty per cent of all rapes in England and Wales are committed against girls under sixteen years old.[127]

Britain's chief prosecutor, Keir Starmer, says nine in ten rapes go unreported.[128]

CHAPTER THIRTY-ONE

FORGOTTEN VICTIMS

'This is my fantasy. He's tied to a chair in a lock-up. Bound and gagged. Terror in his miserable little crying eyes. I'm holding a baseball bat.'

Mr Black closes his eyes, just for a moment. He's there.

He puts his huge hands close together, one above the other, as though he's picked up the bat, weighing it in his hands, ready to swing. They shake, the knuckles are white. The skin looks rough; he is wearing gold rings and an expensive-looking watch. His arms, pressed close to his body, look huge. Veins stand out on his forehead. He's the sort of man for whom everyone starts backing up, right to the edge of the field, when he comes out to bat during sports day's parents' and children's game of rounders.

His voice is low and deep, his accent estuarial.

'He thought he'd got away with it. He thought he was home free. Laughing with his mates about what he'd, they'd done, free of the consequences. But now, now he sees there are consequences. You *do not* get away with this. I'd draw out the moment, savour every second, knowing what was about to come. I'd just wait. Looking at him. Looking for a long time, until I'd had enough.

'Then I'd say something like: "This is what you get for ruining my daughter's life." He ruined her body and mind. He raped her when she was helpless and turned her against me. I see that monster behind her eyes. He is still inside her, is part of her mind – he has changed her into something else – something I don't know, something I don't understand. I could've done exactly that. With the lock-up, you know. But I did the right thing. I told the right people.'

Mr Black had gone to the police station.

'I've had dealings with the police. Some of them are all right; they generally want to do the right thing and nick proper criminals, so I thought this would be just the sort of job they'd want to get their teeth into.'

Mr Black expected, naturally, for the station to empty as police officers stormed out, grateful for the chance to exact justice against such a heinous criminal. A young girl raped by a stream of older men who knew she was a schoolchild. It wasn't every day you heard of that sort of thing, was it?

Instead, they asked him some questions: 'Is your daughter missing? Is she going to make a complaint? How long ago was she raped? She's sixteen, isn't she?'

The answers were, respectively: 'No. I don't know; she won't talk to me. I don't know. Yes.'

She was sixteen, living at home, didn't want to press charges and there was no physical evidence. They told him he could fill out a report. They would take a note of what he had said. They would visit the men concerned and warn them.

Mr Black was incredulous. 'That's all you're going to do?'

'Have you spoken to social services?'

Social services were sympathetic and put together a child protection conference. Mr Black was told that this wasn't the right sort of meeting but they didn't have anything in place to deal with the situation he was facing.

The police told him they were hopeful about making inroads into this gang that had been preying on young girls in the area. The police didn't attend the next child protection conference.

Mr Black is angry. He wants justice.

He lets his arms fall and lets out a single sob.

'I mean, this sort of thing happens to girls whose parents don't love them right? Who don't care or who let them out all hours. I could see it in the eyes of the cops; they looked at me like it was my fault. I know now that this can happen to any girl, of any parent. I feel so helpless. I don't know my daughter anymore, they've broken something in her and I'm damned if I know how to fix it. I wish they were dead. I wish they had never been born. She said that I . . . She told the police . . . that *I* abused her.'

Mr Black's experiences as a parent of a child who's been sexually exploited are by no means unique, and neither are his feelings of frustration and revenge. For example, Suzi held the record for the most missing girl in her town. The police were fed up with looking for her and then bringing her home. They were also fed up with her exasperated parents.

When her father demanded they do something for the umpteenth time, the policeman replied: 'Why can't *you* control *your* daughter? If she were my—'

At this point the father hit the police officer on the chin. The police officer arrested him. The father was later released without charge.

Suzi continued to go missing.

A mother got hold of her thirteen-year-old daughter's phone and wrote down the names, numbers and texts of more than 150 Asian men (one of whom turned out to be a police officer). When she told the police that her daughter had just returned home after having gone missing for five days, and that these men had been abusing her, the police replied that if they took this information they'd be violating the girl's – and the men's – human rights.

Police were called to a disturbance outside a house. A father was demanding that the men inside let his daughter go. Officers went inside and found his daughter hidden under a bed (she had been drugged). The father, who refused to calm down when the officers said they would not be arresting the men, was himself arrested for racial harassment. His daughter, frustrated by this development, ended up being arrested for assault. The police left, leaving other girls behind in the house.

A mother wrote her own unofficial report and sent it to police officers and social workers. She told them that her daughter was taking drugs and having sex with older men. Both police and social services already knew more than the mother, that her daughter had been trafficked across the north-west. They did nothing, leaving the mother with the impression that they had decided her daughter was a 'bad kid'.

When one girl was found lying drunk and passed out on the street, the police fined her mother. The gang who'd raped her had dumped her in the road from a moving car.

Parents are the forgotten victims of child sexual exploitation. CROP, the charity set up by Irene Ivison, is still going strong today (even though vital government funding was cut in 2011). In February 2012 it was renamed Parents Against Child Sexual Exploitation (PACE). It is, as defined by its website, 'the only UK organisation to specialise in working alongside the parents, carers and wider family of child sexual exploitation victims'.

It's a very difficult and very lonely job.*

The authorities put all their focus on the girl, who is often anti-social, uncooperative and aggressive, making any investigation difficult. Parents, siblings, grandparents, aunts and uncles are seen as part of the problem, not part of the solution, and are ignored.

---

*PACE believes, based on limited reporting data, that as many as 10,000 children in the UK may be victims of sexual exploitation.

They are neither listened to, nor included in plans made by agencies for the welfare of their child, nor are they seen as useful in terms of evidence gathering and providing witness testimony to help win prosecution cases.

At the time of writing, PACE, which is based in an office building on the outskirts of Leeds, was working with 128 families, mainly in the north-west, but they receive calls from all over – even from abroad.

'So many parents think they're the only ones going through this but they're not alone,' said Hilary Willmer, the redoubtable seventy-something pioneer and chairperson, who has been with PACE since the beginning.

Dealing with the actual horror of what has happened to their child is only half the story. Reporting it to the police often unleashes more trauma. Once the child is over thirteen, the police can't do anything unless the child makes a complaint, so unless the child is crying rape, the police don't want to know.

They are more likely to arrest these girls for assault and possession of drugs, and will take no notice of parents who can provide descriptions, phone numbers, texts relating to the supply of drugs and sex, and car number plates – all great evidence for an investigating team.

Some police services are changing but still, too often, officers don't take the parents seriously. Hilary cites the case of a father who called to report his child missing at 8 p.m. The police called him back at 1.30 a.m. to say they didn't have anyone available at that time but someone would be around later that day. In another case, a mother reported her daughter's rape to a police station. She was told: 'We don't do rape here. You have to go to another station.'

The fact that the authorities don't understand what is going on can't be overstated.

One white girl, who was sexually abused by Asian men from the age of twelve, was offered language lessons in Urdu and Punjabi by Rotherham council. Social services explained that this was an attempt 'to engage' her in education.[129]

Police officers tend to see a 'troubled girl'. They don't realise that this girl used to get As at school, was very sociable, polite, helpful, etc. They don't see the child behind the damage because they don't talk to the parents.

Specialist child protection teams do not cover these cases.* The parent's first experience of reporting the crime/missing child is usually with a uniformed officer. In one case an officer kept describing the rapist as her daughter's 'boyfriend', as if it was the parents' fault for letting them see him, that they were wasting his time with this 'silly' case.

Schools aren't always much better than the police. One teacher organised a parent–daughter meeting at the school where the pimp's younger brother was studying. Schools write to parents threatening them even though the parents have taken their daughter to the school gate every day. Once they are on the premises, these children are supposed to be in the care of that school. Exclusion simply pushes a girl into the arms of the pimp.

Some schools know what's going on but don't warn parents. They prefer to blame the girls (and thereby the parents) for making bad choices. And caring, intelligent parents with high-flying jobs have been forced to attend parenting classes by their local authority because of their child's 'disruptive behaviour'.

Hit with this double whammy, losing their child to the pimp and no one willing to do anything to help them, parents suffer enormously. As one mother said: 'The worst thing is not being able to control or protect your own daughter. It was so hard to

*With one or two very recent exceptions, described later.

sleep at night. How do you sleep when your thirteen-year-old is out on the street somewhere, and you're not able to protect her? You go over and over it in your mind. Is it something I've done? Have I treated her any differently to my other children?'

The stress of trying to cope with what's happened to their child and trying to protect them – often without the help of the police – comes with tremendous costs. Parents fall behind at work, miss meetings and miss out on what should have been straightforward promotions. In some cases they end up losing their job. Mortgage payments are missed; depression hits and this combined stress sometimes leads to marital breakdowns, affecting the wider family. Siblings often develop behavioural problems.

Some parents become suicidal. One mother thought she had freed her daughter from her abuser, but later found out that her daughter had gone back to him. She gave up and took an overdose of sleeping pills. She survived. Social services saw this attempt as reason enough to take her daughter into care, without exploring the reasons why, making it even easier for her abuser to reach her.

Parents sometimes find their children turn violent (a response to the violence they experience at the hands of their abusers). Fights develop when the child tries to leave the house. They may be sitting down to dinner and a car stops outside, honks its horn and the daughter gets up to run out. The parent grabs her and a punch-up ensues – sometimes the abuser gets involved. Some parents become so frightened of their children that they lock themselves in a room for their own protection.

PACE has spent the last fifteen years doing amazing work, supporting parents and trying to make the police and social services understand what's really going on. They've not only helped kickstart investigations, they've driven them forwards.

However, it's an uphill battle. PACE has worked with over 200 families in the past four years and only two cases have come to court. And, of course, they are only able to help a tiny minority of the thousands of parents across the UK who need their help.

Although children in care homes are seen as easy prey, any child from any family background can be successfully targeted; children on track to get multiple GCSE A grades, children who like to ride ponies, children who help around the house; good, intelligent children from loving, supportive and well-educated families.

It's not unusual for the younger sister to end up following the older sister; in one case PACE dealt with, three girls from the same family fell into the hands of one group of predators. This sort of scenario makes it hard for the authorities to believe that it can be anything but the parents' fault.

And this leads to the vital question: how exactly do these men manage to lure so many children from all sorts of backgrounds with so much success?

2011

The NSPCC reports that:

'An estimated 55,000 children who have experienced sexual abuse receive no therapeutic support each year because of a shortfall in the availability of therapeutic services.

'There is only one therapeutic support programme for every 25,000 children living in the UK and many areas provide no therapeutic provision for sexually abused children at all.'[130]

CHAPTER THIRTY-TWO

A BRIEF INTERVIEW WITH A HIDEOUS MAN

Saeed, a Muslim man in his early thirties, is a council-funded out-reach worker who works with ex-offenders who are Muslim. He's like an unofficial, extra-helpful probation officer who helps these men readjust to a crime-free post-imprisonment life. He has worked with a number of Muslim sex offenders. He wants to keep his real name and location secret, for fear of attacks by extremist groups.

He has promised to make an introduction to a 'hideous man', a key member of a gang who groomed teenage girls. This necessitates a long wait in a café for a taxi, during which time, Saeed explains – with disarming frankness – how these men operate.

'The cops call it grooming,' he says, 'but from what I've discovered, from talking to this bloke in particular, it's more like social engineering – using persuasive language to get someone to do something they might not normally do. It's not like being a pick-up artist; that psychology is wrong for this game. Men who try to pick up girls in bars simply try to follow a certain set of steps that will, hopefully, get the target into bed.

'This stuff is amateur in comparison to what these gangs are trying to achieve. They're playing a long game. What they want to do is socially engineer a girl in a relationship, so that she'll remain loyal to them, no matter what, even after her parents know, so by that time, it's already too late.

'Teenagers are the perfect age because parents think that their daughter's changing behaviour, her general rebelliousness, like staying out late and hanging out with people they might not approve of, is all part of normal teenage rebellion.

'The papers have talked about how easy it is to lure these girls, or make it sound easy – they give them booze, drugs, chat them up and so on. It's not as easy as that. Some girls are too smart or too scared to get involved. Some girls are fully developed physically but emotionally, intellectually and in terms of experience they are blank slates.* The optimum age is fourteen to sixteen. Once they're eighteen to nineteen and have some experience, forget it.

'The guy you're going to meet now, he's twenty-one, well educated and has recently done a short stint for intentionally causing an underage girl to engage in sexual activity. He's got a job, through family connections, in sales, for a large company. He was once, for a year or so, one of the main "chat-up men" for a gang who trafficked girls across the north-west and was probably more skilled at what he did than most. He regrets his actions now but, well, I suppose you can hear it from him.'

A cab pulled up.

'That's him. Come on.'

We sit in the back. The Hideous Man drives. Neither man can see the other's face. He is well spoken and polite. We quickly get on to how he used to find 'targets' as he called them.

'If there's a few of them leaving school, I'll pick the one I want and say something like "Free at last, then?" using my friendliest voice. This is the golden moment. She will judge you in seconds,

---

*A PACE study published in 2005 revealed that 47 per cent of the girls they were working with were aged between fourteen and sixteen, by far the largest age group.

so you have to get everything just right. Your personal appearance, manners and expression have to be just right. Some girls might hold your skin colour or age against you. You can't control this but you can make sure you scrub up well, and give the right kind of eye contact and facial expressions.

'You have to look confident and comfortable. If you don't look comfortable then no one will feel comfortable with you. Less than 10 per cent of normal communication is verbal; everything else lies in body language and vocal tones. If I've done everything right, they respond with a smile. Maybe she'll say something like, "Yeah, that was a tough day."

'I will say: "You know what I like to do after a tough day?"

'"What?"

'"Hang out with my friends, put on a bit of music, have a laugh. We're going to hang out now, you should come."

'She'll look again. She'll see I'm dressed the part. I look appropriate. I'm older, but not too much older, it's a good age difference. Of course they're going to be tempted. Once we're walking and talking I ask them questions, what they're into. Any sisters? Any older brothers? Relationship with mum and dad?

'I'll start praising her, not overdoing it, just enough to give her confidence to keep talking. The more she talks, the more information I'll be able to collect. This is really important. Information is the key to everything. I find out what she's good at, whether it's writing essays or studying chemistry, riding horses or running, drinking or singing. Once you know her accomplishments, you use them to get close to her. Anything she tells me is stored away, ready to be used as our relationship develops.

'One of the most important things is to ask her about friends. Names, ages, anything about them. Then I can approach her mates, say I know a friend of theirs and on I go. Why shouldn't they be friends with me? I'm nice, got money, got access to booze and other boys like me, good times and so on. Once her friends are on board and they are together, they're even more likely to go along with whatever I want. They feel safe; they'll egg each other on and compete for attention.

'The sooner I can take her to a place where I'm well known the better. That way she feels good about me. I'm popular. I'm her guide. She gets used to being under my protection.

'You've got to be natural, relaxed, that's why most guys can't do it. It's like running a con – you've got to be convincing. Girls will notice if you don't believe in yourself so it's important not to overdo it. If you pretend to be something more than what you are, or make promises, at this stage, which can't be kept, then you'll get found out, so keep it simple.

'I used to say I was at college studying business, which I was, and that my family was loaded, so I had plenty of spending money. I believed in everything I was doing, I actually started to think 'I'm going to have a long-term relationship with this girl.'

'I would say right at the start that we had to keep this secret for family reasons. It's a racial thing or parents are frightened of letting you have any fun, they don't understand or know what it's like to be in our shoes.

'If you don't come across as relaxed then there's nothing you can do. It's like dogs – dogs know when people are nervous around them, they won't obey you if they sense this. Girls will sense it straight away and will say, once they're out of earshot, something like: "He gave me the creeps!"

'And you must listen carefully, every time she talks, so no fiddling with the iPhone or drumming your fingers. Do not interrupt and, when appropriate, give them positive feedback.

'Finding out any issues they have isn't usually too hard. After a while you say something like: "You're really beautiful. It's true. Everyone says so. Your life must be perfect." Nobody's life is perfect and it's likely she'll say something like: "My parents don't understand me at all."

'The trick is again to sound sincere. Obviously, she's got to actually be quite good-looking if you're going to tell her she's beautiful, otherwise that line won't work – and you shouldn't go over the top. You could limit it to her eyes or hair, or how smart and together she is.

'Whatever it is she comes out with, if it's her parents for example, then you have to seize on that – say something like: "My parents don't get me either, they always want to control what I do."

'Nothing helps this more than alcohol. Add anything I've mentioned to booze and you can multiply the effects by ten. Get her drunk and she'll tell you things she won't remember. If she hasn't drunk alcohol before, you tell her she's mature enough to try it. You say something like "It feels so good", or "Sounds like a good idea to me", or "Look at the rest of us, we're enjoying it, aren't we?" and back it up with reassurance: "Do you see me falling about, losing control? No. This is good stuff." All they need is a glass or two.

'My role is their fantasy boyfriend. To make it work, I need as much info from them as possible – the sooner I can get them to the "he gets me" stage, the better. Once they're at this stage, I'd be able to fool her parents. I'd be able look them in the eye and tell them what a wonderful daughter they have. If I'd given her permission to talk to her parents about me, she'd have been painting a positive, perfect picture and I'd be able to reinforce this.

'I want her to start feeling that she owes me and ought to do things for me. So you give them presents. We do it in sales every day – a free gift is more likely to get someone to pay attention and respond to your patter by giving you something back. The more value a gift has, and the more unexpected it is, the greater is their sense that they owe you something. So phones are an obvious gift. At the time you say it's nothing but that feeling of owing you something is in them.

'Another way of obligating them is to get them to carry drugs, or something that looks like drugs, which makes her an accessory, so she's "complicit" and will think twice about approaching the police. You just do it casually, as if it's nothing. "Here, pop this in your bag, will you? Got no room in my pockets." It's the least they can do. This also adds to the feeling of commitment. I want to get her to a point where she's given so much to her new relationship that there's no turning back.

'Over time you learn to feed their minds and emotions with actions, words and attitudes that will build the belief system you want, outweighing any evidence that might bring who you are and what you want into doubt. I'll remind her of the good times we had and the clever things she said and did. Positive reinforcement.

'This sounds a bit cultish, but if you can give them a nickname of your choosing it helps build an identity with you and split them further from their family.

'The phone is a powerful tool. You talk every night and text them regularly, though not too much. When you do, show lots of interest in their lives. Remember stuff she's told you before. If she's having arguments with her parents, you side with her and explain why she's right and why they're wrong. As long as she's got her phone with her and it's on, then you're with her too. You can already reach her in her own home and her parents don't even know.

'They're used to being told what to do by an older person and you can use this – as long as you're telling them to do stuff they think they want to do – like have a drink, get into a car, go on a walk, drive, to a party and so on.

'Dealing with the police is easy. They stopped me once and

asked what I was up to with this young girl so late at night. I said: "I'm a friend. I'm just walking her home." I took out my best prop, my student card. I went to a good college. "I've been helping her with a business studies project." They didn't even look at it and waved us on. As long as you have a good explanation and they don't have to do anything, then they're happy.

'Using the right language helps. For example I'll say: "You've got to go to this nightclub." I'm telling, rather than asking if she'd like to go. She's used to doing what I say and I've told her that she *has* to go to this nightclub, so more likely than not she'll go.

'People comply with expectations. Decisions are made on what others expect. Opening car or front doors, you're supposed to climb in or walk through. Handing them a drink, you drink. Weed, you smoke. Bedrooms, you get undressed. If she does refuse, it's easy to get around. For example, say you want a girl to come to a party and she says no. It's: "I'm sorry you won't come. Davina, Becky and Sally [her friends] are coming. They'll be really disappointed not to see you there because they were expecting you but we'll see you next time."

'Once they know their friend is going they change their minds as you start talking about who's going and all the amazing stuff that's going to happen at the party. It's part jealousy and partly because they don't want to miss anything. They can't refuse. It doesn't matter if Davina and her mates are actually going or not.

'When it's safe to say they're your friend, tell them, reinforce it. When you're good friends with someone, you'll help them even when it's difficult and you have to put your own needs to one side – this is very important. The greater the friendship, the fewer boundaries.

'You have to appeal to their interest, not intellect – so knowing what they're into is crucial. Find out what they want from life and see if you can give it to them, or at least help them. They might want love, attention, to connect, to be part of a group, to have fun, to have responsibility. If you're successful at this then they'll never leave you. Be kind just by helping, whether you succeed or not, and they will love you. Get them to think they are in an inner circle of trust.

'Men want sex. Girls want love. I can make them think that sex is love but once we get to the stage where older men are lining up, well, it's pretty obvious what's going on. Before that point, I'd usually talked them into bed but they did it willingly. They were in love. They wanted to, for me.

'After sex you start calling in favours, you press on those weak spots that split them from their family. You let them go home late, get into trouble. Arguments start and once teenagers realise just how much power they can wield, there is no limit to what you can get them to do.

'You just use the right language, using all the techniques you've programmed her with. It all happens naturally. Once her relationship with her family is at breaking point, that's the best time for someone else to have them. They can't go back to their family; they're completely dependent on me and my mates.

'Once they're being taken to shag older blokes, it's time to get nasty. We might have already shown them weapons, perhaps a machete or cricket bat in the car, this way making sure they know we mean business and deal with people who disobey us in violent ways – feeding the fear.

'By now they're dependent on drugs, cigarettes and alcohol and dependent on us to provide them. They need these things to keep getting high, to make them feel better – now there's a price to pay. At the same time they've got no one to turn to if they've broken family ties and old friendships. We tell them no one will believe them – which is usually true.

'Any resistance, we can keep them in a room, make sure they're sleep- or food-deprived. If necessary, there's always blackmail. I say I've got pictures; by now I've usually found out their password and control their Facebook account. They have to do what we want or else pictures will go up on there. I have all the power; they have none. The older ones use heavy intimidation if the girls aren't doing what they're told. Threats of physical pain, threats to family and so on.*

'Money's not the main reason. Few do it for money. People are willing to pay and they do, £10 to £30 a time, but ultimately it's more about the sex. And power. The guy at the top could call on any of these men for a favour and they would do it, whether it's moving drugs or anything. He liked young girls too but this operation was part of a larger picture.

'Why did I do it? Because I liked the challenge, the power and because I wanted to have sex – without my family finding out – and once I knew how it was possible with these girls, it seemed stupid not to. I knew the top guy well through family connections. I was studying business and I'm into self-help books that teach you all these things, so you can build professional relationships. But these things can be applied to all sorts of situations. Everyone thought I was a natural at chatting up girls but it was just because I knew stuff they didn't. The problem was that I made myself indispensable, so they came to depend on me totally to supply them with girls.

'My parents have arranged my marriage. I could have chosen my bride if I'd wanted but you get less support from your family if

*PACE reported that one girl was tortured and hit on the head with a metal rod, burned with an iron, strangled and had a plastic bag put over her head. She was found unconscious and rescued. In another case a girl's baby was kidnapped to force her into prostitution. She was afraid that social services would take her away, so she did what he asked. Younger siblings or other family members have also been kidnapped to force girls into prostitution.

you do that. The smart thing for me is to go along with the arranged marriage, for financial security. It's a good match anyway.

'Some of the guys I worked with were total idiots, but it was like being in a tight-knit crew. We did favours for each other. The guy who ran it, who organised flats and swaps, was respected and influential. That is not to say he was likeable at all, but I still would have done almost anything he said. He almost had me as much under his power as I did those girls.'

2012

In June, the first part of the 'Children's Commissioner's Inquiry into Child Sexual Exploitation in Gangs and Groups' with a special focus on children in care is published.

The deputy children's commissioner, Sue Berelowitz, states: 'As one police officer who was the lead in a very big investigation in a very lovely, leafy, rural part of the country said to me: "There isn't a town, village or hamlet in which children are not being sexually exploited."

'The evidence that has come to the fore during the course of my inquiry is that that, unfortunately, appears to be the case.'[131]

CHAPTER THIRTY-THREE

COLOUR BLIND

Ben

The building, warehouse-sized, white and square, sat incongruously among a row of terraced houses on the outskirts of West London. Inside, twenty teenage boys were sat in a classroom. They were between fourteen and eighteen, all Asian, all with earnest looks on their faces, all intently listening to Naz, who was telling them everything they needed to know about sex.

I was stood to one side. I'd been asked to give a talk about class As, something I do at schools across the UK. I'd come armed, as usual, with my unforgettable slide show of horror, dead junkies (faces obscured), their bodies bloated with gas, still sitting on the chairs on which they'd died and invariably where they'd lain for several days/weeks/months until they were discovered. Junkies don't have friends. It's all part of what heroin does to you. This lecture was held in a community centre and it was free for any lad who wanted to come.

'They just want someone they can speak to frankly and who will be straight with them,' Naz told me on the phone when he booked me. 'These boys are smart and mature but know almost nothing about drugs or sex.' They'd all been excluded from sex education at school on religious grounds.

'We don't talk about sex at home,' one lad told me, 'unless it's about having babies.'

'Then it is just one position they tell us about, missionary, isn't it?' added another.

As for oral and anal sex, forget it.

They rely on older or trailblazing friends, or the Internet. And if they do start Googling terms like 'anal sex' (and although there are many helpful online resources), they could end up looking at porn, where women are objectified, mistreated and abused, and end up with no understanding of sex in terms of a loving relationship.

Naz's mission was to make sure these lads got a rounded education, not only about sex but also to explain why a tiny minority of Asians had recently made headlines for the on-street grooming of schoolgirls for sex.

Naz explained that young Asian men in the UK find themselves living in two worlds. The first involves family, career and/or business and the mosque. In this conservative world where a parent's word is never questioned, there is no sex outside of marriage and no talk of sexual pleasure. Many young men are told from a very young age who they're expected to marry, which might be someone from their family's village back home in Pakistan. Naz tells the boys that about two thirds of British Asians, men and women, marry as virgins.

The second world is the English one of sexual freedom, where binge-drinking on the weekend is socially encouraged and where sex is all about pleasure – whether it is a one-night-stand or a relationship, and where sex is used in advertisements and discussed in magazines full of pictures of semi-naked women, and where porn is easily accessed and widely viewed.

Some Asian men turn their back on this promiscuous world and embrace religion. Some give in to the temptations of Western life and try to exist in both worlds. Some of these men use prostitutes for sex. A tiny, tiny minority become involved in the grooming and exploitation of young girls.

As Naz talked, I began to see similarities between organised grooming and drug dealing. Many councils and police services do not want to admit they have a drugs problem – particularly as it tends to be an expensive problem. It seems to be the same with sexual exploitation. This attitude has helped sexual exploitation take hold, like drugs, and become organised, with the men involved, like drug dealers, familiar with the weakness of the system and the methods they need to employ to trick girls.

Like drug dealers, none of these groups has any sort of moral code. They abuse any girl over whom they are able to exert power, regardless of colour or religion. It's simply a question of availability and accessibility. But, according to data reported in the media, by far the majority of these gangs are made up of Asian men.

In May 2012 *The Times* examined eighteen child sexual exploitation trials going back to 1997. They all related to the on-street grooming of girls aged eleven to sixteen by two or more men and covered Derby, Leeds, Blackpool, Blackburn, Rotherham, Sheffield, Rochdale, Oldham and Birmingham. Fifty-six people were found guilty of crimes including rape, child abduction, indecent assault and sex with a child. Fifty-three of them were Asian.[132]

And in another one of these 'confidential reports' for Rotherham Safeguarding Children Board in 2010, it was noted that the street grooming of young girls had 'cultural characteristics ... which are locally sensitive in terms of diversity'.

It continued: 'There are sensitivities of ethnicity with potential to endanger the harmony of community relationships. Great care will be taken in drafting ... this report to ensure that its findings embrace Rotherham's qualities of diversity. It is imperative that suggestions of a wider cultural phenomenon are avoided.'[133]

Additionally, it seemed that even for alleged crimes that did not make it to court, there was a strong Asian bias. For example:

1. Fifty-four Rotherham children sexually exploited by three brothers from one British Pakistani family, with eighteen stating that one brother was their 'boyfriend' – several of whom said they'd been made pregnant by him.
2. A fourteen-year-old girl allegedly held prisoner in a flat and forced to perform sex acts on five men, four of them Pakistani, plus a thirty-two-year-old Iraqi Kurd asylum seeker.
3. A specialist project identified sixty-one girls who were under the control of three brothers from another British Pakistani family.

In February 2012, a small but enthusiastic demonstration made up of members of the British National Party, the English Defence League, the North West Infidels and the Combined Ex-Forces marched together to bring public attention to the Rochdale trial. They carried banners that read: 'Our Children Are Not Halal Meat'. And hand-painted placards displayed phrases such as: 'Paedo scum'; 'Lock 'em up'; 'Hang 'em'.

Nick Griffin, leader of the BNP and a Member of the European Parliament, posted the following comment on his party's website:

The mass street grooming of young girls from the English community is only being carried out by Muslims. All the paedophile groomers in this particular sort of crime – on the street, in gangs – are Muslims. That's the common denominator.

You only have to read the Koran or look at the Hadith – the expressions of what the Prophet did in his life – to see where Muslim paedophilia comes from . . . Because it's religiously justified so long as it's other people's children and not their own.

Also in February 2012, 150 people took to the streets of Heywood, where many of the crimes took place, and rioted, targeting Asian taxi drivers and takeaways. Police officers faced a hail of bricks when they tried to restore peace.

At the same time, groups of up to a hundred far-right demonstrators staged protests outside the court. Several people were arrested. Two of the six Asian defence barristers pulled out of the trial during the first week, citing concern for their safety.

Part of the reluctance of councils to face the so-called 'race issue' of on-street grooming is the fear of re-igniting a race war. Memories of the Bradford Riots of July 2001 are still strong. The riots, which saw 300 police officers injured and 297 people arrested, were the result of heightened tension between the city's ethnic minority and the city's white majority, exacerbated by confrontations between far-right groups, such as the National Front and the BNP, and the far left, the Anti-Nazi League. Riots also occurred in Oldham and Burnley.

Griffin and the far-right groups were united in their claim that if they weren't there to draw attention to the fact, no newspaper would cover trials that featured what they called 'Muslim paedophile grooming gangs' who were charged with 'countless abhorrent sexually motivated charges against children and minors'.

The BNP had misunderstood what they were protesting about. This was not 'paedophilia'. The vast majority of these men were not attracted to pre-pubescent girls. They wanted to have sex with teenagers with 'adult' bodies. One of very few exceptions was Shabir Ahmed in Rochdale, who also targeted a much younger child.

Also, the comment 'All the paedophile groomers in this particular sort of crime – on the street, in gangs – are Muslims' was incorrect for another reason. Remember the stats from *The Times*? Well, BNP members Ian Hindle, thirty-two, and Andrew Wells, forty-nine (presumably non-Muslim), were two of the only three white offenders among the fifty-six on-street grooming cases the paper examined.

The BNP said it expelled the two after they were jailed for a total of five years and three months in November 2008 for sexual activity with two fourteen-year-old girls in Blackburn. Mr Griffin should therefore rephrase his statement to include members of the BNP.[134]

But, to be fair to the BNP, it would still be incorrect. Evidence from specialist outreach groups from all of the UK reveals that on-street groomers come from all walks of life and are of all colours and creeds.

Wendy Shepherd, child sexual exploitation project manager with Barnardo's in the north of England, said: 'In the North and Midlands many have been British Asians; in Devon it has so far been mainly white men; in Bath and Bristol, Afro-Caribbeans; in London, all ethnic mixes, whites, Iraqis, Kurds, Afghans, Somalis ... The danger with saying that the problem is with one ethnicity is that then people will only be on the lookout for that group – and will risk missing other threats.'[135]

In Devon, nineteen-year-old Jake Ormerod (who is white) was jailed for ten years in 2011 after he admitted thirteen charges of sexual assault against nine girls. Police were looking for more than ten accomplices who were involved in the abuse of more than 139 underage girls in the Torbay area.

Ormerod chatted to girls as they left school and 'friended' them on Facebook, all part of his grooming process, which ended with them coming to his home, where he plied them with alcohol until they were unable to resist his assaults.

Detective Inspector Simon Snell, head of the Child Exploitation Unit for Devon and Cornwall said that: 'He [Ormerod] would prey on young, vulnerable girls, many of whom were frequently missing from home and he would then commit sexual offences against them, often while they were drunk or under the influence of alcohol and cannabis ... He used classic grooming behaviour to make the victim feel as if they are in love with the offender – he then abused them. He is a predatory sexual offender who took advantage of young girls who were vulnerable ... Ormerod is extremely dangerous. He has done a lot of damage. Some of these girls attempted suicide. It has made them ill, it affected them both physically and mentally.'[136]

Unfortunately, in February 2012, as the Rochdale trial was getting under way, Ormerod had his sentence reduced on appeal, from ten to seven years by three of the country's most senior judges, who said the original term was 'excessive'. Ormerod will be out of prison in just three and a half years – but will at least spend seven and a half years under the supervision of the probation service.[137]

In London, where I spent a great deal of time with various outreach groups, there are organised gangs of Area Boys (mixed races), Rastafarians (South London), Yardies (London-wide), Polish gangs (South West and South East, extending into Kent), Bangladeshis (East London) who all groom and exploit girls of all races, using similar methods.

Reports from outreach groups such as Barnardo's in Scotland and Wales reveal that child sexual exploitation is a very real problem but little about the ethnicity of the perpetrators. In Wales, for example, Barnardo's found children being exploited in twenty out of the twenty-one local authorities they profiled (some in very remote areas), identifying a total of 184 separate cases.

Drugs gangs of all ethnicities have started targeting young girls (some of whom are single mums) who have been given a council property, part of a phenomenon described by some outreach workers as 'vulnerable takeovers'. These girls, usually lonely, are looking to connect with someone and make friends. Someone woos them, gets them on (or back on) drugs, moves in and once the girl is dependent, the gang arrives. Then she's trapped, unable to tell anyone because:

a. She will lose her drug supply
b. She will be arrested
c. If she's a mum, she might lose her baby
d. She will be evicted and not rehoused

Outreach groups from around the UK have been reporting cases of child sexual exploitation to the police and social services but most people don't know this because, so far, no one's been listening, and police, politicians and many other groups have been too frightened to talk about the so-called racial issue and have therefore decided to run away from the whole problem – allowing the gangs to take hold.

No one from the BNP was protesting outside Reading Crown Court in October 2012, when a gang of paedophiles was on trial. A former sheep farmer, scout leader, bank manager and soldier in the Household Cavalry (all white) were found guilty of raping children as young as nine in an isolated farmhouse. They filmed, swapped footage of the abuse and sent it to contacts online. The men, Peter Malpas, forty-seven, Anthony Flack, fifty-four, Nicholas Cordery, sixty-three, Simon Wyn-Davies, thirty-eight, were all found guilty and sent to prison.[138]

No one screamed for their heads. No column inches were filled with soul-searching about why white English paedophiles were able to work in gangs to groom and rape children. Is this because, as disgusting as it is, we accept the fact that some men are perverts? That a small, sick part of our population is attracted to small children?

Sexual perversions of all kinds do not recognise colour. The urges that drive men to rape children, whether pre-pubescent or teenage, exist in the same proportion, in all races and cultures – and that includes all religions.

Popular newspaper columnist Melanie Phillips, writing in the *Mail on Sunday* about the Rochdale case, said:

> *While it is the case that in general the overwhelming majority of sex crimes against girls are committed by white men, this particular phenomenon of street gangs in northern towns targeting white girls and passing them around for sex is disproportionately committed by Muslims.*
>
> *The police maintain doggedly that this has nothing to do with race. What a red herring. Of course it doesn't! This is about religion and culture – an unwesternised (sic) Islamic culture which holds that non-Muslims are trash and women are worthless. And so white girls are worthless trash. Which is itself of course a race issue (sic).*[139]

Offenders are Muslim only in name. They drank, took all kinds of drugs, shaved and – most obviously – all had sex with underage girls (while many of them were married). This does not fit the typical Muslim profile. The same goes for white offenders who may class themselves as Church of England, but hardly live by Christian values.

The Rochdale Nine were just perverts who happened to be Asian. As Judge Gerald Clifton sentencing them said: 'Some of you, when arrested, said it [this prosecution] was triggered by race. That is nonsense. What triggered this prosecution was your lust and greed.'[140]

Greater Manchester Police stated that 95 per cent of the men on its register of sex offenders were white. Five per cent were Asian. This is in line with national data. Most abusers are white and most abuse is committed by family members in the family home. However, when it comes to street grooming and sexual exploitation of teenagers, it seems as though Asians are disproportionately represented. One could, as *The Times* has done, make a statistical case for a racial factor. They said their figures were supported by research carried out by the Jill Dando Institute of Security and Crime Science at University College London.

However, Ella Cockbain, one of the academics who carried out the study, said: 'The citations are correct but they have been taken out of context ... Nor do they acknowledge the small sample size of the original research, which focused on just two large cases [involving a total of twenty-five offenders].' The academics were rightly concerned that their research of a small, localised sample was being used to characterise an entire national criminal type.[141]

In June 2011 the government's Child Exploitation and Online Protection Centre (CEOP) published their investigation into localised grooming.[142] They used the broadest possible definition for their study: any situation where a child or young person receives something in exchange for performing sexual favours. CEOP identified 2,379 potential offenders who had been reported for grooming since 2008.

The vast majority were men.

Almost 50 per cent were under twenty-five.

They were only able to identify 940 of these suspects.

358 of these were white (38 per cent).

301 were of 'unknown ethnicity' (32 per cent).

245 were Asian (26 per cent).

29 were black (3 per cent).

7 were Chinese (0.6 per cent).

According to the 2001 census the general population is:

White: 92.1 per cent
Indian or Pakistani: 3.1 per cent
Black: 2 per cent
Other: 1.6 per cent
Mixed: 1.2 per cent

CEOP's figures were reported in the media with various degrees of sensationalism. At first glance it looks like there are proportionally far more Asian men than there should be. Yet the fact that almost one third of the identified pool did not have their ethnicity recorded makes these results impossible to evaluate.

Also, the data was poorly recorded (in police reports and witness statements, for example), inconsistent and incomplete and limited to areas where this data was available (many areas still mistakenly think they don't have a child sexual exploitation problem) and street grooming isn't even an 'official' crime, so the researchers had to judge for themselves.

And CEOP received a limited response, especially children's services and Local Safeguarding Children Boards (LSCBs). Only thirteen out of 433 LSCBs responded to CEOP's request for data. And these were the ones that knew they had a problem and had been involved with investigations in areas such as Greater Manchester.

As CEOP said itself in the report:

Where police, children's services and voluntary sector agencies have worked together, coordinated by the LSCBs, to identify and address child sexual exploitation, a significant number of cases have come to light. However, very few cases are known in areas where agencies do not routinely engage victims and collect data. Agencies which do not

proactively look for child sexual exploitation will as a result fail to
identify it. As a result, the majority of incidents of child sexual
exploitation in the UK are unrecognised and unknown.

Therefore CEOP's assessment was hardly representative of the nature and scale of child sexual exploitation in the UK or, indeed, of the 'localised grooming' model. This supports the theory that, so far, all we can tell is that a small number of Asian men have been identified grooming teenage girls in localised areas in the north and north-west.

East Lancashire police recently compiled stats on grooming. As of September 2012, ten children a week were being reported to police because they were at high risk of sexual exploitation. Between April 2011 and March 2012 there were 1,494 child sexual exploitation referrals in Lancashire; 645 child groomers were identified by Lancashire Police. Seventy-seven per cent of them were classed as white British, 9 per cent were Asian Pakistani and 3 per cent were Asian Indian.[143]

There was a 'perfect storm' in some parts of the north and north-west in that the care system provided a steady stream of vulnerable, mainly white girls from all over the UK to the north-west where they came into contact with closely knit groups of sexually frustrated Asian men (the north-west, relative to the rest of the UK, has a larger concentration of Asian people, for example 11.5 per cent of people in Rochdale are from an Asian background).[144]

There are forty-seven care homes in Rochdale (Haringey in North London, a similar-sized borough, has two private care homes),[145] most of which are in areas where Asian populations have settled, and it is these girls who were preyed upon most and first, where the gangs learned how to operate, before turning their attention to any young girl walking around town and then finally waiting outside school gates.

It's thanks to the fact that these girls were failed at each stage by some care homes, social workers and police officers, that gangs (made up of a tiny minority of the local population) were able to operate unimpeded for more than twenty years, before the true scale of the problem was revealed.

Most outreach groups say they do not find race a useful issue on which to focus. Generalising abusers as being one particular type makes it easier for other abusers who do not fit this profile to continue unnoticed. Far better, they say, to focus on the profiles of the children that end up being abused by these men. That way we can work to prevent it. There's not much point profiling the abusers as we know there have been and always will be a section of the population who are perverts and will do everything they can to get what they want.

We also need to focus on the conditions that give these people the freedom to exploit vulnerable children without fear of retribution. The sooner we do this the better, because right now, too many innocent young people are suffering.

PART IV

2012

In October the government announces that the United Kingdom spent £9 billion on the Olympics. The original estimate, made at the time of the original bid in 2005, was £2.4 billion. Team GB came third in the medal table.[146]

The UK has the highest teenage birth rate in Western Europe. The UK has the highest teenage abortion rate in Western Europe.[147]

Unicef ranks the UK twenty-second out of thirty-five nations measured using their poverty index, with 12.1 per cent of children classified as living in poverty.[148]

There are an estimated 3.5 million children living in poverty in the UK – 1.6 million in severe poverty.[149]

CHAPTER THIRTY-FOUR

THE INVISIBLE WEAPON

Name: Anne
Age: forty-two
Profession: social worker
Location: London, 1997–present.

Your father raped your mother, who, eighteen months later, dropped a cup of boiling water over you. Two seconds later you had third degree burns. You screamed as she covered you in cold wet towels; your skin would have steamed.

I know all about your mum.

She said you had changed her. You were her wake-up call. Her saviour. She stopped taking crack, stopped smoking weed. Broke free from her pimp. Was making a go of it. Wanted to be a good mother to you and nothing more.

Your grandma said she'd never manage.

Your mother, only sixteen, was amazed by you. A boy. She'd wanted a little boy. She was going to bring you up right, to be a real man, not like your dad. She couldn't wait.

Still you screamed.

Your skin was cold. Why were you still screaming?

The nappy. She forgot about your nappy; boiling water had got inside. It steamed when she removed it.

An ambulance took you to the hospital, where a team was waiting. The doctors knew that water transfers heat to skin twenty times faster than air. They knew that the depth of the burn is dependent on temperature, contact time and medium. They knew that toxic agents released by inflammation, caused by the burn, cause most of the tissue damage. They knew that babies have very thin skin. They knew the scald would not look that dramatic. It's not like flames, which blacken, blister and boil the skin's liquids. They knew it would be deep.

You screamed.

They worked.

A doctor spoke to your mother. She was thin, hollow-cheeked, found it hard to understand when the doctor explained how serious this was.

He did not know your mother's history but doubted her ability. He called social services.

I rushed straight over, even though it was too late.

Your father is a rapist. Your mother only one of his victims. You arrived too soon. You weren't supposed to be here. But you are, and this is what happened.

Thoughts that keep me sane:

You will grow up somewhere else.

You will never know I stood here.

You will forget this.

Natalie

When Anne appeared at the door, I could tell something was amiss.

'Can I come in? Bloody shit day.'

We walked through to the lounge and I put the kettle on.

My first six months were almost up. It had been tougher than I thought but I loved the work, I'd built up trust with so many girls and we were managing to help keep most of them safe.

I asked Anne what was wrong.

'You really don't want to know.'

'I do. Even though I don't, if you see what I mean.'

'I've just come from the hospital, where I've spent the last hour waiting for news on a three-month-old baby.'

She told me what happened.

I sat quietly for a moment afterwards. 'Well, there's not much you can add to that except to say, yes, that counts as a bloody shit day.'

'I've really had enough. I've been making mistakes, missing stuff.'

'What do you mean?'

'I put Janine in care. I missed Sandra's lies. And they're just two of my mistakes we know about. What else have I done?'

'You couldn't have known Sandra was lying, and you didn't know what was going to happen to Janine. We all know there's a heavy psychic price to pay doing this job, and a big part of that is that children you try to save still end up getting hurt whatever you try and do. Sometimes, it's the system we need to blame, not individuals.'

Anne nodded, but uncertainly.

'I would say I have something to cheer you up,' I continued, 'but I'm not sure what you'll make of it.'

'Go on, try me.'

'You know Hannah?'

'The black girl on the estate? Raped? The one with the ongoing gang problem?'

'That's the one. She's pregnant.'

'Seriously? That's meant to cheer me up?'

'And the father is an ex-member of Racist Attack.'

'Oh good grief.'

'No, you'd think it was a bad thing but amazingly it was consensual. They're in love. He's sticking around and because of the baby the gang are leaving Hannah alone. You should see them together, it's like Romeo and Juliet, but with a happy ending.'

'My goodness. Hope among the ruins. I'd pay to see the night Hannah introduced the little racist to her mum: "Mother, I'd like you to meet the father of my child, he was a Nazi once but he's all right now."'

Beatrice exploded into the room.

'Brannigan's just arrived!'

'Oh, Christ,' I said, getting up quickly.

'Who's Brannigan?' Anne asked.

'A chief superintendent who's decided, in the wake of the news going mad about these girls in Rochdale, to come here and learn something about child sexual exploitation. Feels more like an inspection. Want to enjoy the show?'

'Sure, why not? It's not every day you get to meet a chief superintendent.'

Chief Superintendent Brannigan was in full dress uniform, shiny silver buttons, polished peaked cap. He looked extremely out of place in our informal building. And it was soon clear that he had very different ideas about teenage girls and sexual exploitation.

Inevitably the chat rapidly moved into issues we'd been facing with regards to gang violence.

'Rest assured we have a policy of zero tolerance towards guns. Anyone found in possession of a gun will face a long prison sentence.'

'Does that include girls?' Miranda asked.

'It's regardless of sex.'

'But what if a girl is coerced into holding a gun for a gang?' Anne asked.

'Zero tolerance means just that. If she knows what's good for her, she will refuse to hold the gun. Those who store weapons for others are committing a crime, as well as helping others to commit theirs.'

'Chief Superintendent Brannigan,' Beatrice said, 'do you know which weapon cannot be detected during a stop and search?'

'I'm sorry?'

'Which weapon cannot be detected during a stop and search? Or a metal detector, for that matter.'

Brannigan looked uncomfortable.

'Give up?'

'I suppose, yes.'

'The answer is rape. You might be doing a good job looking for knives and guns but what about the weapons you can't see?'

Brannigan still looked perplexed.

'Let me give you a real-life example,' Beatrice said. 'Charlotte, who was twelve, went to a "good" school because her mum was keen to have her educated away from the area she lived in. But she couldn't escape the gangs and they used her to sell crack. When she was thirteen the police arrested her and confiscated the drugs she was supposed to sell. When she returned home, the gang kidnapped her and gang-raped her as punishment. This was how Charlotte lost her virginity.

'Saying no to the gang for Charlotte is like her asking to be gang-raped. When the gang tells her to hold anything, whether it's drugs, guns, stolen property, she does it, no question. And you're saying the police response will be to put her in prison?'

Brannigan nodded. 'I understand what you're saying but—'

'All I'm saying,' Beatrice continued, 'is that when you arrest a young girl for carrying a weapon or drugs, there might be a good reason why. It might be worth asking us, or another charity with our experience to talk to her, to get the whole story. In my opinion "zero tolerance" means "100 per cent ignorance", that you're blinkering yourself to the circumstances that put the young person in that position.'

'I think what Beatrice is saying,' Miranda added with a slight smile, 'is that you have to look at what might be behind the crimes. The other day, I got a call from one of our girls. She'd been arrested and charged with assault after she attacked a fellow passenger on an Underground train. What looked like a straight-forward case of assault was in fact much more complicated. She'd been drugged and raped not long before, had fallen asleep on the train, had a nightmare she was being attacked again and woke up hitting the passenger next to her. She needed therapy, not a court date.

'We're playing a difficult game here,' Miranda continued. 'There are so many things we need to do to help these girls and police policy is not always helpful. From what the girls tell us about dealings with the police, officers use inappropriate language and clearly have certain stereotypical pictures of teenage girls who find themselves in trouble. Police officers tend to downplay the severity of sexual assault and exploitation, because they think the girl consented.

'Young people don't always distinguish between caring and con-trolling behaviours, which is just one reason why they don't always think they've been abused. What chance do they have if the police can't see past this? They're not protecting themselves, they can't because they don't realise they need protecting or if they do they don't know how. Even if young people can't or don't try to avoid exploitative situations, they are still in no way at fault.

'It's always the men – and some women – using them who are responsible for the sexual exploitation. I'd like you to tell your offi-cers that sexual exploitation is not simply "selling sex"; it means that the young person has been tricked or forced into sex and we need to help her break free.

'The girls come here because they're told we can be trusted and they come back to us because we prove that to be true. You've got to get to the stage where the police can say the same thing.'

'Thank you so much,' Brannigan said. 'It's been educational.'

He left promising he would re-educate his officers.

Once he'd gone, Anne looked at Beatrice. 'You were amazing! His face was a picture!'

Beatrice smiled. 'I've been waiting to do that for years.'

'Where's Mary?' I asked. 'She'll be sorry to have missed that.'

Mary was with Ginger in one of the counselling rooms.

Parks are supposed to be happy places but Ginger finds it hard to go near any green space now. Just the sight of a play area with swings and slides and those little plastic animals on springs is enough to make her feel sick. If she sees a skate park, then she starts shaking. One summer evening last year, Ginger was gang-raped by a gang in an East London skate park.

The park had once contained a community centre that used to be open until 10 p.m. every night. It had been closed. Cutbacks. When councils look at something like a community centre, they see costs, not savings. They see salaries, maintenance and services. This is one of society's many crime-related dichotomies: councils and police cite lack of funds but the government insists savings must be made and budgets are therefore cut.

Closing non-essential services like community centres and youth services in general saves money in the short term but, in the long term, the costs can quickly add up when considering police resources, associated crime, associated drug use, new addictions, crimes, court cases, care homes, prison time, etc.

In the North London borough of Haringey, every last youth club was shut in 2011. Cuts of £41 million to the council's overall budget led to the youth services budget being reduced by 75 per cent. The August 2011 riots erupted in places like Haringey, where there were few or no youth services.[150]

Doug Nicholls, from Unite, told the BBC that at least 20 per cent of youth centres in England and Wales would close in 2012 and that 3,000 youth workers (40 per cent of the total) would lose their jobs by the end of the year.[151]

He was right.

Meanwhile, Jonathan Toy, head of community safety and enforcement at Southwark council in South London, said local authorities were being forced to reduce their efforts to stop gang violence.

Every time there's a murder, however, the investigation costs £1.5 million.[152] This is the crime dichotomy in action – cutbacks lead to costs. Contrary to what the politicians say saving money isn't the only answer. Spending it wisely is.

Mary thinks we should tell the deficit to get stuffed; some things are just too important. Community centres are able to reach children who need help. They are cheap, effective and run by dedicated, well-trained front-line staff with a passion for what they do. They know when children are falling down and know where to send them – whether to social services or outreach charities like us. Ultimately, if you send young people out onto the streets with nothing to do, and with nowhere to go apart from the mall and the multiplex, then you're feeding the problem.

You can see the effect of the cuts everywhere, from the riots to the rapes. Ginger's local community centre went. Now the warden just opens the gate at dawn and closes it at dusk, a gate that is easily scaled by anyone with two arms and two legs.

So, along with the community centre went the homework club, the photography projects, the drama group, the music project, film editing and the football club that worked with other community centres to hold tournaments in neutral areas.

The space around it, the park and the skate park were still accessible, except it became a haven for bored kids and then gangs who used the space to smoke cannabis, drink, fight, stash weapons (increased stop and searches means blades are hidden under bushes and in this case, inside one of the ramps), take and sell drugs and have sex.

'I liked school,' Ginger told Mary. 'I come from a single-parent family but my childhood was great. Mum was great. I never knew my dad, so I didn't miss him. There was nothing to miss, not even a void because I didn't know any different other than being with Mum. I didn't mind not having brothers and sisters. My friends always moaned about their siblings, what bullies they were.

'Mum was a nurse in an old people's home. She was working a lot of shifts. She said I was old enough to be trusted. I told her it was fine if she worked late. I liked being alone and I had lots of homework to do.

'That summer I started hanging out with my friends at the skate park. It was great. We got drunk and smoked a bit of weed, let the lads try and chat us up, have a laugh. Then one day one of the lads there said he had something to show me. He'd made a room under one of the ramps. He jammed in a long screwdriver and lifted out a side panel and you could climb in. Inside there was a space, about six feet high, two feet wide and eight feet long and very dark.'

When Ginger was inside he molested her. She tried to fight him off but other lads climbed in. She didn't know how many. They raped her. Afterwards they waited for her outside her home. She was in their gang now, they said. Every now and again she was taken into the 'hide', sometimes by much older men.

She was terrified; she couldn't tell anyone. She'd seen the weapons; they all knew where she lived, some went to the same school. Thanks to her mum's job, Ginger was able to hide it from her.

Ginger wanted to get free of the gang. 'I just want it to stop. Things have been happening that I don't understand. I have nightmares and panic attacks; I even puked up in my sleep once.'

At least, Mary thought, Ginger wasn't pregnant.

But it was only a matter of time.

2012

October: Keir Starmer, QC, Director of Public Prosecutions, admits that a generation of girls has been betrayed by the justice system's flawed approach to sexual exploitation.

'If we're honest it's the approach to the victims, the credibility issue, that caused these cases not to be prosecuted in the past. There was a lack of understanding.'[153]

The following month the second part of the Children's Commissioner's Inquiry into Child Sexual Exploitation in Gangs and Groups is published. The report's authors report that there were 2,409 child victims of sex crimes committed by gangs or groups of men during a fourteen-month period from 2010 to 2011.

The report also estimates that a further 16,500 young people had displayed high-risk signs of exploitation.[154]

CHAPTER THIRTY-FIVE

TERMINATION DAY

Natalie

I emerged from the stairs into our reception and stopped in surprise.

Mika was waiting for me. Nothing unusual about that because I was expecting her, but this was the first time I'd seen her without jewellery and make-up. She looked so young, so vulnerable, like she actually was fourteen.

Mika was seventeen weeks pregnant. Today was termination day.

In preparation she had followed the instructions, showered, drunk only water and left her jewellery and make-up and taken the dilators.

'Not easy, leaving without make-up,' she said with a weak smile, 'I feel naked without it.'

This wasn't the girl I was used to dealing with. Mika was normally exuberant, rude, fearless, fuck-you-for-tomorrow-we-die kind of girl.

'How are you?'

'OK, I suppose. I've spent so long dreading this. I spent all day every day thinking about it. I'm knackered. It'll be a relief when it's over. Then I can start living again. Really.'

Another weak smile.

I'd thrown just about every contraception device I knew about at Mika, but there was little room for caution in her chaotic life.

We walked to the clinic in silence through the noisy streets. She seemed calm.

We entered the reception. A nurse greeted Mika straight away and started to usher her through into a side office.

Mika spoke quickly. 'I want Natalie with me.'

The nurse was called Selina; she had a beautiful voice, she told me later she was from Ghana. She seemed totally relaxed and sympathetic. She'd been through this with a hundred girls already this year but never let slip any sign that this had become routine.

'It's not possible for Natalie to be with you during the medical examination and the procedure itself but she's very welcome to stay here.'

'I understand.'

'Can I just confirm your ID?'

Mika gave her name, address and date of birth.

'You've taken the dilators?'

'Yeah.'

The nurse checked Mika's blood test results then took her medical history.

'I know you've been asked this before but we're busybodies here and double-check everything. Any allergies?'

'No.'

'Taking any other medication?'

'No.'

'Do you have any of these conditions?'

Selina passed a card with a list of illnesses, from diabetes to heart disease.

'No.'

'Family history of any of these conditions?'

'No.'

'Ever had a surgical procedure before?'

'No.'

'Well, everything looks just fine. Is there anything you want to ask me?'

Mika shook her head.

'You understand that this procedure will terminate your pregnancy.'

'Yes.'

'And, finally, I know you've answered this question before, but we're such busybodies we need to hear it again. Can you confirm for me your reasons?'

'I am on my own and am too young to have a baby. I have no one to help me. I can't finish school if I have the baby.'

Pregnancy had changed Mika. She'd slowed down and had even turned up more regularly at school.

'Thank you, Mika. If you just sign the consent form to state that you are aware of the procedure, risks and complications and that you request the operation to take place, then we're all finished. I'll just file this paperwork, check with the doctor and I'll be back with your gown and you can get changed. I'll look after your clothes and bag and give them to you afterwards, OK?'

'Yeah.'

'I've brought a cardigan for Mika,' I said. 'While she waits, it's quite cold in there, when you're sitting in the gown, with the air conditioning on.'

I knew this from having been a few times now. A few of the girls said they were really cold while waiting for the doctor.

'Of course, no problem,' Selina said. 'I'll be back in two minutes.'

I looked at Mika and smiled. 'OK?'

'Yeah. Bit nervous.'

'To be expected.'

I was feeling anxious, so goodness knows what it was like for

Mika. My butterflies were so bad that when Selina came through the door a minute later I almost jumped out of my seat.

'Ready, Mika?'

She nodded.

'See you after,' she said.

'I'll be here.'

I watched her leave, then found my way down to an empty waiting room, got myself a drink of water and sat down.

No going back now.

Mika's pimp had sent her by minicab to an anonymous hotel, part of a multinational chain. In her hand was a slip of paper with the room number and a mobile phone number. The gazes of poorly paid reception and security staff remained fastened to computer and video screens respectively, as Mika, drunk, staggered to the lift with bottles of fizzy wine clinking in plastic bags. Money had been paid.

Mika knocked on the door. A man older than her father opened it. There were others behind him.

She was raped. Mika stopped hearing the men once she had drunk enough. She let them do whatever. Couldn't stop them if she tried. Every so often the pain made her cry out.

They didn't even let her clean up. Just got her clothes back on, more or less, escorted her to the same minicab that had brought her there. Then they went home, some to wives and children.

Mika went to the doctor first. She couldn't tell the doctor how she got pregnant. The doctor would want to report it. Mika just wanted the baby gone.

The doctor disagreed. 'What about adoption?' she asked. 'I see so many couples who want kids and can't.'

Mika left and came to see me.

*

Mika is lying on a bed.

The doctor arrives, a young man. He uses an ultrasound to confirm the age of the foetus. The monitor screen and sound of the heartbeat is hidden from Mika. Not something you want to see or hear at this stage.

The doctor studies Mika's cervix and uterus. He confirms that this isn't an ectopic pregnancy, where the fertilised egg has implanted outside the uterus.

The anaesthetist, a woman, enters and prepares the intravenous line. She is friendly.

The anaesthetic is released. Mika enters a twilight state as the anaesthetic, an intravenous sedation, makes her feel like she's floating. She doesn't feel the local anaesthetic being injected into her cervix.

A small, plastic suction tube connected to a small but powerful pump is inserted into Mika's womb. The foetus is broken apart and removed, along with surrounding tissue. The doctor checks and double checks he has everything.

Until you're in this situation you can't judge what's right or wrong. You can't have an opinion. You can't judge any teenager who has had an abortion, because unless you've lived in the world inside her skull, you can't know how it feels to be in this situation, at this age, with a certain set of options. Mika was one of thousands of teenage girls who go through this experience every year in the UK.

Almost 190,000 abortions were carried out in 2010. The latest you can have an abortion is twenty-four weeks – almost six months – through forced miscarriage. Most late abortions (3,000 at nineteen to twenty-four weeks) are performed on teenagers. Teenage pregnancy in the UK is the highest in Western Europe. Of pregnant teenagers aged sixteen and under 62.5 per cent opt for abortion.[155]

Since the government introduced Teenage Pregnancy Coordinators (TPCs) ten years ago, teen pregnancy fell year after year. The latest data for 2010 (it takes two years for the Office for National Statistics to collect and publish this data) shows the under-eighteen conception rate for 2010 is the lowest since 1969 at 35.5 conceptions per 1,000 women aged fifteen to seventeen – down to 34,633 in 2010, down 9.5 per cent on 2009.[156]

TPCs provided advice on sexual health, gave girls confidence to insist on contraception and not to feel pressured into sex. They targeted those most at risk as well as those girls who'd already had abortions. A third of all abortions carried out in England and Wales are repeats (64,300 out of 189,574 in 2010). Earlier this year I took a fourteen-year-old girl to have her third termination.[157]

TPCs brought together the work of local authorities, Primary Care Trusts (PCTs) and voluntary sector services and were starting to make a difference in the levels of teenage pregnancy in England. They were abolished in 2011. The Teenage Pregnancy National Support Team, which provided free consultancy-style support to those working on the issue locally, has also been closed.[158] The government is trying to save money – but we all know it costs a lot of money to look after teenage single mums and their children. We will only truly know the effect of these cuts in the coming years.

A lot more teenagers have already started coming to us who want to have an abortion.

We don't judge. We talk it through, make a list of pros and cons. Make it real. Teenagers take longer to reach a decision because they feel they have no one to talk to, that it's too scary, that they are unable to resolve the Catch 22 of not wanting to have an abortion while at the same time knowing they can't look after a baby. Some girls develop post-traumatic stress disorder after abortion and it helps enormously if someone is around afterwards to talk it through.

Mika and I walked slowly back to Ennett House. She hadn't wanted to tell her mum and we respected that.

While Mika stretched out on the sofa in the lounge, I prepared some soup in the kitchen. She hadn't eaten for twelve hours.

'How long can I stay?'

'Take all the time you need.'

'Thanks.'

When I came in with the soup she was sitting on her hands, staring into space, still dazed from the unreal feeling of the anaesthetic.

'It's OK. It's over. You can get on with your life now.'

Mika nodded. 'I know.'

She paused for a while.

'Natalie,' she said softly, 'I would have killed myself if I'd not been able to do this. And I wouldn't have done it without you.'

We sat quietly for a moment, eating the soup.

'I didn't believe the test,' Mika said. 'I hoped it would go away and I wouldn't have to make a decision. I can't make decisions. I always get them wrong.'

'That's not true. You were not in control of the situation that led you here. Others made decisions for you and forced you to do what they wanted. Making a decision like this sets you free.'

'I see what you mean, kind of. I didn't decide to have sex with those men in the hotel. They decided they were going to have me. My doctor didn't want me to decide. She wanted to decide for me. She wanted me to have the baby because she didn't believe in abortion and I could have given it to a couple that really wanted a baby and couldn't have one.

'They slag off teenage mums in the press but maybe they didn't decide to get pregnant. Maybe they didn't decide to use contraception because they weren't expecting to have sex. Maybe they weren't allowed to decide to have an abortion. People will look at them like dirt anyway, like it was their fault. But you helped me make the right decision. I didn't want to bring a child into a life without hope.'

Mika stayed until the end of the day. Eventually, it was time for her to go.

'I call you a bit later, to check you're all right.'

'Thanks.'

'Remember, any bleeding or pain then you need to call me and you need to go back to the clinic, OK?'

'I know, thanks.'

I can see Mika's got what it takes to do something with her life (and I think I'm the only one, but then I'm the one who has spent most time with her).

I've since seen it in others who've made it. I feel so angry that instead of having an education – the thing that gives you your best shot in life – girls like Mika are being raped, enduring abortions and fighting addiction and yet society blames them, as if this was the life they'd chosen.

2012

October: David Crompton, the Chief Constable of South Yorkshire Police, appears before a parliamentary inquiry into agencies' handling of street-grooming sex crimes.

When MPs ask him how organised networks of sex offenders in Rotherham were able to get away with so many crimes for more than a decade, the chief constable replies that in 2010, 'given the intelligence about the level of potential offending, we simply didn't have sufficient resource devoted to this particular activity' ... this had 'contributed to some of the difficulties that spanned a number of years' but it was 'important to say that the situation now is very different from a few years ago'.

The MPs ask for prosecution figures for 2012.

The chief constable is forced to admit there have been none.

Number of prosecutions in Rotherham from 1996 to 2012 = 1.[159]

CHAPTER THIRTY-SIX

BIG DAY OUT

Natalie

Every once in a while, Miranda badgered various bigwigs for a treat for the girls.

These rare treats, usually a day trip, were, occasionally, life-changing events for some of the girls. Even though most of them lived in central London, they'd never walked along the South Bank, never crossed the wibbly-wobbly footbridge that crosses the Thames and connects St Paul's to the Tate Modern, let alone been inside either of those buildings.

This year Miranda managed to get hold of fifteen VIP tickets to the London 2012 Paralympics. The girls who wanted to come, and that was nearly all of them, put their names in a hat and we drew them at random. Gloria, Sandra, Janine, Mika, Mariam and Hannah's names were among the lucky ones.

Come the day, Miranda, Beatrice, Mary and I were waiting nervously for the girls to arrive. They weren't exactly known for being on time. And they were also supposed to come 'dressed appropriately' and be on their best behaviour.

All of them showed up early.

We set off in a small coach in the sunshine, the girls laughing and joking. For a while they were free, safe, taken care of and about to see, we hoped, something truly inspirational. Changes that had been hard to see were suddenly clarified when all the girls were together.

Gloria, free of crack, and back at home, was still coming to see us. The hollowed-out crack look had faded from her face and although school had proven difficult, some wonderful teachers were helping her every step of the way.

As for Mika, I pushed hard for social services to go to court to get a secure order and she was eventually placed in a secure unit outside of London, with no access to transport. Mika needed to learn to develop appropriate relationships with a peer group and the best way to do this was in a therapeutic setting.

Early visits from her family hadn't gone well. Her father had to be dragged along, and then only said things designed to upset her. I travelled to see Mika every week and kept saying the same thing to her team – when she's ready to move on, do not, under any circumstances, place her anywhere in London.

Despite her family's continued rejection Mika not only made friends, she started to show an interest in education. She also discovered both a love and talent for music. Needless to say, the local police were as delighted as I was. Countless hours were saved, freeing them up to respond to other crimes.

Mariam was on course to get a whole heap of GCSEs, and was planning to go to college.

Hannah, four months pregnant and still with her lover, the former member of Racist Attack, was studying hard for her GCSEs.

Nikki suffered from panic attacks and although we had no proof I neither trusted nor liked her mother one bit. For now though Anne was on her case and watching Nikki's mother like a hawk.

Sandra's return to her family was complete; she said she wanted to work in child protection.

Janine was still with her wonderful foster family and was healing, although on bad days she had threatened to burn off her tattoos with acid. Miranda had since found a laser treatment centre prepared to organise NHS funding for their removal, considering the exceptional circumstances in which Janine got them. The work was long and painful but, in the end, extraordinarily effective.

We were making a difference.

In a way, all we did was to be there for them. We listened, believed and helped. That's all they needed. They wanted what everyone else did – a chance for a decent life – and that meant an end to violence, drugs and gangs.

And if we put in time *and* money, then the rewards will be enormous for society. We just won't necessarily know about them. And this is a problem for governments who like to show voters reports about how much money they've saved, because it's difficult to measure crimes that haven't been committed.

In 2011, children's charity Barnardo's tried to find out. Barnardo's has been providing services to prevent, and get young people away from, sexual exploitation for sixteen years and currently runs twenty services providing interventions for young people who have either been sexually exploited, or are at risk of sexual exploitation. Between 2009 and 2010, Barnardo's worked with 1,098 young people across the UK.

They wanted to know what difference their interventions made, financially and socially, and so measured four outcomes associated with sexual exploitation to which they could assign a monetary value:

Reduced missing episodes
Reduced alcohol and drug abuse
Improved engagement in education, training or employment
Reduced accommodation and housing need

They examined 539 cases where the outcome was known. The average age was sixteen, ranging between ten and eighteen years old. Eighty-five per cent were female, 75 per cent were white British, 3 per cent were parents and 25 per cent were looked-after children.

They found that intervention:

1. Reduced the risk of sexual exploitation by more than 50 per cent
2. Reduced missing episodes by 75 per cent[160]

Costing child sexual exploitation is tricky. As the effects may last for years, or a lifetime (the sooner you can get to them the more likely they are to recover and require less support throughout their lives), there are many factors that are simply too complex to even estimate, such as education, state benefits, tax losses, lost private earnings and social exclusion, all of which can affect each other. Then, there are factors such as the increased risk of accidents for missing persons or increased crime, which also cannot be measured with any certainty.

Barnardo's simply looked at the cost of an average missing episode to the police (about £1,054, according to Lancashire Constabulary) and compared this with the results of their study and found that for every £1 Barnardo's spent, they saved the police between £6 and £12.[161]

This is just for the police.

If you look at a child who runs away 30, 40 or 50 times – and this happens frequently – then the savings from looking out for just one child could run into several hundred thousand pounds. And, not only do the interventions save money, they also hugely reduce the chances of a child becoming a victim of sexual exploitation.

The Children's Society analysed the costs of children running away from care homes. They stated that early intervention in terms of preventing runaways could result in savings to public services of up to £300,000 per child.[162]

We haven't learned from history. From the start of the twentieth century, people have campaigned to end the sexual exploitation of children. Media attention comes in waves as the phenomenon is 'rediscovered' every decade or so, through scandals like the Rochdale case. Each time, governments of all parties made efforts but ultimately failed to deal with the problem, to give the right people the knowledge and power to protect children.

Lancashire Police recently set up a unique pilot project called Engage, based in Blackburn. Engage brings together a range of services – police, social workers, nurses, sexual health and drugs workers and PACE parents – to prevent, protect and prosecute. In just one year, Engage discovered a total of 100 offences of child abduction, rape and sexual activity with minors involving 36 individuals. They rescued 80 children in four years. Many of these girls are back at school.

This sounds like something that needs to be rolled out across the UK. Any society that fails to learn from its past will repeat its mistakes. We're still right at the start of dealing with a problem that should not even exist in the twenty-first century.

We have to accept that a significant proportion of the UK's population abuses thousands of children every day. Until we do, and until we start changing our attitudes towards so-called 'troubled children', we are all guilty of neglect.

'She's so tiny.'

'And the pool's massive!'

'Imagine being that small . . .'

Ellie Simmonds, aged just seventeen, was about to swim in the

400 metres freestyle final. She had achondroplasia, which meant that she was only four feet tall.

When the starting buzzer went the whole place exploded. To my amazement (I'm not a sports fan), I found myself joining in, screaming like an insane person and had to apologise to a man in the row in front of me when I bashed his head with my programme. The girls, meanwhile, had started synchronising their screams to urge Ellie on.

From the start the race was dominated by the world-record holder seventeen-year-old American Victoria Arlen, who had been left partially paralysed in 2006 by a virus that affected her spinal cord.

The competition fell away length by length. Ellie was the only one able to hold on and fought to get close, but Victoria held the lead through the halfway point and then drew away by a body length in the last third.

We cheered at the top of our voices and Ellie started inching back; on the final turn they were fingertip to fingertip. Driven by the crowd's energy, Ellie started driving forward, catching Victoria inch by inch, and she touched the wall just one second ahead, breaking the world record by an incredible five seconds.

We celebrated like we'd just won the gold ourselves.

The Paralympics showed what happens when the country throws itself behind something. If only the same effort could be made to help girls like these, to end abuse, to keep girls safe and with their families, looking forward to the future, then, as a nation, we could be truly proud.

As far as I am concerned, they are already champions – at surviving.

Despite everything, they are still hopeful for the future, and we owe it to them to make sure they get the future they deserve.

*

Ben

Sylvia's drop-in centre has gone. The community centre has gone.

The shooting gallery is still open. Fat Bob's is still open, even after Ever Ready Eddie raided his place as a matter of principle. Bob was bailed and open for business the next day. Elton's crew hasn't yet cropped up on anyone's radar, however, so that's something.

My Magic Bus is still hanging in by the skin of its rusty bumpers. Sylvia retrained and joined me to carry out tidying-up medical care to those kids who end up on the wrong side of the local militia; just small stitches, bandages and antiseptic, but it saves them from waiting for hours in A&E, if they would have bothered to go at all.

These kids are marooned from normal society. For them, life is not unlike *Lord of the Flies*; they have their own rules, codes and hierarchy. They self-police. With clusters of kids gathered around the Magic Bus, Carol, thirteen, told me how she had a row with another older girl, new to the estate, and within half an hour that girl had a gun in her face.

'I didn't have any problems after that,' she said with a smile.

Andy approached. He was holding his arm awkwardly.

'All right, Ben?'

'Not so bad, Andy. Yourself?'

'Can I see the nurse?'

'What's wrong?'

He rolled up his sleeve. There was a deep cut on the top of his forearm; exposed muscle glistened. It had stopped bleeding but the fleshy gash made my stomach turn a quick flip.

'Sylvia!'

Sylvia appeared from inside. Looked at me then Andy. 'Right then, young man,' she said, 'I think you might need a hospital visit for that.'

'Please,' Andy said. He was ready to run.

I leaned in close to Sylvia and whispered: 'We have painkillers, don't we? Antiseptic, bandages and stitches?'

Sylvia nodded. 'Yes, but—'

'Let's get him fixed up first and ask questions later. He isn't going to want to risk the hospital. To him that means police, social services and a possible care home. Andy isn't going to let that happen.'

Sylvia stood back. 'Right, young man. Step inside my operating theatre and let's see if we can't stick you back together again. You got any pins and needles in your fingers?'

Andy shook his head. 'Nah, it's just sore.'

I followed inside and sat in the seat behind as Sylvia got to work. 'What happened, mate?' I asked softly.

'Got mugged.'

'By whom?'

Andy shrugged. You don't tell.

'What for?'

'The stash. Someone had been watching, knew what I did. They were waiting when I got a load for Fat Bob. I tried to stop them and they cut me.'

'How many?'

'Four, I think.'

'Fat Bob know?'

'Yeah.'

'And?'

'He let me off paying him back. But I can't run for him no more.'

Once the stitches were in, Andy had some spagbol and went back out into the world with more problems than any kid should have to face.

'What the hell do we do?' I asked when he had gone.

'Turn up tomorrow,' Sylvia replied, 'and the day after that, and the day after that.'

The next day a girl just like Nikki showed up. Exploited and beaten badly enough to need stitches over her eye and a trip to the dentist.

'Where are you from?' Sylvia asked as she worked with her needle and thread.

'Nowhere,' the girl said. 'I'm just a nowhere girl.'

She was right. These girls feel as though they have nowhere to go. There are so many of them out there who need our help. They are on the run, all of them escaping, whether through drugs, drink, gangs or sexual exploitation.

Thousands of them. From towns, cities and hamlets all over the UK. Twelve, thirteen, fourteen, fifteen, sixteen; every age.

They run to escape their childhoods. They run when they cannot take it anymore. Together, they would fill twenty large comprehensive schools.

They beg. They rob people, shops, businesses. They buy and sell drugs. They sell themselves. They buy and sell one another. They cheat, they steal. They run, again and again.

They cry. They get angry. They do not understand. They are not nice to look at, deal with or think about. Nobody knows what to do.

Police ignore them. People ignore them. The system ignores them.

Some of them die. Some are murdered. Some of them commit suicide. Some of them vanish.

Thousands are raped.

Some go home. Some stay in special homes. Some stay in shelters.

Some turn eighteen and it is even harder for people to understand.

They go to prison. There is no escape.

Society ignores them and society pays. Society wishes the problem would go away.

END NOTE

If you have been the victim of sexual abuse, whether yesterday or twenty years ago, it's vital to report it. Even if you don't want to follow it up with a criminal investigation, you hold valuable criminal intelligence that could be used to help protect other children. Also, by coming forward, you will have taken the first step on the road to achieving some kind of closure. You can do this by contacting your local police (or anonymously via Crimestoppers), local social services and various voluntary organisations.

Childline: childline.org.uk 0800 1111
Crimestoppers: crimestoppers-uk.org 0800 555 111
NSPCC: nspc.org.uk 0800 800 5000
Parents Against Child Exploitation (PACE) paceuk.info
    0113 2403040

NOTES

INTRODUCTION

1 Social workers put off by high-profile whistleblowing cases, communitycare.co.uk, 1 November 2012.

1885

1 'The Maiden Tribute of Modern Babylon I: the Report of our Secret Commission', W. T. Stead (*Pall Mall Gazette*, 6 July 1885).

1908

2 *Child's Guardian*, 1912, XXVI (11), p.126; 'Cleansing the Portals of Life: The venereal disease campaign of the early 20th century', in Langan, M., and Schwarz, B., *Crises in the British State 1880–1930*, (HarperCollins, 1985).

3 *Knowledge of Evil: Child Prostitution and Child Sexual Abuse in Twentieth-Century England*, Alyson Brown and David Barrett (Willan, 2002), p.82–3.

CHAPTER 2 – GIRL NO. 1

4 'Youth Gangs, Sexual Violence and Sexual Exploitation', A Scoping Exercise for the Office of the Children's Commissioner for England, Professor J. J. Pearce & Professor J. M. Pitts, University of Bedfordshire Institute for Applied Social Research, March 2011.

1913

5 *Child's Guardian*, September 1913 XXVII (9), pp.103–4.

CHAPTER 3

6 'Rehab centre forced to shut: The UK's only residential centre for young people whose lives are blighted by drugs and alcohol has been forced to close its doors', Rachel Williams, *Guardian*, 3 March 2010.

7 Drug Misuse Declared: Findings from the 2010/11 British Crime Survey England and Wales, Kevin Smith and John Flatley (eds), July 2011

8 'Are some children's homes putting profit before child protection?', Simon Cox, BBC Radio 4's *The Report*, 5 July 2012.

9 *The Crime Factory*, Officer 'A' (Mainstream Publishing, 2012), p.96.

10 'Kicking the habit: How important are teen rehab centres?', Dan Cairns, BBC News, 4 August 2011.

11 Ibid.

1922

12 *Prostitution, a Survey and a Challenge*, G. M. Hall (London: Williams and Northgate, 1933), p.26.
13 'The Grave Sex Plague', Max Pemberton, *Weekly Dispatch*, 2 June 1917.
14 *Knowledge of Evil: Child Prostitution and Child Sexual Abuse in Twentieth-Century England*, Alyson Brown and David Barrett (Willan, 2002), p.78.

1936

15 'Mystery of Britain's Vanished Girls', *Daily Express*, 22 May 1936.
16 *Tit-Bits* magazine, 2 March 1935.

CHAPTER FIVE

17 'Homelessness: end of the line for the bendy-bus rough sleepers', Patrick Butler, guardian.co.uk, 9 December 2011.

1938

18 *The Shield* V (3) December 1937.

CHAPTER SIX

19 'Shot teenager "a victim of gang war" by Sri Carmichael and Justin Davenport', *Daily Mail*, 16 October 2007.
See also londonstreetgangs blog: https://sites.google.com/site/londonstreetgangs/gang-lists/south-london-gangs/t-block-original-greenside-bangers
20 'Youth Gangs, Sexual Violence and Sexual Exploitation, A Scoping Exercise for the Office of the Children's Commissioner for England', Professor J. J. Pearce & Professor J. M. Pitts, University of Bedfordshire Institute for Applied Social Research, March 2011.
21 Ibid.

1943

22 L. Fairfield, 'Notes on Prostitution', *British Journal of Criminology* 9, 1959, p.170.

CHAPTER SEVEN

23 'Refuges for young runaways', Camilla Pemberton, *Community Care* magazine, 30 April 2010.

1948

24 *Knowledge of Evil: Child Prostitution and Child Sexual Abuse in Twentieth-Century England*, Alyson Brown and David Barrett (Willan, 2002), p.87.

CHAPTER EIGHT

25 'Khyra Ishaq social worker had 50 cases on the go', Molly Garboden, *Community Care* magazine, 30 July 2010.

1952

26 *Knowledge of Evil: Child Prostitution and Child Sexual Abuse in Twentieth-Century England*, Alyson Brown and David Barrett (Willan, 2002), p.137.

1959

27 *Knowledge of Evil: Child Prostitution and Child Sexual Abuse in Twentieth-Century England*, Alyson Brown and David Barrett (Willan, 2002), pp.128–33.

1969

28 'Schoolgirls on the Game', *People*, 26 October 1969.

1976

29 *Knowledge of Evil: Child Prostitution and Child Sexual Abuse in Twentieth-Century England*, Alyson Brown and David Barrett (Willan, 2002), Chapter 7.

1976

30 *Knowledge of Evil: Child Prostitution and Child Sexual Abuse in Twentieth-Century England*, Alyson Brown and David Barrett (Willan, 2002), p.160.

1976

31 *Sunday Times*, 4 April 1976, p.3, column h.

1978

32 'The Sour Side of Sixteen: Schoolgirls on the Streets', *The Times*, 12 February 1978, p.12, column a.

1984

33 P. Ayre and D. Barrett, 'Young People and Prostitution: an end to the beginning?', *Children & Society*, 14: 48–59, 2000.

34 *Knowledge of Evil: Child Prostitution and Child Sexual Abuse in Twentieth-Century England*, Alyson Brown and David Barrett (Willan, 2002), p.177.

1990

35 Melrose, M., and D. Barrett 1999. 'Not much juvenile justice in these neighbourhoods: A report on a study of juvenile prostitution.' Paper presented at British Criminology Conference, Liverpool, 13–16 July.

1991

36 'Children's homes "powerless" to protect the vulnerable from predatory sex gangs', Andrew Norfolk, *The Times*, 9 May 2012.

1997

37 'The new Labour government ...': 'Safeguarding Children Involved in Prostitution: Supplementary Guidance to Working Together to Safeguard Children', Department of Health, Home Office, Department for Education and Employment and National Assembly for Wales: London. http://www.dh.gov.uk/en/Publicationsandstatistics/Publications/PublicationsPolicyAndGuidance/DH_4006037

38 'Three quarters of ...': 'Findings – Monitoring Poverty and Social Exclusion', Joseph Rowntree Foundation (York: Joseph Rowntree Foundation, 1998).

1999

39 'Exit Strategy', S. Wellard, *Community Care* magazine, 17 February 1999. http://www.communitycare.co.uk/Articles/18/05/2000/6600/Exit-strategy.htm

2003

40 'Charlene Downes murder detective forced to resign', BBC News online, 24 December 2011. http://www.bbc.co.uk/news/uk-england-lancashire-16325953
'Police rapped for blunders in murder case of girl "turned into kebab meat"', Graham Smith, *Daily Mail*, 16 October 2009. http://www.dailymail.co.uk/news/article-1220815/Police-disciplined-blunders-murder-case-girl-turned-kebabs.html

2003

41 '"Overdose" girl was in care', Alexandra Frean, *The Times*, 2 October 2003.
'Scandal of care firms that failed to protect girls from grooming: Teenager in children's home died from overdose after being targeted for sex', James Tozer, Daniel Martin and Nazia Parveen, *Daily Mail*, 11 May 2012.
'Dead at 15 – care girl who sold body to buy heroin', Damon Wilkinson and Helen Johnson, *Rochdale Observer*, 2 March 2007.

2004

42 'The NSPCC "Street Matters" Project in London', N. Patel and J. Pearce, in M. Melrose and D. Barrett (eds), *Anchors in Floating Lives:*

Interventions with Young People Sexually Abused Through Prostitution (Russell House Publishing, Lyme Regis, 2004).

'Sex in the city: mapping commercial sex across London', S. Dickson, The Poppy Project, London, 2004.

43 'Rochdale grooming trial: Asian grooming gangs, the uncomfortable issue', Nigel Bunyan, *Telegraph*, 8 May 2012.

CHAPTER TWENTY-THREE

44 House of Commons oral evidence taken before the Home Affairs Committee, Localised Child Grooming, 3 July 2012, Tim Loughton MP.

45 DfE (March 2012) Children's Homes in England Data Pack, London: HM Government. 1,810 children's homes were registered with Ofsted on 30 September 2011. Of these, 439 (24 per cent) were local authority run and 1,371 (76 per cent) were in the private or voluntary sector.

46 'Concern at venture capitalists who make millions out of children in care', Andrew Norfolk, *The Times*, 2 July 2012.

47 Ibid.

48 Report from the Joint Inquiry into Children Who Go Missing from Care, June 2012, p.22.

49 Ibid., p.32, paragraph 104.

50 'Children in care are "living near sex offenders"', Andrew Woodcock, *Independent*, 3 July 2012.

51 Report from the Joint Inquiry into Children Who Go Missing from Care, June 2012, p.20, para 47.

52 Ibid.

53 Ibid., p.34, para 116.

54 Ibid., p.35, para 118.

55 Quote on Ofsted Website, News Section, 'Children and Families Services', last accessed 8 January 2013.

56 Report from the Joint Inquiry into Children Who Go Missing from Care, June 2012, Foreword, p.3.

57 Ibid., p.11, para 3.

58 'What happens when someone goes missing?', Louise Coletta, BBC News, 24 August 2012.

59 Ibid.

60 Report from the Joint Inquiry into Children Who Go Missing from Care, June 2012, p.12, para 7.
See also: 'What's Going on to Safeguard Children and Young People from Sexual Exploitation?' Sue Jago, with Lorena Arocha, Isabelle Brodie, Margaret Melrose, Jenny Pearce and Camille Warrington, University of Bedfordshire, October 2011.

61 Ibid., p.12, para 9.

62 Ibid., p.26, para 79.

63 Ibid., Executive Summary, p.9.

64 Ibid., p.16, para 27.

65 'Protecting vulnerable girls at Clare Lodge secure centre. A key facility for vulnerable girls is under the threat of closure despite its vital contribution', Camilla Pemberton, *Community Care*, 25 January 2011.

66 'David Cameron faces a fresh revolt as sacked ministers go on the attack', *Evening Standard*, 11 September 2012.

2006

67 'Teenage car crash tragedy "was most distressing case in my career" says expert', Alice McKeegan, *Manchester Evening News*, 13 October 2010.

2007

68 'Sex grooming scandal inside a seaside town by Andrew Norfolk', *The Times*, 7 April 2011.

69 'Blackpool Council social worker delays "risked harm to children"', BBC News Online, 13 July 2012.

CHAPTER TWENTY-FIVE

70 'Five Rotherham men jailed for child sex offences', BBC News Online, 4 November 2010.

2008

71 Rochdale Neighbourhood Renewal Strategy Conference
    Rochdale Federation of Tenants & Residents Association
    http://www.housingnews.co.uk/enews/site.asp?ID=7184&view=
    1&UserID=32236&UserEmail=lorna@spinmedia.co.uk

CHAPTER TWENTY-SIX

72 'Policeman yawned loudly as girl, 15, described how she was forced to have sex', Andrew Norfolk, *The Times*, 28 September 2012.
    'Teenage girls suffer as we look the other way', Jenny McCartney, *Telegraph*, 29 September 2012.

73 'Rochdale child sex grooming case originally dropped', BBC News Online, 9 May 2012.

74 '"Child sex victims were prostitutes with enough business acumen to win *The Apprentice*", man at centre of sex gang trial tells court', Jamie McGinnes, *Daily Mail*, 8 May 2012.

75 'Rapist who told child victims to call him "Daddy" gets 19 years', Andrew Norfolk, *The Times*, 22 June 2012.

76 'Rochdale sex gang leader is jailed for "years of rape"', Paul Stokes, *The Times*, 3 August 2012.

77 'Councillors give their backing to "hard working family man" accused in Rochdale "grooming" case', John Scheerhout, *Manchester Evening News*, 18 April 2012.

78 'Police and care blunders led to years of abuse', Andrew Norfolk, *The Times*, 8 May 2012.

79 'The venture capitalists and the scandal-hit children's homes', Cahal Milmo, *Independent*, 24 May 2012.
  'Scandal of care firms that failed to protect girls from grooming: Teenager in children's home died from overdose after being targeted for sex', James Tozer, Daniel Martin and Nazia Parveen, *Daily Mail*, 11 May 2012.

80 'Are some children's homes putting profit before child protection?', Simon Cox, BBC Radio 4's *The Report*, 5 July 2012.

81 'Police and care blunders led to years of abuse', Andrew Norfolk, *The Times*, 8 May 2012.

82 Ibid.

2009

83 'Barnardo's reported ...': 'Bradford councillor calls for investigation over child trafficking claims', *Bradford Telegraph and Argus*, 25 September 2012.
  http://www.thetelegraphandargus.co.uk/news/9946648.print/

84 'Charlotte's school ...': 'Notes, reports and meetings, but still no action to save girl from sex gang', Andrew Norfolk, *The Times*, 22 November 2011.

CHAPTER TWENTY-SEVEN

85 For the definitive account of Fiona Ivison's case, see *Fiona's Story: A Tragedy of Our Times*, Irene Ivison (Virago Press, 1997).

2010

86 'Ofsted carries out ...': 'Ofsted: Leeds Council failing to sufficiently fund child protection', Judy Cooper, *Community Care*, 1 February 2010.
  http://www.communitycare.co.uk/Articles/01/02/2010/113695/ofsted-rates-leeds-councils-child-safeguarding-as-inadequate.htm

87 'One month later ...': 'Raped, pimped and driven to suicide: the 16-year-old girl failed at every turn', Andrew Norfolk, *The Times*, 21 November 2011.

CHAPTER TWENTY-EIGHT

88 'Spending your 4th of July as a "child prostitute" – or victim?', *Washington Times* Communities, 4 July 2012, Speaking Out by Holly Smith.

89 'Irene Ivison: Mother, Woman and Campaigner. A Tribute', Adele L. Weir, CROP publication, 2002.

90 Ibid.

91 Ibid.
92 Ibid.

2010

93 'Soldier spared jail for sex with 13-year-old after judge ruled "she made the running"', *Telegraph*, 8 January 2010.
'Ex-soldier, 41, who had sex with 13-year-old girl spared jail as woman judge says teenager "did most of the running"', Arthur Martin, *Daily Mail*, 8 January 2010.

CHAPTER TWENTY-NINE

94 'Murdered girl was victim of Pakistani sex grooming gang', Andrew Norfolk, *The Times*, 2 December 2011.
95 Rotherham Safeguarding Children Board, Serious Case Review Overview Report. In respect of: Child S, Produced by Professor Pat Cantrill, April 2011, p.57, paragraph 1.
96 Ibid., p.40, paragraphs 3 and 4.
97 'Groomed for sex then thrown into a canal and killed: Life for man who murdered white girl for "shaming" Asian family', Paul Sims, *Daily Mail*, 22 December 2011.
98 Rotherham Safeguarding Children Board, Serious Case Review Overview Report. In respect of: Child S, Produced by Professor Pat Cantrill, April 2011, p.57, paragraph 1.
99 Ibid., p.112, paragraph 4.
100 Ibid., p.72, paragraph 5.
101 'Social workers hid fact they knew teenage mother was at risk from sex grooming gangs SIX YEARS before she was brutally murdered', Daniel Miller, *Daily Mail*, 7 June 2012.
102 Rotherham Safeguarding Children Board, Serious Case Review Overview Report. In respect of: Child S, Produced by Professor Pat Cantrill, April 2011, p.40, paragraph 7 to p.41, paragraph 1.
103 Ibid., p.41, paragraph 3.
104 Ibid., p.43, paragraph 6.
105 Ibid., p.43, paragraph 5 and 7.
106 Ibid., p.44, paragraph 2.
107 Ibid., p.44, paragraph 8 to p.45, paragraph 5.
108 Ibid., Section 3.6, p.113.
109 Ibid., p.45, paragraphs 3 and 4.
110 Ibid., p.59, paragraph 2.
111 'White teenage mother stabbed to death and dumped in canal after having baby with married Muslim', *Daily Mail*, 13 May 2011.
112 Ibid.

2010

113 'English Defence League supporters attack police at Bradford rally', Matthew Taylor and Martin Wainwright, *Observer*, 28 August 2010.

114 'Protecting Our Children', English Defence League, 4 October 2012. http://englishdefenceleague.org/edl-news-2/1806-protecting-our-children

CHAPTER THIRTY

115 'White teenage mother stabbed to death and dumped in canal after having baby with married Muslim', *Daily Mail*, 13 May 2011.

116 'Groomed for sex at 12, stabbed to death at 17: Shocking life of white teenage mother murdered after Asian lover rejected her child', Rob Cooper, *Daily Mail*, 2 December 2011.

117 Rotherham Safeguarding Children Board, Serious Case Review Overview Report. In respect of: Child S, Produced by Professor Pat Cantrill April 2011, p.112, paragraph 4 and p.47, paragraph 5.

118 Ibid., pp.41–2.

119 Ibid., p.48, paragraph 1.

120 Ibid., p.144, paragraph 4.

121 'Officials hid vital facts about men suspected of grooming girl for sex', Andrew Norfolk, *The Times*, 7 June 2012.

122 'Police files reveal vast child protection scandal', Andrew Norfolk, *The Times*, 24 September 2012.

123 Rotherham MBC statement, rotherham.gov.uk, 25 September 2012.

124 Ibid.

125 *The Times* Leader: Telling the Truth: 7 June 2012.
'Officials hid vital facts about men suspected of grooming girl for sex', Andrew Norfolk, *The Times*, 7 June 2012.

2011

126 'Revealed: the horror of the 5,000 children under 16 raped every year', Denis Campbell, *Observer*, 14 May 2006.

127 Statistics on child sexual abuse, NSPCC, June 2012.

128 http://www.nspcc.org.uk/Inform/resourcesforprofessionals/sexualabuse/statistics_wda87833.html

129 'Police files reveal vast child protection scandal', Andrew Norfolk, *The Times*, 24 September 2012

2011

130 Statistics on child sexual abuse, NSPCC, June 2012
http://www.nspcc.org.uk/Inform/resourcesforprofessionals/sexualabuse/statistics_wda87833.html

2012

131 'MPs to investigate deputy children's commissioner's claims', BBC News Online, 13 June 2012. http://www.bbc.co.uk/news/uk-politics-18422204

CHAPTER THIRTY-THREE

132 'The 17 cases identified by *The Times* which showed a pattern of exploitation by *Times* Staff', *The Times*, 5 January 2011.

133 'Police files reveal vast child protection scandal', Andrew Norfolk, *The Times*, 24 September 2012.

134 'Blackburn men jailed for sex offences "were thrown out of BNP"', Tom Moseley, *Lancashire Telegraph*, 23 November 2008.
'The 17 cases identified by *The Times* which showed a pattern of exploitation by *Times* Staff', *The Times*, 5 January 2011.

135 'Child sex grooming: the Asian question. Special Report day one: As nine men are jailed for a total of 77 years for abusing young girls, what do we actually know about the cultural side of such crimes?', Paul Vallely, *Independent*, 10 May 2012.

136 'Paedophile, 19, jailed for his part in ring that abused 139 victims as young as 11 in seaside tourist resort', Luke Salkeld, *Daily Mail*, 9 July 2011.

137 'Teenage paedophile who groomed up to 139 girls as young as 11 on Facebook has sentence REDUCED by top judges', Luke Salkeld and Richard Hartley-Parkinson, *Daily Mail*, 29 February 2012.

138 'Man jailed for "paedophile parties"', PA News, 15 October 2012.

139 'The Rochdale sex ring shows the horrific consequences of Britain's "Islamophobia" witch-hunt' by Melanie Phillips, *Daily Mail*, 9 May 2012.

140 'Rochdale grooming trial: Nine men jailed', BBC News, 9 May 2012.

141 'Child sex grooming: the Asian question. Special Report day one: As nine men are jailed for a total of 77 years for abusing young girls, what do we actually know about the cultural side of such crimes?', Paul Vallely, *Independent*, 10 May 2012.

142 'Out of Mind, Out of Sight', Executive Summary, CEOP thematic assessment, June 2011.

143 'Ten children a week in danger of sexual exploitation in East Lancs', *Lancashire Telegraph*, 17 September 2012.

144 UK 2001 Census.

145 'How the Rochdale grooming case exposed British prejudice', Daniel Trilling, *New Statesman*, 15 August 2012.

2012

146 'London 2012: Olympics and Paralympics £377m under budget', BBC News Online, 23 October 2012. http://www.bbc.co.uk/sport/0/olympics/20041426

147 Family Planning Association Teenage Pregnancy Factsheet: http://www.fpa.org.uk/professionals/factsheets/teenagepregnancy

148 'Child poverty in UK set to increase as result of austerity drive', says Unicef, Amelia Gentleman, *Guardian*, 29 May 2012.

149 'Child Poverty in 2012: It shouldn't happen here', Save the Children, September 2012
www.savethechildren.org.uk/resources/online-library/child-poverty-2012-it-shouldnt-happen-here

CHAPTER THIRTY-FOUR

150 'Tottenham riot: Our community was dying ... now it's dead', Ryan Parry, *Daily Mirror*, 8 August 2011.

151 'Unite union stages rally against youth service cuts', BBC News, 12 February 2011.

152 'Farewell youth clubs, hello street life – and gang warfare', Alexandra Topping, *Guardian*, 29 July 2011.

2012

153 'We failed grooming victims, law chief Keir Starmer admits', Andrew Norfolk, *The Times*, 24 October 2012.

154 'Media prejudice' claim as child-sex report turns a blind eye to Asian gangs, Andrew Norfolk, *The Times*, 21 November 2012

CHAPTER THIRTY-FIVE

155 'Cuts threaten to undo progress on reducing teenage pregnancies', Rachel Williams, *Guardian*, 9 August 2011.

156 Ibid.

157 Ibid.

158 Ibid.

2012

159 'Police chief admits force has failed to charge sex groomers', Andrew Norfolk, *The Times*, 17 October 2012.
'South Yorkshire Police admits no new prosecutions of child sex abusers in Rotherham', Rosa Prince, *Telegraph*, 16 October 2012.

CHAPTER THIRTY-SIX

160 An assessment of the potential savings from Barnardo's interventions for young people who have been sexually exploited, Pro Bono Economics and Barnardo's, September 2011.
161 Ibid.
162 Make Runaways Safe Campaign Publication, Children's Society.